THIRD EDITION

# EXCEPTIONAL LEADERSHIP

## 16 CRITICAL COMPETENCIES
## FOR HEALTHCARE EXECUTIVES

WELL-CULTIVATED SELF-AWARENESS

COMPELLING VISION

MASTERFUL EXECUTION

A REAL WAY WITH PEOPLE

CARSON F. DYE   ANDREW N. GARMAN

HAP

ACHE Management Series

Your board, staff, or clients may also benefit from this book's insight. For information on quantity discounts, contact the Health Administration Press Marketing Manager at (312) 424-9450.

**Library of Congress Cataloging-in-Publication Data**

Names: Dye, Carson F., author. | Garman, Andrew N., author.
Title: Exceptional leadership : 16 critical competencies for healthcare
  executives / Carson F. Dye, Andrew N. Garman.
Other titles: Management series (Ann Arbor, Mich.)
Description: Third edition. | Chicago, IL : Health Administration Press,
  [2024] | Series: ACHE management series | Includes bibliographical
  references and index. | Summary: "Exceptional Leadership describes the
  professional and personal skills and behaviors that managers need to
  lead successfully and thrive in healthcare's high-stakes environment.
  The book offers a leadership competency model based on four themes:
  well-cultivated self-awareness, compelling vision, a real way with
  people, and masterful execution. Each competency is covered in its own
  chapter that defines it, provides examples and advice, and outlines
  common skill deficits"-- Provided by publisher.
Identifiers: LCCN 2023054682 | ISBN 9781640554429 (trade paperback ; alk.
  paper) | ISBN 9781640554436 (ebook) | ISBN 9781640554443 (epub)
Subjects: MESH: Health Services Administration | Leadership | Professional
  Competence | Quality of Health Care
Classification: LCC RA971 | NLM W 84.1 | DDC 362.1068--dc23/eng/20240112
LC record available at https://lccn.loc.gov/2023054682

The paper used in this publication meets the minimum requirements of American National Standard for Information Sciences—Permanence of Paper for Printed Library Materials, ANSI Z39.48-1984. ♾ ™

Manuscript editor: Sharon Sofinski; Cover designer: Mark Oberkrom; Layout: PerfecType

Found an error or a typo? We want to know! Please e-mail it to hapbooks@ache.org, mentioning the book's title and putting "Book Error" in the subject line.

For photocopying and copyright information, please contact Copyright Clearance Center at www.copyright.com or at (978) 750-8400.

Health Administration Press
A division of the Foundation of the
  American College of Healthcare Executives
300 S. Riverside Plaza, Suite 1900
Chicago, IL 60606-6698
(312) 424-2800

For the many truly exceptional leaders with whom I have worked and recruited over the years
*Carson F. Dye*

For every healthcare leader striving to make the world a healthier place for the generations to come. Thank you for helping us heal our future.
*Andrew N. Garman*

# Table of Contents

## Part IV: Masterful Execution—The Fourth Cornerstone

## Part V: Putting the Competencies to Work

# *Foreword*

As we shift our leadership focus toward addressing the multitude of challenges in the post-pandemic landscape, the next edition of the Dye–Garman *Exceptional Leadership: 16 Critical Competencies for Healthcare Executives* is a valuable guide. I have often pondered whether leaders are born or made, and upon reviewing the third edition, I remain convinced that this book, with its solid framework and guidance, can empower leaders of varying aptitudes to become exceptional. It offers a proven framework to elevate leaders from their current strengths and abilities to extraordinary levels by utilizing the best-practice tools outlined within the book for assessing and enhancing critical success skills.

In this updated version of the extremely popular *Exceptional Leadership: 16 Critical Competencies for Healthcare Executives*, Carson Dye and Andrew Garman provide a contemporary perspective on the pressing demands of leadership in today's world. The third edition offers refreshed case studies accompanied by thought-provoking discussion questions and a self-reflection guide. Equally important is the inclusion of updated chapters designed to assist leaders in navigating the challenges brought on by the pandemic, as well as a guide for cultivating and retaining robust teams—undoubtedly one of today's greatest leadership challenges.

The new edition remains highly relevant in a time when the need for extraordinary, even courageous leaders is more crucial than ever. Having an updated perspective to steer the development of leaders is truly beneficial. The Dye–Garman model suggests that while the 16 competencies have remained consistent, evaluating them within the context of today's landscape is imperative. I am particularly impressed by the practical tools featured, such as the updated case studies and mini-cases with discussion questions. In addition, the focus on Diversity, Equity, Inclusion, and Belonging concepts is especially pertinent as leaders strive to attract and retain top talent. These resources enable leaders to explore real-world examples, leveraging their leadership skills and utilizing the competencies as a guide to become exceptional leaders.

In the words of Maya Angelou, "People may forget what you said, people will forget what you did, but they will never forget how you made them feel." Exceptional leaders create an environment where teams can shine and truly belong. In *Exceptional Leadership: 16 Critical Competencies for Healthcare Executives*, Dye and Garman offer us a competency model that will allow us to become the best leaders we can be and drive the positive we aspire to see.

*Denise Brooks-Williams, FACHE*
*EVP and Chief Executive Officer of*
*Care Delivery Operations Henry Ford Health*

# Foreword

OVER THE PAST decade, the rate of change in healthcare is at an unprecedented pace. Significant changes in payment policies, increased consolidation, entry of nontraditional players into the healthcare space, workforce shortages, advances in technology including telehealth and artificial technology, alongside the increases in natural disasters and public health emergencies, underscore the need for exceptional leadership to successfully navigate these changes. Carson Dye and Andy Garman's third edition of *Exceptional Leadership: 16 Critical Competencies for Healthcare Executives* provides an updated view on their highly regarded competency model on the critically important competencies necessary for exceptional leadership.

In academia, we strive to balance theory, history, and analytical and evaluative techniques with practical applications to prepare healthcare leaders. Our goal is to prepare, mentor, and coach students to take on these roles. Despite our best efforts, too often students wonder whether they have "what it takes" to be a leader. Through case study vignettes, this book helps demystify what it takes to be a leader by providing a practical guide to emerging *and* seasoned leaders. It does so by distilling leadership to behaviors, and behaviors are areas that we can all work to hone and improve regardless of our stage in career. It underscores the notion that leaders are not born nor fit squarely into one mold. Rather, developing leadership competencies is a lifelong journey built on enhancing self-awareness, developing a vision, strengthening relational and interpersonal skills, and enhancing impact through effective implementation and execution.

Dye and Garman offer an important framework for exceptional leadership that will be a valuable resource for early careerists and lifelong learners alike. As I write this, I am preparing for a new role and am appreciative of the opportunity to learn new and important insights this book offers. Instructors, students, and practitioners will undoubtedly find this easy to navigate, practical, and engaging textbook a valuable resource that they can use inside and outside of the classroom.

*Paula H. Song, PhD, Interim Dean,*
*College of Health Professions,*
*Richard M. Bracken Chair of Health Administration,*
*Virginia Commonwealth University*

# *Preface*

THERE ARE GOOD leaders, then there are *exceptional leaders.*

We wrote this sentence for our first and second editions (2006 and 2015). Since then, the amount of change in healthcare leadership development has been amazing, especially as it relates to the use of competencies. When we wrote the first edition, leadership competencies were not used in a systematic way in many healthcare organizations; by the time of the second edition, most organizations had started to use competencies in some way. The conversation and work around getting a better understanding of leadership keeps growing, and organizations have become more advanced in their approach to leadership development. Sadly, the COVID-19 pandemic upended leadership development within almost all organizations, including healthcare. Happily, as many of these organizations rebuild their approaches to leadership development, they are finding a wealth of new tools to make these initiatives more tailored, efficient, and impactful. Even though the industry still has a lot to improve, we are excited by how far it has come and its future potential. We are particularly energized by how much traction strategic talent management has gained, with leadership competencies providing an organizing framework. The most advanced of these high-performance work systems touch almost every aspect of management practices, including hiring, selection, development, performance management, promotions, and even job design. Competencies help by providing a common behavioral language for clearly communicating performance needs. And this clarity makes a difference in organizational performance—quality, patient safety, employee engagement, financial results, and community impact.

For most of us, identifying an exceptional leader is easier than explaining what makes that person exceptional. The answer to "What makes a leader exceptional?" is simple: competencies. Because we explain the term *competencies* in the Introduction, we give just a basic definition here. Leadership competencies are a set of skills, knowledge, values, and traits that guide a leader's performance, behavior, interaction, and decisions.

Any leadership book will tell you *how* to make a leader exceptional. This book offers that and more: it tells you *what* makes a leader exceptional. We define these competencies and fully explain what they mean.

In 2006, for our first edition, we set out to identify these 16 competencies for three reasons:

1. Many good leaders in healthcare really want to be great leaders, and they want it for the right reason—to make a real difference to the patients and communities they serve.
2. Most healthcare leaders do not have many mentors, do not attend many leadership programs, or are not given meaningful skill-development opportunities very often.
3. In this time often marked by the war for talent, leaders need to be better at assessing the skills and competencies of other leaders, especially those they are hiring.

At the writing of this third edition, the whole health ecosystem is going through the biggest changes it has seen in more than 50 years. Some leaders are becoming fatigued by the challenges they face, but others are excited to see the biggest opportunities in their careers to be part of remaking the entire healthcare system into a far more powerful delivery system for human health and community vitality. Also, as we think about the original reasons for our selection of the 16 competencies, we find that those reasons continue to guide our opinions.

We chose the 16 competencies for our model because (a) they are the ones most often identified by search committees as separating exceptional leaders from good leaders; (b) they relate well to other highly regarded competency sets that we have developed and/or reviewed; and (c) they drive the most effective leadership success that we have seen. And since the first and second editions, we have found that many organizations have adopted these 16 competencies both for their organizational competencies and as a curriculum guide for their internal leadership development programs. Even though their uses may have changed over the years, the competencies themselves have not. They are still the most in-demand competencies in healthcare—still the markers of exceptional leadership.

## WHY ANOTHER BOOK ON LEADERSHIP?

We asked this question in 2006 and 2015 when we wrote the first and second editions; the question remains very relevant today. Many more books have been added to the vast library of leadership literature. But many of them still belong to what Hogan and Kaiser (2005, 171) call the "troubadour" literature, or books that fill the business sections of airport bookstores. We agree with their statement that, "Despite its popularity, the troubadour tradition is a vast collection of opinions with very little supporting evidence; it is entertaining but unreliable." We did not list any titles, but we know our readers will get the point.

## Healthcare Leadership Is Different

Although many leadership issues are common across industries, healthcare has many unique leadership challenges. The relationships, life-and-death nature of the work, emotional demands, and financial challenges in this industry are different from those in other fields. COVID-19 also brought enormous challenges to healthcare, and its shock waves will echo in the field for many years to come. Because of these unique qualities, the healthcare field needs its leaders to have a different approach as well. The competencies in this book give healthcare leaders this edge.

## Healthcare Needs Great Leaders

As the healthcare industry faces the big changes brought about by COVID-19, labor shortages, value-based reimbursement, population health management, and cost and capacity pressures, as well as the coming changes from personalized medicine, consumer-driven care, and heightening expectations from our communities and other stakeholders, one of the biggest imperatives of the next decade in healthcare will be preparing leaders to handle the system changes these opportunities and challenges will bring. All of these challenges will continue in this high-stakes environment, where disruptive innovations can change the future of a healthcare organization in a heartbeat.

## The Science of Leadership Keeps Evolving

Although there has been a lot of progress in the past decade in the science of leadership assessment and development, extracting insights from the scientific literature remains difficult, and the relative value of different service vendors is hard to evaluate. Bookstores are full of books on leadership, but most reflect the views of a single successful leader, author, or firm, and many are just stories or personal observations not grounded in the growing scientific knowledge base.

In this book, wherever possible, we ground each area of leadership performance with contemporary research. In doing so, we give you the most advanced thinking on how to improve in these competencies.

## Leadership Competencies Are Not All Equally Important

When we wrote the first edition of this book, leadership competencies were not commonly used in the healthcare sector. But since then, many consulting firms, healthcare organizations, and professional associations have developed their own leadership competency models. If we compiled all the competencies from these models, we would end up with hundreds of them.

Having too many competencies is not useful for development planning. It is also not helpful for selecting leaders for different roles. We are not saying that there are only 16 competencies that matter. But we do believe that these are the ones that make the most difference between good leaders and great leaders. That's why we focus on these 16 competencies that seem to distinguish between good leadership and great leadership. If your goal is to be an exceptional leader, these are the competencies you need to master.

## Having a Leadership Competency Model Does Not Guarantee Success

Another concern with competency models is that some people put too much emphasis on them. We agree that having and using a good model is critical for improving organizational performance through leadership. But adopting a competency model does not move leadership forward all on its own. Ulrich, Zenger, and Smallwood (1999, 27) wrote about the "search for a 'holy grail' of leadership attributes" and how adopting one does not necessarily mean that leadership issues are resolved. The Exceptional Leadership Competency Model presented in this book is a practical and focused tool, but we don't claim that it is the end-all, be-all tool of leadership development.

## Leadership Development Is *Your* Responsibility

Exceptional leaders take responsibility for their own development. They don't wait for their superiors to coach them or for their organizations to provide them with opportunities. If you want to be an exceptional leader, you have to learn your development needs and find your own ways to improve on them.

## WHAT WILL YOU GAIN FROM READING THIS BOOK?

Our goal is to show you the competencies that define an exceptional leader. Throughout the book we give you tools to help you and your team develop your leadership potential and improve your organization's performance.

## A Deeper Understanding of Leadership

By reading and reflecting on each of the 16 competencies, you will gain additional insight into leadership and learn the key qualities that make leaders highly effective.

## Guidance in Coaching and Developing Skills

This book gives you practical suggestions for developing leadership skills that you can apply right away. You can use this book to plan your own development or to support others in their development. Executive coaches can use the material to help guide and shape the behavior of leaders they are coaching. Executives can use the discussion to advise and mentor their direct reports on their leadership behavior.

## Guidelines for Assessing Executive Candidates

This book is an excellent guide for assessing candidates for executive leadership roles. You can use the 16 competencies as a benchmark to create interview questions and evaluate leadership capability.

## Counsel on Avoiding Derailment

No one sets out to derail their career on purpose. But career derailments often happen. Skill deficits in any of these areas can slow down or even disrupt your leadership career. Knowing what you need to improve can help you avoid derailing your own career.

## Guidance for Physician Leadership Development

Many organizations have recognized the importance of developing physician leaders and giving them more leadership roles. This book can serve as an excellent introduction to the key behaviors of effective physician leaders.

## A Foundation for Customized Leadership Competency Models

Because the competencies in this book focus on exceptional leadership, you may find them useful as a starting point to create your own competency models.

## A Practical Foundation for Teaching Leadership

The material in this book is suitable for academic instruction—for example, as a supplement to theory-based texts. You can use the competencies as stand-alone topics, and the vignettes at the start of each chapter as conversation starters. The self-assessment and development tips also work well for career-development planning assignments. Additionally, this book can be the basis for peer-led leadership-development meetings in practice settings.

## RESOURCES FOR INSTRUCTORS

If you use this book as part of a leadership or management course, you can access excellent resources for instructors. The book's contents are built around a major case study (St. Nicholas Health System) that is followed throughout the book. This case study is complex enough to give instructors many options for using it. Sprinkled throughout the book are many questions that can be used during classroom discussion. Also, each chapter in the first four parts of the book has short case studies at its end: answer guides are available in the instructor resources. The instructor resources also include an extensive set of PowerPoints and additional discussion questions and answer guides. If you adopt this book for use in a course, resources can be requested by e-mailing hapbooks@ache.org.

*Carson F. Dye*
*Andrew N. Garman*

## REFERENCES

Hogan, R., and R. B. Kaiser. 2005. "What We Know About Leadership." *Review of General Psychology* 9 (2): 169–80.

Ulrich, D., J. Zenger, and N. Smallwood. 1999. *Results-Based Leadership*. Boston: Harvard Business School Press.

# Acknowledgments

So many people deserve mention for their role in this book. It is truly the culmination of many years of interactions in the living laboratory of leadership. My executive search career gives me almost daily interaction with exceptional leaders, and I am so privileged to have worked with so many great organizations. I hope the lack of a long litany of names from clients, candidates, and working peers does not cause concern; there are simply too many to name. Moreover, I was blessed to have worked for and with many exceptional leaders in my 20 years in four hospitals/health systems.

Let me begin with special recognition for my partner and coauthor, Andy Garman. This is our fourth book collaboration, and I truly appreciate his ability to stay grounded, to bring an appropriate academic eye and mind to our work, and to focus on what counts. His insights about leadership are really profound. This third edition has been a challenging endeavor for him because it hit him in the midst of significant work demands, but he met the challenge. Thanks, Andy—I think our team approach produces an incredibly solid product. I also thank you for your rigor in your work and your eye for detail.

As more of my work—and avocation as well—morphs into the physician leadership realm, there are many physician leaders to thank. And several of them helped in a direct way with the physician leadership chapter: John Byrnes, MD; Kathleen Forbes, MD; Kevin Casey, DO; Lily Henson, MD; Saria Saccocio, MD; Doug Spotts, MD; and Scott Ransom, DO. This chapter truly represents the "voice of the physician" and I think greatly benefits as a result.

I continue to be indebted to Jacque Sokolov, MD, my coauthor on *Developing Physician Leaders for Successful Clinical Integration* (Health Administration Press, 2013). A number of other physician leaders with whom I have worked closely have also given me thoughts and ideas, and I thank them—Imran Andrabi, MD; John Baniewicz, MD; Jeremy Blanchard, MD; Bhagwan Satiani, MD; David Tam, MD; Davin Turner, DO; and Raul Zambrano, MD.

The book has been the anchor for an online program at the American College of Healthcare Executives since its first publication, and I want to thank the many participants who provided suggestions that helped frame the third edition.

My respect and appreciation for the staff of Health Administration Press never seems to end. It is so clear to me that our field is blessed to have this publisher serving us.

My daughter Emily Dye is always great help with models and graphs and the visual "things." She also works in the healthcare field and has had many interactions with some truly exceptional leaders. Also, my daughter Liesl continues to provide great input on thoughts and logic. I am also deeply appreciative of the rest of my family—wife Joaquina; two other great daughters, Carly and Blakely; and sons-in-law Jeremy, Phil, and Nick.

—*Carson F. Dye*


As I reflect on this revision, I am struck by how much the world has changed since we worked on the second edition in 2015, including people's expectations of our healthcare leaders. Extrapolating these trends forward, I anticipate challenging times ahead, with the importance of capable, values-driven leadership only increasing. It has been gratifying to watch Carson's work in this area flourish, and I am glad to have made a contribution to its scientific foundations through this collaboration. Thank you, Carson, for all you do to bring this wisdom to the field through your work.

I am only able to make these types of contributions because of the support of the people and organizations who help me pay my bills. I am particularly grateful to the leadership of RUSH, RUSH University, the College of Health Sciences, and the Health Systems Management department for providing such a supportive environment to work in since 1998, and to the International Hospital Federation's Geneva Sustainability Centre, which is one of my greatest sources of hope for the future.

Thanks, as always, to the American College of Healthcare Executives for championing healthcare management as a profession, with its own unique competencies, values, responsibilities, and contributions to pursuing a high-value learning health system. Another special thanks to the many leaders who have willingly contributed their time and expertise to the leadership research projects we have pursued over the years.

This revision benefited tremendously from the editorial guidance of our colleagues at Health Administration Press. Thank you very much once again for all your help, support, and patience.

Lastly, I am grateful to my wife Debbie for being the wonderful person she is and joining me as we walk each other home; and to our children, Emily and Tyler, for being the wonderful people they are, and for all I know they will do to heal our future.

—*Andy Garman*

# *Introduction*

WE CAN ALL think of people who seem to have been born to lead. They are the ones who stand out in every organization because they have a knack for making things happen and achieving anything they set their mind to. We often expect these leaders to succeed long before we see their performance results.

Many other leaders become exceptional over time, through hard work and self-development. They recognize their strengths and development needs, gain the experience they need, and find mentors who can help them make the most of these crucible experiences.

For both types of leaders—the "born" and the "made"—the path to exceptional leadership is faster with a good roadmap. A good competency model (see Exhibit 1) provides this roadmap.

One of the main reasons competencies work so well is that they are practical and observable. Dye (2023) wrote that the competency theory of leadership actually "enables leaders to 'see' the behaviors ideal for competent leadership.

---

**Exhibit 1  What Is a Competency?**

Competency has many definitions, but David McClelland's 1973 article is widely considered the original and most authoritative source. When he wrote this article, intelligence and skills tests were the main tools used to make selection decisions. McClelland's work aimed to go beyond a narrow, skills-based definition of success and explore broader, underlying characteristics of individuals that could predict success.

In short, competencies are a broad collection of knowledge, skills, abilities, and characteristics. They include values (such as ethics and integrity), cognitive skills (such as thinking and problem solving), interpersonal skills (such as communicating and listening), embracing diversity (such as tolerance and respect), and change management (such as strategic planning and risk taking).

As deeper-level constructs, competencies are not something learned from a one-day training workshop or a class. They involve gradual improvements over time as a result of mindful practice, feedback, and more practice.

---

For example, the trait theory of leadership states that a leader is an effective communicator; the competency theory provides specific behavioral examples of what effective communication is." This is why many organizations have adopted the use of competencies.

Competencies can also help people who are in charge of selecting leaders. They can use competencies to evaluate and hire candidates based on their performance and potential. A bad hiring decision at the senior level can be disastrous for any organization, and a clear understanding of exactly what comprises highly effective leadership will minimize this risk.

## EXCEPTIONAL LEADERSHIP COMPETENCY MODEL

This book is based on the 16 leadership competencies that we have identified as essential to exceptional leadership in healthcare. We arrived at this list through the following steps:

1. We reviewed the competency lists that boards and executives used in their executive searches.
2. We narrowed down the list to the competencies that consistently distinguished the leaders who were considered the best performers—those who made the final rounds and who were usually hired.
3. We interviewed experienced search consultants (with over 100 years of combined search experience) who specialized in healthcare. We asked each of them the following questions:
   - What are the most important competencies your clients look for when hiring new executives?
   - Think of the three best executives you have ever placed in your search careers. What leadership competencies did these leaders have that set them apart from the rest?

Each of the competencies we retained were identified by multiple search consultants.

4. We also asked similar questions about leadership competencies to healthcare chief executive officers (CEOs) and executive coaches.
5. To refine our definitions of these 16 competencies, we compared them with systematic reviews of leadership research as well as the competency lists of well-known consulting firms.

Our end goal was to develop a competency model that was focused enough to help aspiring exceptional leaders concentrate on their most important development opportunities and rich enough to be revisited many times in the years to come.

After two decades of use, examination, and application, the 16 competencies have stood the test of time. To confirm the accuracy and relevance of the competency model for this third edition, we:

- interviewed several CEOs and other senior healthcare leaders, human resource executives, and leadership development executives about their use and acceptance of the competencies in the model;
- reviewed uses of the model with organizations and with executive search and consulting firms;
- considered the many comments of support for the 16 competencies we have received over these years from individual readers; and
- commissioned a multivariate correlation of the model with a well-known leadership personality assessment tool of an international organizational psychology firm.

Since the first and second editions of the book were published in 2006 and 2015, this competency model has been widely adopted and adapted. It has been the basis for several leadership development programs, some sponsored by the American College of Healthcare Executives and some by other associations and individual healthcare organizations. The authors have received messages from many individuals who said the book deepened their personal understanding of leadership and improved their leadership skills. Several organizations have used the book as the core curriculum in internal physician leadership programs. A number of colleges and universities have used the book as a text for leadership classes and other related courses. Consulting and executive search firms have used the model to evaluate leadership and assess candidates for leadership positions. Outplacement firms have used the book to help advise their clients. The model has been used in several settings for physician leadership assessment and development. The competencies have been used in many situations as a foundation for developing behavioral interview questions in selection situations. The responses from many of these individuals have been positive about the effectiveness, relevance, and application of this leadership competency model. One review summarized the thoughts of many others: "The book is concise and very clearly structured, making it a quick and enjoyable read for executives in just about any industry." Another review praised "the way the charts that were highlighted explained the good as well as the bad points for each point that was being explained in that chapter."

The use of leadership competency models has also been shown to be a hallmark of excellent companies in many industries. A comprehensive study of numerous organizations done by Hewitt (Gandossy et al. 2007) showed that those companies with better financial performance were likely to use competencies as the basis for succession management, external hiring, and inside promotions.

One of the main motivations for the authors to develop the Exceptional Leadership Competency Model in the first edition was their concern that most competency models had lists of competencies that were far too long to be practical. At that time, two of the commercially available competency models from consulting firms had competencies numbering 68 and 128. We felt that those lists were unmanageable and, in some cases, specific competencies were redundant. Interestingly, since the publication of the first book, most competency models have *shortened* their lists, which has made them more user-friendly. *Talent management* has also become a popular term in all industries, and most of these programs are built on competency frameworks. A 2011 study by the RBL Group of firms such as IBM, General Mills, Procter & Gamble, PepsiCo, and Eli Lilly concluded, "Top companies have a defined competency model that describes a unified theory of what leaders at their organization should know, be, and do. And they use their competency models in all phases of talent and leadership development." To be functional, competency models have to be concise enough to be usable and targeted enough to have meaning.

## AN OVERVIEW OF THE FOUR CORNERSTONES AND THE 16 COMPETENCIES

We have organized the 16 competencies into four domains, which we call the *cornerstones* of exceptional leadership:

Cornerstone 1: Well-Cultivated Self-Awareness
Cornerstone 2: Compelling Vision
Cornerstone 3: A Real Way With People
Cornerstone 4: Masterful Execution

These cornerstones support our leadership model and are placed on a foundation of a healthy self-concept, which is discussed later in this introduction. Exhibit 2 illustrates this foundation model.

**Exhibit 2  The Four Cornerstones and Healthy Self-Concept Foundation**

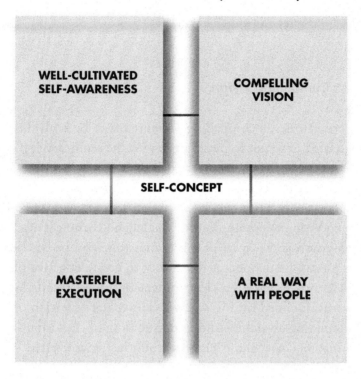

## Cornerstone 1: Well-Cultivated Self-Awareness

*Self-awareness* means knowing yourself as a leader—especially your strengths, limitations, hot buttons, and blind spots. Developing self-awareness requires leaders to think and feel on two levels. First, leaders must develop the ability to gather accurate, high-quality feedback from the work environment. Second, leaders must reflect with an open mind on what that feedback means to them and to their leadership performance.

While these processes may sound simple, in reality they are not. We all get some feedback from the environment, and we all accept it with some open-mindedness. The extent of both this environment and our openness makes the difference between good leadership and exceptional leadership. Exceptional leaders make sure their environment is rich in feedback (see Chapter 20 for tips on how to create a feedback-rich environment) and internalize the feedback they receive.

High performance in the area of self-awareness also involves mastering two competencies: Leading With Conviction and Using Emotional Intelligence. You can think of personal conviction as the driving force that guides you in serving a larger purpose; emotional intelligence, on the other hand, involves the management of that purpose in the relationships you create.

## Cornerstone 2: Compelling Vision

Of the four cornerstones, a compelling *vision* tends to be both the most visible and the most related to senior leadership roles. At the senior level, if leaders reach their limits before achieving their career goals, it is usually because they have not mastered one or more of the competencies in this cornerstone.

Three competencies make up this cornerstone associated with exceptional leadership: Developing Vision, Communicating Vision, and Earning Trust And Loyalty.

Developing vision is the heart of this cornerstone and begins this section of the book. Vision can be defined as the ability to create effective plans for your organization's future, based on a clear understanding of trends, uncertainties, risks, and rewards. Defined in this way, we can separate creation of vision from the process of building awareness and understanding of the vision (i.e., communicating vision) as well as gaining support from the "unconverted" (i.e., earning trust and loyalty).

## Cornerstone 3: A Real Way With People

This cornerstone relates to implementation—making things happen through people and through process.

*Interpersonal relations* are a key part of the leader's role, and most leaders who have some experience already have a fairly well-developed set of interpersonal skills. At a minimum, most leaders understand that you can attract more flies with honey than with vinegar, that people care about more than just their paycheck, and that interpersonal conflicts rarely resolve themselves on their own. That said, our experience leads us to conclude that (1) outstanding leaders usually have outstanding interpersonal skills, and (2) most leaders have some room for growth in the area of interpersonal relations.

The interpersonal domain can be divided into five competencies: Listening Like You Mean It, Giving Great Feedback, Mentoring, Developing High-Performing Teams, and Energizing Staff.

In each case, our focus is on how to refine an already strong skill set to the level of outstanding performance. We start this section with a chapter on listening, which in many ways is the unifying characteristic of this cornerstone. In describing what makes an executive effective, Peter Drucker (2004) identified eight practices and just one rule: "Listen first, speak last."

## Cornerstone 4: Masterful Execution

The final cornerstone involves *execution*—where the rubber meets the road in getting activities assigned to strategies, decisions made, tasks accomplished, and agendas advanced.

Leaders are ultimately judged by what they get done. Regardless of the leadership competencies they display, the true measure of their impact is the success they bring to their organizations.

Although success in execution is strongly influenced by the quality of a leader's working relationships, it is also influenced by the approaches the leader uses. The six competencies that best distinguish the highest performing leaders in this domain are Generating Informal Power, Building True Consensus, Mindful Decision Making, Driving Results, Stimulating Creativity, and Cultivating Adaptability. We examine each of these in turn.

The model is illustrated in Exhibit 3 where the 16 competencies are shown in each of their cornerstones.

## HOW IS THIS BOOK STRUCTURED?

The book has five parts. The first four introduce each of the 16 competencies in the leadership competency model. For individuals wishing to enhance their leadership performance, these four parts provide for a very introspective look at the specific competencies and give personalized counsel in each. The fifth part is more macro in scope and looks at the competency model within the context of the organization. The book opens with the introduction of the St. Nicholas Health System Case Study. The case is intended to provide a context in which to place the leadership competencies. It provides a context for the vignettes that open each chapter and can be used to help tie all of the concepts together. However, each of the chapters can also stand alone; they can be read without the benefit of the introductory case, and in any sequence the reader chooses.

**Exhibit 3 Exceptional Leadership Competency Model**

Each chapter is organized around the following sections:

- *Opening vignette.* This section provides an example of the type of situation in which leaders can shine if they demonstrate a mastery of the competency.
- *Definition of the competency.* This section explains what the competency is and why it is so important.
- *How highly effective leaders demonstrate the competency.* Here we describe, in specific details, what extraordinary leadership looks like when the competency is mastered.
- *When the competency is not all it could be.* Here we describe the common skill deficits that prevent good leaders from being great leaders in this competency.
- *Misuse and overuse: how the competency can work against you.* Sometimes leaders get into trouble because they overdo it. Here we describe what problems can arise for overdoing or misusing a given competency.

- *Finding role models.* One of the very best ways to learn new skills is to find a master to help you. In this section, we tell you where you are most likely to find people who have mastered the competency.
- *Additional opportunities for personal development.* Not all leadership development is equally effective. Here we provide options for developing a competency area, focusing on what has been shown to work best and what our colleagues and clients tell us has been most helpful to them.
- *Think About It.* These brief sections provide additional opportunities for reflection and study for each competency and are provided at the end of each competency chapter.

The final section, Putting the Competencies to Work, provides practical tools for using the competency model to drive improved leadership performance. Chapter 17, Systems Approaches to Leadership Development, summarizes the evidence base supporting high-performance leadership development systems. Chapter 18, Leadership Coaches, provides insight into the world of executive coaching and gives specific tips on how to select, use, and best benefit from coaching. Chapter 19, Mentors: How to Find and Work with Them, presents ways to best benefit from the use of mentors. Chapter 20, Developing a Feedback-Rich Working Environment, describes how to upgrade one's workplace and work culture to maximize its learning value. Chapter 21, Physician Leadership Development and Competencies, addresses the rapidly evolving world of physician leadership and presents special circumstances that surround the movement into leadership by physicians. Finally, Chapter 22, Final Questions About the Exceptional Leadership Model, discusses how different competency models can be "mapped" or compared to one another, and explores some of the questions about leadership competency models that arose from readers of the first two editions. The first 16 chapters look at leadership from the perspective of what an individual does as a leader and are well suited for individual growth as well as coaching and leadership development within a larger organizational context. The final six chapters address many of the broader and more contemporary issues that surround the practice of using leadership competency models.

## Appendixes

In the appendixes, we have assembled a wealth of additional tools to help you along the path of personal development.

Appendix A provides a set of self-reflection questions, which can help you prioritize your development by assessing your strengths and development needs. Appendix B provides a framework for structuring, implementing, and monitoring your leadership self-development plan. Appendix C provides behavioral interview questions that can be used in interviewing and assessing candidates for leadership positions.

## SELF-CONCEPT: THE FOUNDATION

As with physical cornerstones, the four cornerstones of exceptional leadership need a solid foundation. In the case of leadership, this foundation is a healthy self-concept.

### The Critical Importance of Self-Concept

To be an exceptional leader and to perform at the highest level, it is vital that you have a healthy *self-concept*. Having a healthy self-concept means you agree with each of the following:

- You are satisfied with your place in the world and feel that you have a purpose in life.
- You feel a sense of control over your life and destiny.
- You are confident in your ability to achieve what you set out to do.
- You have a positive self-image.
- You feel comfortable with how you relate to others.

More simply, self-concept is your own understanding of and comfort level about yourself. Some people may refer to self-concept as self-esteem, or self-confidence, or self-worth. Regardless of the terminology, the message is the same: If you are content and happy with who you are and what you have accomplished, you are comfortable with others as well and are fully accepting of their achievements and contributions, regardless of whether those contributions may be considered to be of higher value than yours.

We have been disappointed in the lack of attention that this topic receives. Most leadership development courses and their content material focus mainly on behaviors and competencies. Without a healthy self-concept, the other leadership competencies at best will feel unnatural and at worst will never be mastered.

In the words of one well-known CEO, "I can usually tell more about leaders and their potential through learning how they perceive themselves than in any other way." Leaders with a positive self-concept do not have to tear down others to bring themselves up. They rarely yell, scream, or curse, and they do not feel the need to play political games for their own gain. Their value systems foster a positive regard for others because they first have a high, but appropriate, regard for themselves.

We consider positive self-concept a prerequisite for exceptional leadership because it influences every aspect of a leader's effectiveness. Self-concept makes its most visible difference in the way leaders handle success and failure and work with others.

### Successes and Failures

Highly effective leaders are driven to achieve, but they also have control over their drive. They enjoy their accomplishments and take pride in them. Failures and setbacks may upset them, but they do not tear them apart.

Leaders with a poor self-concept see accomplishments as simple milestones—expected points of passage on the way to other landmarks. They rarely appreciate praise given to their organization or community. These leaders are often said to be out to prove something.

A similar phenomenon occurs with failures. Leaders with high self-regard view their failures in a balanced way—sure, there is pain in failing, but there is also the chance to learn from mistakes. Failures will not stop great leaders from making bold decisions in the future; instead, these leaders will continue to move forward but do so in a more informed way. Leaders with low self-regard do not see failures in the same way. They blame failures on others and on bad luck, and they seldom learn from such mistakes.

## Working with Others

The more accepting leaders are of themselves, the better they are at accepting others. A leader's ability to accept others creates a climate of psychological safety in the workplace. A safe climate allows people to receive and use constructive feedback better because they will not be distracted by feelings of personal vulnerability. Conversely, if people feel that their job is at risk, they are much more likely to act defensively, with self-preservation as their main goal and the good of the team or organization as a secondary consideration.

A healthy self-concept also helps to encourage and embrace diversity in the workplace. Leaders who have a solid self-concept are more tolerant and accepting of people who have different backgrounds and beliefs. One of the hallmarks of exceptional leadership is the willingness and ability to assemble teams made up of diverse individuals. These leaders know that having such a team is a great advantage. Today's great leaders must continually incorporate diversity initiatives into their strategies; a strong self-concept makes doing this much easier.

Make no mistake: leaders can go far *without* a healthy self-concept. We have observed several leaders who have a low sense of self-worth but still reach top positions in healthcare. They may even be successful throughout their entire careers. In fact, some are driven overachievers, and others are absolute perfectionists or are compulsively controlling. However, these leaders' achievements typically come at the expense of others. They use tactics such as fear, intimidation, and political manipulation that can damage an otherwise positive organizational culture. Their direct reports are unlikely to reach their full potential, and there are limits on how far people will follow these kinds of leaders.

We are clearly not alone in this perspective. A stream of research has emerged that links self-regard to effectiveness. Numerous studies have found significant connections between self-concept (termed "core self-evaluations" in the social sciences) and job performance, job satisfaction, and thriving at work (Judge and Bono 2000; Kleine, Rudolph, and Zacher 2019; Wu and Griffen 2011). Perhaps even more telling is that self-concept may also determine how much mentoring leaders receive during their career (Hezlett 2003), how effectively leaders can hear and use feedback on their performance (Bono and Colbert 2005), how well they do in training programs (Stanhope, Pond, and Surface 2012), and how capable leaders are to recognize and pursue strategic opportunities on behalf of their organizations (Hiller and Hambrick 2005).

## What to Do if Your Self-Concept Needs Strengthening

If you think your self-concept foundation could use some work, we recommend that you make this work your top leadership development priority. That might mean putting this book aside for a while, or at least not starting with these competencies as your main focus. A positive self-concept is not something you can get from a book, but we can suggest some helpful first steps.

### Consider How You Feel About Yourself

Are you satisfied with your life? Do you enjoy who you are, or do you have a persistent sense of regret? What about your career? Do you feel proud of your achievements, or bad about the opportunities you may have missed? When you accomplish something, can you take pride in it, or do you tend to see every achievement as nothing more than a step toward some bigger goal? When you fail at something, can you embrace the lessons learned, or do you just blame yourself for trying in the first place? When someone else disappoints you, are you able to see their side, or do you find yourself quickly turning against them? If you were to learn that this day was your last, would you feel you had lived your life well?

The more personal discomfort you have with yourself, the more room you have to grow in the area of self-concept, and the more likely it is that this development should be your first priority.

### Ask Those Closest to You for Their Candid Feedback

Consult a significant other, family member, or spiritual confidante to seek their opinion of your self-concept. Listen to them with an open mind, and try to accept what they say as accurate. Often the people who know us well know us better than we know ourselves. Remember also that perceptions are often more important than reality.

### Build on Your Positive Qualities

Focus on your positive physical, mental, and emotional qualities. What are you good at? What do you do well? What do you like about yourself? Use these positive concepts to balance out the aspects you feel less positive about. List your accomplishments. Celebrate achievements. Congratulate yourself on things you do well.

### Seek to Understand Your "Dark" Side

Having a healthy self-concept does not mean that you have no weak spots or hot buttons. But it does mean that you recognize your vulnerabilities so that you can prevent them from undermining you. Understanding your "dark" side requires the discipline to face your vulnerabilities, examine how they may have interfered with your effectiveness in the past, and learn how to spot the warning signs and what to do when you see them.

### Enlist Some Help

Unlike the competencies in this book, self-concept may *not* work as well as a self-development project. Getting help from a coach, spiritual counselor, therapist, or other professional with specialized training can make a big difference in the speed of your progress.

## A FINAL WORD

With a mastery of these competencies, you will have the potential to be an effective leader; however, you should be prepared for the process to take a lot of time and effort (see Exhibit 4). To master these leadership competencies, you will need to invest time to reflect on how you practice each competency. You may also need to develop and maintain reliable and accurate feedback mechanisms in your workplace.

**Exhibit 4  Is a Competent Leader an Effective Leader?**

Not necessarily. Competence is best described as the *capacity* to perform. To translate competency into *actual* performance requires both motivation and opportunity. Putting in the time and energy required for success requires motivation; we all face barriers to success, but exceptional leaders overcome these barriers more often. Opportunity relates to the environment in which leadership takes place; some environments are conducive to successful leadership, while others are not. We have seen exceptional leaders enter organizations and then leave because the environments were not set up to allow them to be successful.

That said, our experience tells us you do get what you give. If you put in the time and effort, you can become a more successful leader. In the process, your ability to help others and your organization will expand along with your influence. In short, it is time well spent.

---

You will also need to master the ability to maintain your ground during times of substantial turbulence.

We wish you the best on your self-development and your career, and we hope you find this book to be a helpful guide along the way

## REFERENCES

Bono, J. E., and A. E. Colbert. 2005. "Understanding Responses to Multi-Source Feedback: The Role of Core Self-Evaluations." *Personnel Psychology* 58: 171–203.

Drucker, P. F. 2004. "What Makes an Effective Executive?" *Harvard Business Review* 82 (6): 58–63.

Dye, C. 2023. *Leadership in Healthcare: Essential Values and Skills*, 4th ed. Chicago: Health Administration Press.

Gandossy, R., M. Salob, S. Greenslade, J. Younger, and R. Guarnieri. 2007. "The Top Companies for Leaders 2007." Hewitt & Associates in partnership with *Fortune* and the RBL group. Lincolnshire, IL: Hewitt & Associates.

Hezlett, S. A. 2003. "Who Receives Mentoring? A Meta-Analysis of Employee Demographic, Career History, and Individual Differences Correlates." Unpublished doctoral dissertation, University of Minnesota, Minneapolis.

Hiller, N. J., and D. C. Hambrick. 2005. "Conceptualizing Executive Hubris: The Role of (Hyper-) Core Self-Evaluations in Strategic Decision-Making." *Strategic Management Journal* 26: 297–319.

Judge, T. A., and J. E. Bono. 2000. "Relationship of Core Self-Evaluation Traits—Self-Esteem, Generalized Self-Efficacy, Locus of Control, and Emotional Stability—with Job Satisfaction and Job Performance: A Meta-Analysis." *Journal of Applied Psychology* 86 (1): 80–92.

Kleine, A., C. Rudolph, and H. Zacher. 2019. "Thriving at Work: A Meta-analysis." *Journal of Organizational Behavior* 40 (9–10): 973–99.

McClelland, D. C. 1973. "Testing for Competence Rather Than 'Intelligence.'" *American Psychologist* 28 (1): 1–14.

The RBL Group. 2011. "Top Companies for Leaders." http://rblip. s3.amazonaws .com/Articles/top-companies-2011-research%20report.pdf.

Stanhope, D. S., S. B. Pond III, and E. A. Surface. 2012. "Core Self-Evaluations and Training Effectiveness: Prediction Through Motivational Intervening Mechanisms." *Journal of Applied Psychology* 98 (5): 820–31.

Wu, C.-H., and M. A. Griffen. 2011. "Longitudinal Relationships Between Core Self-Evaluations and Job Satisfaction." *Journal of Applied Psychology* 97 (2): 331–42.

# St. Nicholas Health System Case Study

THE FOLLOWING CASE study will be used throughout the book to introduce many specific aspects of competencies. This opening portion provides substantive background on the organization and its leadership team. Please note that the case is fictional, and any similarities to real events, locations, or individuals, living or deceased, are purely coincidental.

## INTRODUCTION

The St. Nicholas Health System is a prominent integrated health delivery system that comprises the following components:

- St. Nicholas Medical Center, which has 525 beds
- Suburban Western Health Center, which has 225 beds
- Suburban East Health Center, which has 185 beds
- Three small rural hospitals, all at least an hour drive away
- The St. Nicholas Medical Group, which has 630 employed physicians and 90 advanced practitioners
- St. Nicholas Health Plan, with almost 500,000 covered lives
- St. Nicholas Ambulatory Care Company, which was established in the past year and includes home care and visiting nurse services, two freestanding emergency departments (EDs), three urgent care centers, two health centers, multiple outpatient clinic locations, a durable medical equipment company, several ambulatory pharmacies, and a hospice program.

St. Nicholas operates in Barkley, a bustling city of 3.5 million people and a highly competitive healthcare market. Barkley is an economically vibrant city, and its residents appreciate its many parks and proximity to a large lakefront. As in many large US cities, however, there are significant health and life expectancy disparities between different neighborhoods. To help address these issues, St. Nicholas has implemented several community programs aimed at addressing social determinants of health. Although the city's population has remained relatively stable, there is a growing influx of immigrants from regions impacted by climate change.

## ORGANIZATIONAL STRUCTURE

The health system's executive leadership group (ELG), led by CEO Elizabeth Parris, is detailed in Exhibit 1.

The ELG holds scheduled meetings every other week on Tuesdays from 7:30 to 11:30 a.m. with a predetermined agenda that is focused 80 percent on tactical operations and 20 percent on strategic initiatives. Parris chairs the meetings, and in her absence, Miguel Jimenez takes over. The agenda items are covered first, with Parris's report always first on the list. If time allows, the group moves around the table, allowing each individual time to discuss additional items. Some of the group members have tactfully remarked to one another that the meeting is primarily a "show and tell" session, and that missing it is not a significant issue.

Among the many types of dynamics inside the group is the fact that following every Tuesday meeting, many of the group members spend additional time splintering off into different sub-groups to discuss additional topics. Two of these sub-groups have become very close-knit and frequently spend time together outside of work, including going to lunch and socializing with their significant others. One of these groups is composed of CFO Samantha Stoman, senior VP of business development Dave Damron, and executive director of the employed physician practices Dr. Maria Borman. The other group consists of COO Miguel Jimenez, senior VP of medical affairs Dr. Howard James, and VP of legal services Terry Tolls.

The Suburban West and East hospitals are crucial to the success of the system and are both profitable. However, their administrators, Mary Moses and Wayne Walters, respectively, do not feel fully integrated into the executive group. They have great autonomy in managing their operations and focus mainly on internal matters. They are in regular contact with Dr. Borman concerning the physicians employed by the network. In addition, the three rural hospitals managed by Duhal Malinka have minimal involvement with the system and operate independently due to their geographical distance. Although there has been some discussion of having Malinka oversee the two suburban hospitals, Jimenez has been quietly vying to have them report to him directly because of their closer ties to the downtown medical center.

At St. Nicholas, executives and their direct reports collaborate extensively to achieve their goals. Parris is a hands-off leader who takes most of her counsel from Dr. James, Stoman, and Damron.

**Exhibit 1 Organizational Chart for St. Nicholas Senior Leadership**

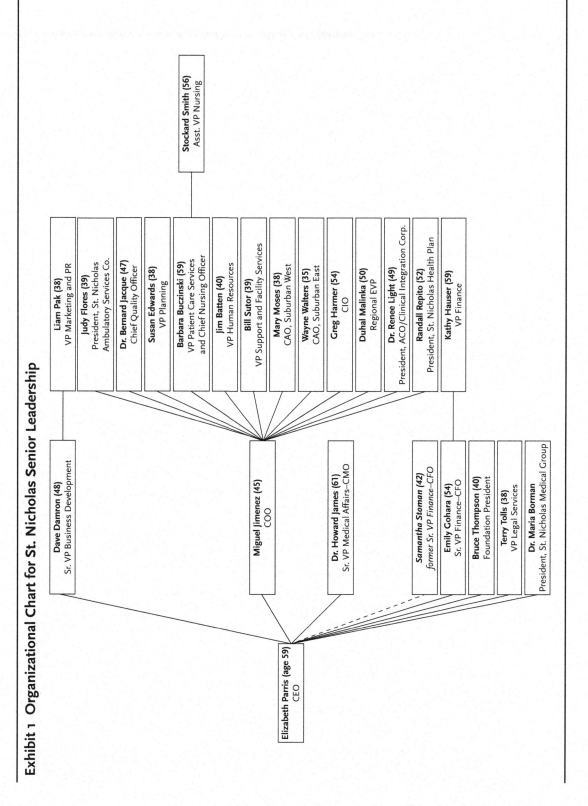

Parris schedules biweekly meetings with her direct reports but interacts with Dr. James much more frequently and visits Stoman's office daily. Although she does not often have lunch, she will go to a long lunch every week or so with Damron.

The entire executive leadership group has been employed at St. Nicholas for at least three years. Parris has been at St. Nicholas for eight years, the last three as CEO. The previous CEO had been in the position for 20 years.

Some of the executives—such as VP of support services Bill Sutor, VP of finance Kathy Hauser, VP of planning Susan Edwards, assistant VP of nursing Stockard Smith, and VP of patient care services Barbara Buczinski—have been with St. Nicholas for more than 20 years and have never worked for any other healthcare organization.

## STRATEGIC CONTEXT

St. Nicholas's current context includes the following trends:

### Demographics and Community

◆ Population growth and diversification that has historically tracked the national average, and has more recently begun increasing
◆ An elderly population that is growing faster than the national average
◆ A thriving urban university community, including two Commission on Accreditation of Healthcare Management Education–accredited master's programs, one in a school of public health and health professions and the other in a business school
◆ Significant city and state deficits, caused in part by pension-related financial obligations (city and state) as well as a history of privatization decisions driven by short-term financial needs (city)
◆ Ongoing civic efforts to position the city as a national leader in innovation and sustainability.

### Operations and Staffing

◆ An up-to-date electronic medical record system (EMR) and a strong cybersecurity track record
◆ Significant growth in employed physicians (currently 75 percent of medical staff is employed, and half of the independents have some type of arrangement

with the system, such as co-management models) with plans to increase the number of employed physicians substantially in the next two years
- Relatively low turnover in comparison to other health systems of its size, with many long-term employees, and relatively little unionization
- A tightening labor market, such that recruiting is becoming one of the largest constraints on future growth
- Increasing pressure for the demographic profile of St. Nicholas leaders and providers to better reflect the communities they serve
- Increasing expectations from current and prospective employees to support work–life balance

## Business

- A two-year trend of 4 percent declines in inpatient admissions
- Twenty percent growth in year-over-year ED visits (including the freestanding EDs) prior to COVID and flat since then
- Significant growth in ambulatory encounters and explosive growth in telehealth
- Significant growth in competition from nontraditional providers, particularly in primary care
- Increasing attention from the capital markets to how the organization represents its corporate social responsibilities, as well as perceived risks associated with environmental, social, and governance (ESG) considerations.

## Strategic

- Involvement of the St. Nicholas Health Plan in the health insurance exchanges, the state Medicaid program, and the development of a clinical integration corporation
- Consolidation of multiple employed physician offices into larger ambulatory buildings
- Pursuing expanded use of data analytics and the transparency of data between health plans, providers, and employers
- Considering a tiered and narrow network to offer to several local large employers
- Beginning involvement in some multi-payer collaboratives
- Pursuing increased growth in the post-acute market

As of now, the Barkley market is dominated by three major healthcare systems. St. Nicholas has a strong presence in inpatient care, particularly in heart, vascular, and orthopedic services. However, the system has lost its primary oncology physician group to one of its competitors, resulting in a decline in its cancer services. It is worth noting that St. Nicholas is the sole healthcare system in the Barkley region that operates its own health plan. Additionally, the system has experience working with Medicare Advantage plans.

Following a recent update of its strategic plan, St. Nicholas's major current strategic initiatives include:

- Bundled payment programs in heart and orthopedics with four large employers
- Physician-led clinical integration corporation
- Focus on increased growth of Medicare Advantage plans
- Value-based payment program trial
- Population health initiatives
- Continuum of care project, including emphasis on reduction in readmissions and building stronger ties to nonacute care lines of business
- Targeted quality improvement programs
- Expansion of physician leadership dyadic models
- Growing physician employment by 25 percent; employed physicians will represent 90 percent of the medical staff
- A comprehensive employee engagement and recruiting plan, including pursuit of "best places to work" designations as well as education partnerships to address areas of high workforce need
- Major work transformation projects in nursing and other clinical areas
- LEAN projects in all inpatient facilities

## TEAM DYNAMICS

As our case opens, CEO Elizabeth Parris has recently announced to the ELG that Samantha Stoman, the senior VP of finance, is leaving to join HealthAmerica, a $15 billion health system in the Southeast, as its senior VP and CFO. Stoman was in charge of managed care contracting during her tenure at the organization. Dave Damron, the senior VP of business development, has expressed interest in taking over the managed care function after Stoman's departure. Meanwhile, Kathy Hauser, the VP of finance, has approached Parris to express her interest in the CFO role.

After a thorough search, an external candidate, Emily Gohara, was hired as the new senior VP of finance and CFO. Gohara was selected over two other external candidates who were also strong contenders; Hauser was eliminated from consideration in the first round of interviews. Although not openly discussed among the ELG, many preferred the other external candidates to Gohara. Some believed that the main reason she got the final offer was that she worked for a CEO who was Parris's former mentor. They also felt that the interview process was based more on personal fit than professional skills. Jim Batten, the VP of human resources, had recommended to Parris that they use a leadership competency model in the selection process but had not been able to implement one in time.

Parris hoped that hiring Gohara would bring some fresh perspectives to the team and help them prepare for St. Nicholas's future. She knew that some of the team members were not supportive of Gohara's appointment, but she did not expect the decision to affect the team's cohesion and collaboration so much. In discussing the team's new dynamics with Batten, they decided the timing was right to implement the more comprehensive approach to team and leadership development they had been talking about for years.

## INDIVIDUAL STYLES AND APPROACHES IN THE SENIOR TEAM

Several weeks after Gohara started as CFO, Batten presented a comprehensive proposal to the senior team to begin integrating leadership competencies as well as a greater focus on individual work styles into St. Nicholas's talent management program. Batten gave the following remarks to the group:

> Today I am introducing a new talent management program that will align all our efforts with our strategic goals. We have done some of this work before, but we have not connected the dots or linked them to our business objectives. To get there, we'll need to base our talent management decisions on a clear set of organizational competencies, and match competencies to positions. Having a competency model will help us communicate better about performance and how to improve it. The competency model we will be using reflects the latest leadership research and provides practical and observable behavioral indicators. This will help us set clearer and more consistent standards for success, enhance our understanding and evaluation of leadership, and ultimately help reduce the risk of making avoidable hiring and promotion mistakes.
>
> In addition to competencies, our team will also benefit from knowing more about our individual work styles. That's why I asked you to complete the style assessment before our meeting today. The assessment is based on

the DISC model, which some of you may have seen before. In your packets you will find the results of your own assessment, as well as the results from the rest of the team.

The survey Batten had them take was based on the DISC model with its four styles summarized below:

I. Dominance D
II. Influence I
III. Steadiness S
IV. Conscientiousness C

**Dominance:** A more direct style in terms of interactions with others; more of a driver and at times, demanding; goal orientation and results are hallmarks of this style, with some risk of too little attention to individual interests and needs of others.

**Influence:** A friendly and outgoing style, very people-focused; gets things done through the quality of relationships they are able to cultivate; some risk of being viewed as soft or easy to persuade.

**Steadiness:** A style focused on sincerity and stability; loyal to the organization and its mission as well as trusted colleagues; values traditions; some risk of having too little focus on the need for evolution and change.

**Conscientiousness:** An analytical, meticulous, and controlled style; attentive to detail; tends to be highly organized; some risk of spending too much time "in the weeds" or having difficulty communicating with people less knowledgeable about a given area.

Equipped with this work style information, as well as an understanding that St. Nicholas would be adopting a leadership competency model, the senior team began to reflect on recent experiences from which they might be able to learn through the use of these new tools.

# A Look at the St. Nicholas Senior Management Group and Their Work Styles

| Executive | Title | Work Style |
|-----------|-------|------------|
| Elizabeth Parris | CEO | C |
| Dr. Howard James | Senior VP, Medical Affairs | S |
| Miguel Jimenez | COO | D |
| Samantha Stoman | Former Senior VP, Finance | D |
| Emily Gohara | New Senior VP, Finance | C |
| Kathy Hauser | VP, Finance | D |
| Dave Damron | Senior VP, Business Development | D |
| Susan Edwards | VP, Planning | C |
| Liam Pak | VP, Marketing and Public Relations | I |
| Dr. Bernard Jacque | Chief Quality Officer | C |
| Barbara Buczinski | VP, Patient Care Services | S |
| Stockard Smith | Assistant VP, Nursing | I |
| Jim Batten | VP, Human Resources | C |
| Bruce Thompson | Foundation President | I |
| Terry Tolls | VP, Legal Services | C |
| Bill Sutor | VP, Support and Facility Services | S |
| Mary Moses | Administrator, Suburban West | S |
| Wayne Walters | Administrator, Suburban East | I |
| Judy Flores | President, St. Nicholas Ambulatory Services | I |
| Dr. Maria Borman | President, St. Nicholas Medical Group | D |
| Greg Harmer | CIO | C |
| Duhal Malinka | Regional Executive VP | C |
| Dr. Renee Light | President, ACO/Clinical Integration Corp. | D |
| Randall Repito | President, St. Nicholas Health Plan | C |

# Part I

# WELL-CULTIVATED
# SELF-AWARENESS—
# THE FIRST CORNERSTONE

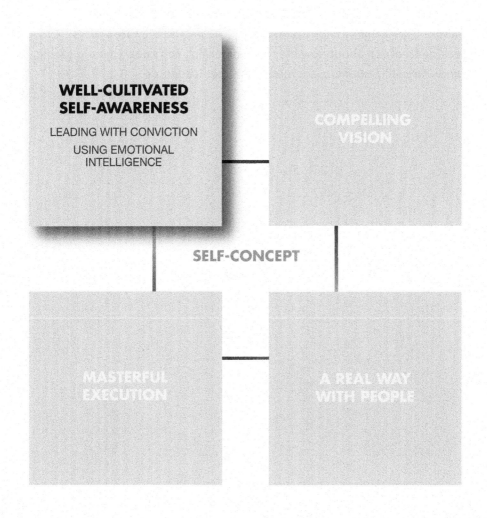

THE FIRST CORNERSTONE, a Well-Cultivated Self-Awareness, is the basis of all leadership competency development. Knowing yourself and acting in an authentic way are essential to consistently ethical leadership. One CEO once commented, "Self-awareness means that you have a good understanding of what you have and what you don't have." Of the 16 competencies, the two that comprise this cornerstone—Leading With Conviction and Using Emotional Intelligence—are the most inwardly focused. The word *insight* comes to mind when thinking about the skill sets described in this section. Socrates is credited with saying "know thyself," which is a good theme to keep in mind when studying these competencies.

> In my experience, the best leaders I have worked with really know themselves—their strengths and weaknesses—and they are always seeking feedback about how they are perceived. You know that old saying, "know thyself"? I think it is a mark of a great leader.
>
> *Health System CEO*

# CHAPTER ONE

# Competency 1: Leading With Conviction

Elizabeth Parris had been tossing and turning since 2:45 a.m., haunted by the decision she had to make about the health system's new executive vice president and chief operating officer (COO). As president of an organization that had outgrown its management structure, Parris needed someone who could handle the day-to-day operations and free up her time for strategic planning and board relations. The organization was facing many operational and tactical challenges, and Parris had been overwhelmed by them for too long. Hiring an executive VP/COO would allow her to delegate these tasks and focus on the external roles that were becoming ever more important.

The health system was far along in the search process and had narrowed the field to two candidates: Miguel Jimenez and Akira French. Parris had invited her executive team members to join the interviews and wanted their feedback. She believed Jimenez was the right person for the job. Although he had not been in a similar position previously, he had a variety of experiences that gave him strong operations and turnaround exposure. A creative thinker, Jimenez had worked in many different types of complex organizations, and he had always brought a sense of urgency and personal commitment to excellence. He had also achieved impressive results with a variety of approaches. Parris was confident that Jimenez would do whatever it took to make the organization run as efficiently as possible. This was evident in his accomplishments and was confirmed by his references.

The only problem? None of Parris's team members supported Jimenez.

*(continued)*

(continued from previous page)

In his interviews with the executives, Jiminez made it clear that he was focused on results. He said he would treat people fairly, but he would not hesitate to let people go if he thought it would serve the organization's needs. Across the board, the executives felt threatened by Jimenez.

When they realized Parris was leaning toward Jimenez, they tried to persuade her to choose French instead. Unlike Jimenez, French had already done this job in another system. She also had more years of work experience. During her on-site interview, she had done a far better job of establishing rapport with the team—everything from learning about their career goals to finding out about their history with the organization. She praised their work and expressed enthusiasm about their future. But French had her own drawbacks. She lacked Jimenez's sense of urgency, she preferred gradual changes over radical ones, and she would be slow to change management if needed. Her results reflected this—they were decent but not outstanding. In short, Parris thought that French would probably do fine in the role, but Jimenez could do much better.

Parris's entire leadership team was against her on this one. Some of them had hinted that they would quit if Jimenez was hired. One had implied that Parris was being sexist in her decision. All were waiting for her to make an announcement that morning.

This vignette shows Elizabeth Parris grappling with a tough decision involving, among other elements, conflicting values. The scene, a sleepless night, is one when internal dilemmas are often most clear. The distractions and intrusions of the workday are there only as memories, which allows the real internal struggles to emerge.

## WHAT IS LEADING WITH CONVICTION, AND WHY DOES IT MATTER?

Leading With Conviction is the competency that is most central to the leadership role. The highest-performing leaders we have encountered all have a strong sense of their personal convictions. These convictions suggest to them how the world should be. They see their leadership role as moving an organization from its current state to its ideal state. Personal conviction is closely linked to vision, another key leadership competency (discussed in Chapter 3).

**Leading With Conviction** means you are aware of and connected to your values and beliefs, are not afraid to take a lonely or unpopular stance if necessary, are comfortable in tough situations, can be trusted to stay consistent even in stressful circumstances, are clear about where you stand, and will face difficult challenges with poise and self-assurance.

For exceptional leaders, strong personal conviction is derived from various sources, including religious beliefs, deeply held connections to community, and a fundamental sense of morality—that is, what is right and wrong. All of these values are often, though not always, instilled at an early age by important caregivers and role models. More than merely a compass, personal conviction provides leaders with the strength to carry on when they may feel they are the only person behind a cause or a goal. Perhaps most important, the strength of personal convictions helps highly effective leaders deal with the inevitable setbacks and professional disappointments that come with the role.

## HOW HIGHLY EFFECTIVE LEADERS LEAD WITH CONVICTION

Everyone has some sense of personal conviction or some guiding set of principles that they follow. Decision making of any kind would not be possible without it—without a standard or metric by which to judge options, one option would never be better than another one. Exceptional leaders, however, more often use their personal conviction in their decisions. Several qualities of these leaders are as follows.

### Showing Conviction

Highly effective leaders with strong personal conviction express their moral and ethical principles through the work they do. They are aware of their values and beliefs and are comfortable discussing them. Their colleagues and direct reports, if asked, would describe these leaders with phrases such as "highly principled," "standing up for what they believe in," and "walking their talk."

### Keeping Conviction in Check

While these highly effective leaders hold powerful convictions, they are also able to keep them appropriately in check. In addition, although they feel their convictions throughout their work, they are simultaneously able to recognize their convictions as personal and not universal. They are willing to blend the views and convictions of others into their decisions. They recognize their beliefs as "right for me" but not right in the absolute sense. While they may take delight in sharing their views, they are not overzealous missionaries out to convert their direct reports and peers. They view others' efforts to find their own individual larger purposes as virtuous in their own right, seeing this process as more important than the conclusions that are drawn.

### Keeping Ethics in Mind

Highly effective leaders are well known for having high integrity and ethics. They recognize the ethical dimension of most decisions, and they are not afraid to ensure ethical issues are understood before a decision is implemented.

## WHEN LEADING WITH CONVICTION IS NOT ALL IT COULD BE

Less effective leaders do not use their conviction to its full potential. As a source of guidance, conviction may sometimes serve as a flashlight when a lighthouse is needed. It may influence thinking but fail to guide decision making. It may steer leaders in a virtuous direction at first but will ultimately succumb to external pressures. Here are some common reasons that Leading With Conviction falls short.

### Conflicted Convictions

Although leadership roles inevitably involve compromise, leaders who lack strong personal conviction may find that the direction their organization is taking frequently changes course. They may agree to one direction in a physician meeting and then reverse the direction when under pressure from board members. Other times, they may give up individual goals for the sake of the team, and the team for the sake of the organization. They may ignore social goals when the hospital faces a financial crisis using the argument "no margin, no mission." The high speed of decisions and trade-offs in a leadership role can leave a leader little time for reflection and integration to the point where she begins to lose her sense of identity and becomes unsure about her own beliefs.

## Lacking Conviction

Some leaders deal with their personal trade-offs by avoiding them. They convince themselves their ideals are not so important, or they avoid thinking about them altogether. For others, the ideals may not have been strong to begin with. As they advance in their careers, these leaders do little to nurture their beliefs, thinking their life is easier that way.

In well-run organizations, leaders can still care about their personal values and contribute significantly to the organizational objectives. Well-designed incentives and careful monitoring can align personal values well enough that organizational goals are not compromised. However, such leaders do not perform to their full potential. Their direct reports see their relationships as transactional and have little motivation to work beyond the point of expected accomplishment.

## Disconnection Between Conviction and Work

Other leaders have strong personal values but choose not to let these values show in their work roles, or they miss the chances to support their values through their work. We have encountered many such leaders—all talented individuals—who stop themselves at midlevel roles, gradually losing their interest in work while increasing their involvement in outside activities. They may pursue noble social causes, such as founding and running volunteer organizations, while at work they perform at an acceptable but not outstanding level.

Even more worrisome are leaders who simply lose hope of making a difference in their organizational roles. In this category, we find leaders who are suffering from executive burnout—those who may have had admirable but unrealistic ideas about what they could achieve in their senior roles but who find they are unable to adjust their expectations and fully engage in the considerable good they *can* do. They have truly "retired on the job."

## Overfocusing on Personal Goals

A final area where personal conviction can be harmful involves letting personal goals become the *raison d'être*. In this type of environment, staff have little interest in helping each other, and leaders see their position mainly as a means for personal achievement. Leaders who allow this to happen find that organizational goals are neglected and that leadership teams have members who engage in destructive politics and act selfishly.

## MISUSE AND OVERUSE: HOW LEADING WITH CONVICTION CAN BACKFIRE ON YOU

Although strong convictions can drive leaders and their teams to deliver outstanding performance, they can also have a serious downside when overused, leading to one or more of the following patterns.

### Dismissing Other Perspectives

This can happen if leaders truly think their views are the only right ones. This pattern is often linked to zealous religious beliefs; however, in reality, such an attitude usually says more about the individuals than the religion they claim to follow. In extreme cases, these leaders may regularly make statements such as "I answer only to God" as a way of claiming moral superiority rather than engaging constructively in the face of conflict.

More commonly, these less effective leaders may say things such as "This is a matter only the board and I would fully understand." Such a rigid attitude tends to directly hinder the leader's ability to build and maintain effective working relationships. Regardless of their other skills, such leaders typically find themselves unable to climb many rungs on the corporate ladder. Leaders who place such a high value on their own opinions also often cut off creative input from their team members.

## Failing to Own One's Perspectives

A more subtle but related challenge comes from the nature of the leadership role as a position of implied authority. Leaders can fall into the trap of treating their personal convictions as correct by virtue of their leadership role—"I'm right because I'm the boss." Such an attitude, while perhaps not openly hostile to others' perspectives, nonetheless fails to recognize and respect others' views as valid. Leaders who follow this pattern also run the risk of creating a team of "yes people" and stifling team creativity. Groups led by such leaders rarely venture outside the box and almost never engage in innovative problem solving. In the end, valuable opportunities to develop understanding and trust through the experiences of work may be lost at the expense of higher performance.

## Being Too Judgmental

Moral thinking and judgments become dangerous the moment they enter the interpersonal realm. Internally, statements about what one "should" or "must" do may reflect personal conviction, but externally, they may come across as moral superiority, scolding, and holier-than-thou.

Leaders who are hard on themselves often struggle to avoid being just as hard on their direct reports, their peers, or, even worse, their superiors. People in general have a low tolerance for being considered morally inferior. Leaders do not get to make the mistake of being too judgmental many times before it comes back to bite them.

So why would a leader make this mistake, not once, but repeatedly? Because convictions can create blind spots. When a decision is proposed or an action is taken that runs against what the leader stands for, he can be thrown into a moral outrage that prevents him from seeing the appropriate considerations of interpersonal judgment. The leader then does not think about consequences, reactions, or impressions. Instead, he is consumed by indignation. He will react defensively and out of concern, but the tone will come across as a sermon or a lecture.

**Misuse and Overuse: How Leading With Conviction Can Work Against You**

Here are some signs that a leader may be overusing or misusing their conviction:

- Dismissing other perspectives
  - Leaders view their beliefs as the only valid ones.
  - Leaders dismiss or ignore other viewpoints that differ from their own.
- Failing to own one's perspectives
  - Leaders consider themselves to be right because of their authority or expertise.
  - Leaders surround themselves with "yes people" who do not challenge the leader or think creatively.
- Being too judgmental
  - Conviction comes across as a sermon rather than a point of view.
  - People who disagree with the leader are labeled as immoral, unethical, or incompetent.

## LEADING EFFECTIVELY WITH PERSONAL CONVICTION

### Finding Role Models

As with all of the competencies discussed in this book, you can take two approaches to finding good mentors who will help you live by your personal convictions. The first is to look for people with a strong reputation for living by their principles. You can ask yourself or others questions like:

- Do you know anyone who really lives by her principles?
- If you had a moral dilemma at work and wanted to talk to a mentor about it, who is the first person you would want to call?
- Who is the best person at expressing his or her convictions without sounding judgmental or arrogant?

The second approach is to look for people whose profession or occupation requires them to master this competency to succeed. For example, you can find people who lead with conviction in faith-based organizations, religious leaders who have become effective in secular settings, or leaders of organizations that have a strong social mission (e.g., nonprofits, charities, social enterprises).

## Additional Opportunities for Personal Development

Strength in personal conviction comes from knowing yourself and your principles. You can enhance your self-awareness and alignment with the greater good by joining organizations that foster these qualities (e.g., social service organizations, religious groups, other mission-driven associations). Another helpful exercise is to conduct a personal inventory of your convictions; Carson Dye's (2023) book *Leadership in Healthcare: Essential Values and Skills* provides a useful approach. However, if you need to focus your efforts on a particular deficiency, here are some suggestions:

### Reconnect with Yourself

If you feel disconnected from your personal convictions, we recommend revisiting your "origin story"—the reasons why you chose healthcare as a career in the first place. You might even consider digging up the essay you wrote for graduate school admission, or recall the first healthcare leadership role you took. Reminding yourself of what motivated you to enter healthcare can help you become a more authentic and inspiring leader to others. This is especially important in the post-COVID world, when many providers find themselves in need of professional renewal.

Make time to reflect on your work. You can do this at the end of the day, at the end of the week, or on an as-needed basis, depending on the challenges you face. Reflection time, whether alone or with a trusted colleague or loved one, can help you stay in touch with your personal convictions.

### Broaden Your Horizons

A powerful way to gain a sense of your personal conviction is to expose yourself to a different context or culture. When we look into the histories of breakthrough leaders, we notice that many have lived, at some point in their lives, within a culture different from their own. This experience can help leaders develop a deeper understanding of themselves because it enables them to come into regular contact with their own convictions.

Travel is a great way to expand your perspective; however, if this is not feasible for you, consider reaching out to individuals or groups who have different worldviews. If you can think of a group you "just can't understand," they are probably an ideal choice. A good exercise is to put yourself in situations where your only goal is to be more open to others' opinions—for example, by visiting another religion's place of worship or the rally of a competing political party. Learn to recognize within yourself when you begin to close down to the opinions of others or to react with hostility. Chapter 6, "Listening Like You Mean It," offers more helpful tips on how to improve your receptivity to others' ideas.

If you need to become more open-minded about other opinions and perspectives, challenge yourself to question your own assumptions and biases in settings outside of work, where the stakes are lower. Have conversations with people who have very different views from yours, and try to summarize their perspectives aloud before you respond with your own. Make it a point to give others' perspectives center stage once in a while. Catch yourself when you want to say, "Do it because I said so," and challenge yourself to come up with a clearer rationale for the course of action.

### Focus on the Common Good over Personal Goals

If others perceive you as focusing too much on your own goals, we recommend you take this feedback seriously. You may be creating a negative work environment—no one will go the extra mile for leaders they see as just out for themselves. Start by taking an honest look at your motives. What do you hope your achievements will do for you? What will be "enough," and what does "enough" look like? Leaders who can face these questions can start to develop a healthier and more fulfilling sense of personal conviction.

## SUMMARY

Leading With Conviction plays a central role in exceptional leadership, and it is worth your time to master it. Doing so requires work on self-awareness as well as becoming mindful of how you translate your personal convictions into leadership actions.

---

### Think About It

VP of human resources Jim Batten was having a discussion with Bill Sutor, VP of support and facility services, about self-awareness in leadership. Sutor argued that too much conviction could turn a leader into a dictator. He cited the example of the Jonestown massacre and said that he thought leaders who pushed too hard were no better than Jim Jones. Batten argued that this viewpoint was extreme. Sutor asked Batten what controls could be put into place by an organization to ensure that this would not happen.

*(continued)*

---

*(continued from previous page)*

- What would you say to Sutor?
- What measures do you think can be taken to ensure that a single leader's personal conviction does not lead an organization astray?
- Most organizations have chief compliance officers. Should one of the roles of this position be to oversee the directives given by leadership that might not align with the values of the organization?

## Think About It

Some organizations have codes of ethics. You can find the Code of Ethics of the American College of Healthcare Executives at https://www.ache.org/about-ache/our-story/our-commitments/ethics/ache-code-of-ethics.

- How can these codes help prevent abuse in the area of personal conviction?
- How might these ethical guides become more relevant and influential in the daily operations of an organization?

## REFERENCE

Dye, C. 2023. *Leadership in Healthcare: Essential Values and Skills*, 4th ed. Chicago: Health Administration Press.

# CHAPTER TWO

# Competency 2: Using Emotional Intelligence

Several years ago, two members of the senior team at St. Nicholas Health System had the following conversation.

"Our new CFO, Emily Gohara, is a pro at reading people and connecting with them. She always keeps her cool. She is nothing like Kathy Hauser. Kathy was on Samantha Stoman's team, and she got away with a lot of bad behavior. Kathy thinks she is a great leader, but everyone is scared of her. She has been losing it more often ever since she was turned down for the CFO job. Who knew she had such a short fuse? She only cares about herself. I know she is smart and has done some great things for our health system, but she is just too wrapped up in herself."

"We had a similar situation a few years ago when Dave Damron was passed over for promotion. I think he deserved the promotion, but he handled it well. We all thought he would leave after being passed over, but he stayed, became an even better team player, and was very supportive of his new boss. He really showed great poise. I am sure that it was one of the main reasons that Liz Parris promoted him as soon as the job opened up again. And he is getting great results. I think he has been a real asset for us lately. Now if only Kathy Hauser would grow up a bit."

A year later, Gohara and Parris fired Hauser because she could not adapt to the new changes in the finance team.

THIS VIGNETTE ILLUSTRATES a common pattern in leadership roles: Drive and skills are enough to earn a promotion but not enough to keep it. Long-term effectiveness depends on the quality of the leader's working relationships, which are in turn a function of the leader's capacity to understand and work effectively with emotions—of others as well as themselves.

## WHAT IS EMOTIONAL INTELLIGENCE, AND WHY DOES IT MATTER?

*Emotional intelligence* is a construct that ties together a number of interpersonal skills. Although the idea has its roots in academia, its popularity in relation to managing people began with author Daniel Goleman (2005). Some people think emotional intelligence is just about having good social skills, but that's not the whole story. Emotional intelligence also means knowing and handling one's own emotions while understanding and working with other people's emotions. Besides reading others, the most effective leaders have a deep awareness of their own emotions.

> **Using Emotional Intelligence** means you recognize personal strengths and weaknesses; see the links between feelings and behaviors; manage impulsive feelings and distressing emotions; are attentive to emotional cues; show sensitivity and respect for others; challenge bias and intolerance; collaborate and share; communicate openly; and can handle conflict, difficult people, and tense situations effectively. A person's emotional intelligence is sometimes referred to as his emotional intelligence quotient, or EQ.

## HOW HIGHLY EFFECTIVE LEADERS USE EMOTIONAL INTELLIGENCE

Leaders regularly find themselves in circumstances where emotions run hot. An emotional charge can be a productive energy source, and emotional intelligence can spell the difference between putting this energy to good use and watching it burn out of control. Exceptional leaders learn to manage these emotional charges in themselves and others, so that the energy is channeled most productively. They do so through developing greater self-awareness as well as through a more attuned sensitivity toward the emotional responses of others. Some of the ways in which emotional intelligence needs to guide leadership decision making are described in the following balancing acts.

## Acting with Self-Interest Versus Acting with Selfless Interest

A fundamental polarity in leadership involves the balance between self-interest (what you do to serve your own needs) and selfless interest (what you do to serve the needs of others or the needs of the organization). Balance means both sets of needs are adequately served. If too much emphasis is placed on the selfish side, your influence in the organization may erode or fail to develop in the first place. If too much emphasis is placed on the selfless side, the responsibilities of your role will erode your familial relationships, health, and well-being.

Most leaders have vulnerabilities, or blind spots, on either side of the balance. On the selfish side, we have the temptations associated with leadership roles. As you reach higher levels, your ability to influence the resources you receive, even your own salary, expands, and the line between purposeful influence and influence for its own sake becomes difficult to see. Others, such as your direct reports, will feel greater pressure to curry your favor and to convince you that everything is going great (regardless of how things are really going). The selfish temptation is to lose your objectivity and begin believing your own press releases.

However, danger lurks on the selfless side, too. As your influence and resources increase with higher-level positions, you will be approached with greater frequency to contribute to causes of all types. You will have expanded opportunities to do good on behalf of your organization and to support pet causes, which may or may not align with your organization's goals. A soft spot can quickly become an Achilles' heel.

This is where cultivating self-awareness comes in. Effective leaders use their self-awareness to identify and overcome their blind spots, enabling them to keep an objective, optimal balance.

## Engaging Others Versus Maintaining Distance

Being "one of the gang" is difficult for the CEO or other leader. Leaders must master a healthy balance between engaging the people they work with and maintaining a distance from them.

An imbalance on either side of this continuum diminishes the leader's effectiveness. If too much distance exists, coworkers will find it difficult to trust you. A lack of engagement with direct reports can create an emotionally cold environment that people do not look forward to coming to and are eager to leave at the end of the day. Without getting occasional messages of approval, some direct reports will suspect the worst and assume the distance is a signal of personal vulnerability.

Not getting along with your coworkers can be bad, but being too friendly can be worse. Some leaders use work relationships to fill emotional needs that go beyond their work goals. If leaders need constant approval from the people they work with, they may be too quick to give in to requests from direct reports or, alternatively, may shamelessly suck up to their bosses. Another common pattern is possessiveness around working relationships, in which leaders not only fail to facilitate but also actively block the development of social networks that do not pass through them. These leaders may also hold too tightly onto "their" talent, which can impair the career development of their direct reports and will make these leaders look less collaborative.

Exceptional leaders exhibit enough engagement that relationships of trust, familiarity, and comfort can evolve. On the other hand, these leaders keep enough distance that they can pursue with some objectivity the kinds of candid feedback, appraisals, and personnel changes that may be in the best interests of the organization's goals.

### Trusting in Self Versus Trusting in Others

Trust is another area where leaders need to find the right balance. Leaders who trust too much give away tasks to others and forget about them. If the work does not get done or does not get done properly, they will be quick to pass along blame and will have trouble recognizing their own failure to provide supportive check-ins and other monitoring.

On the other hand, some leaders trust themselves too much and others too little. This is a more common pattern of performance problems, perhaps in part because it tends to get leaders in less immediate trouble than the former pattern. Leaders who do not learn to place adequate trust in others will either fail to delegate, creating a growth-stifling work environment in which no high-potential employee will stay for long, or underdelegate, giving tasks to others but then checking in so frequently and with such force that the tasks require twice the work that they should.

Highly effective leaders achieve an optimal balance of trust by delegating important aspects of work to others while continuing to monitor that work in ways that are respectful and nonintrusive.

## WHEN POSSESSING EMOTIONAL INTELLIGENCE IS NOT ALL IT COULD BE

Less effective leaders do not use the full extent of their emotional intelligence. Ways in which they fall short of accomplishing this competency involve the following.

## Lacking Concern for Others

At times, leaders may lack an appropriate level of concern for others. They may get so wrapped up in working toward the organizational mission that they fail to recognize the individual needs of others around them. At other times, leaders may simply be so self-absorbed that they fundamentally have no respect for others.

## Needing Approval

Some leaders are overly concerned with how they are perceived by others. Their need for approval prevents their personal conviction from driving their principles and actions. A common example is found in CEOs who are confident and self-assured until they get in front of their boards, where they will quickly back down if challenged. Other common examples include leaders who are so concerned with others' approval that they are unwilling to make tough decisions that might offend some of their team members. These leaders are sometimes described as "country-club managers."

## Being Volatile

Leaders who are passionate about their jobs will occasionally be upset—maybe very upset—by the decisions or actions of others that frustrate their goals. Strength in leadership comes not from stifling these emotions but rather from controlling them. Leaders are described as volatile if others cannot predict what will set them off or if their emotions seem to control them.

## Mistrusting Others

Highly effective leaders who have a strong grasp of emotional intelligence are willing to trust others. They delegate often and regularly and help others develop. They share both responsibility and accountability. It is rarely said of them that they have to check everything before anything is done. Leaders should work hard to communicate the big picture and learn how to empower others.

**When Possessing Emotional Intelligence Is Not All It Could Be**

When emotional intelligence is not as strong as it could be, a leader may be described in the following ways:

- Lacking concern for others
  - Individual needs of others are not recognized.
  - Self-absorption prevents the leader from recognizing and respecting others' views.
- Needing approval
  - Action is driven by approval-seeking rather than personal conviction.
- Being volatile
  - Emotions are in control of the leader rather than the leader being in control of his emotions.
  - Staff feel they cannot predict what will set off their leader on any given day.
- Mistrusting others
  - Everything has to go through the leader before anything can get done.
  - Work is not delegated, and staff are not empowered.

## MISUSE AND OVERUSE: HOW EMOTIONAL INTELLIGENCE CAN WORK AGAINST YOU

Can you be too emotionally intelligent? Perhaps not. However, emotional intelligence definitely can be misapplied and at the expense of higher performance in the following ways.

### Getting By on One's Good Graces

Emotional intelligence tends to be highly prized in senior leadership roles; all else being equal, leaders with higher EQs (emotional intelligence quotient) will be more favored for promotion or, in the case of downsizing, more likely to be retained. We all share a bias to want to work with colleagues who are agreeable, and no one knows how to be agreeable better than a high-EQ leader.

Conversely, high-EQ leaders may also be particularly adept at convincing others to overlook their underperformance. High-EQ leaders can be less effective in other areas and will suffer fewer confrontations about it. They tend to have political networks that are far stronger than those of their peers and can tap them for support whenever poor performance becomes a concern. Some leaders have held on to senior roles for long periods through little more than their good graces and social ties.

## Overextending the Emotional Role

Some leaders with high EQs enjoy the emotional aspects of their work to the point that they may actually foster a volatile work environment. For these leaders, the patterns of creating an emotional crisis and then working through and repairing relationships provide greater familiarity and comfort than a more stable environment. However, needlessly volatile environments unnecessarily draw attention away from the pursuit of organizational goals.

For some leaders, serving as on-call negotiators or interpersonal problem solvers can be gratifying roles. These leaders may be reluctant to let others work challenges out for themselves or, in the case of direct reports, work with them to develop their own emotional intelligence.

## Avoiding Noninterpersonal Aspects of Work

Some high-EQ leaders focus too much time on the interpersonal aspects of their roles. These parts of their roles are where they get the most positive feedback, but they may not be adding the most value. For example, more time than necessary may be taken up maintaining work ties (e.g., somehow always finding the time to attend every social event, no matter how far-flung) or processing interpersonal exchanges that may not need the level of scrutiny they receive, when the time would be better spent addressing other critical elements of the leader's role (e.g., budgeting, planning).

---

### Misuse and Overuse: How Possessing Emotional Intelligence Can Work Against You

If a person overuses this competency, the following problems can result:
- Getting by on one's good graces
  - Formidable social networks prevent performance problems from being addressed.
  - Underperformance is often overlooked and rarely confronted.

*(continued)*

---

*(continued from previous page)*

- Overextending the emotional role
  - Contribution as a facilitator, negotiator, or interpersonal problem solver becomes oversubscribed.
  - Direct reports are not encouraged to work through their own challenges or develop their own emotional intelligence.
- Avoiding noninterpersonal aspects of work
  - Social aspects of the role are overemphasized.
  - The less people-focused, more mundane but still critical aspects of the role are neglected.

## HOW TO ENHANCE EMOTIONAL INTELLIGENCE

### Finding Role Models

High-EQ leaders tend to be found in the greatest numbers in human resources, pastoral care, counseling, and social service roles. In these roles a higher EQ is a more central requirement for effectiveness, opportunities to develop and hone these skills are more frequent, and the skill set is tested more routinely. Whatever the challenges you face in your working environment, chances are people in these types of roles have seen it and worse. (A caveat: Not *all* such individuals have a high EQ; the notes about overuse earlier in the chapter also apply to individuals in these groups. Be sure a potential mentor has a reputation as both an effective leader and having a high EQ.)

### Additional Opportunities for Personal Development

Although many books, seminars, and courses cover this topic, the best way to improve your EQ is to improve the quality of the feedback you receive about yourself and your relationships. The opposite of self-awareness is blind spots, and we all have them to some degree. The only way to uncover these blind spots is to receive feedback about them and to be willing to internalize what that feedback means.

You can improve the quality of the feedback you receive in a variety of ways:

- Develop more structured ways of getting feedback (e.g., use 360-degree programs, ask subordinates to provide input to third parties about how they feel about you).

- Improve your ability to hear feedback (e.g., work with a facilitator or a coach).
- Create a climate more conducive to feedback (e.g., conduct staff training or build feedback reviews into the ongoing work that you do).
- Make meaningful rounds (not just brief drop-in visits) and ensure that they are truly listening tours viewed as helpful by the people visited.

Chapter 20, "Developing a Feedback-Rich Environment," provides additional suggestions on how to hard-wire some of these activities into your workplace. Another suggestion that has been used in the literature on this topic for some time is the Johari Window (see Exhibit 2.1), which is discussed in some detail in *Leadership in Healthcare: Essential Values and Skills* (Dye 2023). This concept helps leaders better identify blind spots and develop ways to address them. For the more ambitious reader, the writings of Daniel Goleman (1995, 2000, 2005, 2011a) provide highly accessible and practical summaries of the broad research base on which emotional intelligence concepts are based.

The Johari Window, which was named after the first names of its inventors, Joseph Luft and Harry Ingham from Westinghouse, describes the process of human interaction. A four-paned "window" divides awareness into four quadrants: open, hidden, blind, and unknown. The lines dividing the four panes can move as awareness changes. The four quadrants represent the following:

**Exhibit 2.1 Johari Window**

| | Known to Self | Not Known to Self |
|---|---|---|
| Known to Others | OPEN | BLIND |
| Not Known to Others | HIDDEN | UNKNOWN |

- The *open* section represents what you and others know about yourself. The knowledge that this window represents includes facts, feelings, wants, needs, and desires. As you continue to get to know people, the sections move to place more information into the open window.
- The *blind* section represents what others know about you but that you are unaware of. Blind spots can affect the level of trust between individuals; the challenge here is to get this information out in the open.
- The *hidden* section represents what you know about yourself but others do not know. With higher EQ comes a more refined understanding of what you should keep hidden and what you should disclose to build trust with others.
- The *unknown* section represents what neither you nor others know about you. Growing in this area is the most sensitive but often the most helpful for higher-level leadership growth.

## SUMMARY

Leaders' effectiveness depends heavily on their ability to get things done through their relationships with others. Most of the challenges healthcare leaders face involve the need to influence people they have little to no formal authority over. Doing so effectively requires a solid understanding of others' needs and desires, as well as an ongoing monitoring of where they are emotionally with respect to a given task or initiative. Doing so exceptionally requires an even deeper understanding of others and oneself, so that this emotional intelligence can be put to its best use.

### Think About It

Emotional intelligence seems to relate to self-awareness. Daniel Goleman (2005, 43) defined the term *self-awareness* as "having a deep understanding of one's emotions, as well as one's strengths and limitations and one's values and motives."

- What are some of the specific organizational mechanisms and tools that can help leaders become more self-aware?

## Think About It

VP of patient care services Barbara Buczinski returned from a national nursing executive meeting where she attended a workshop on the "bright side" and "dark side" aspects of leadership. References that she brought back to St. Nicholas included:

Furnham, A. 2022. "Bright and Dark Side of Personality." In *Overcoming Bad Leadership in Organizations*, edited by D. Lusk and T. L. Hayes, 12–13. Oxford: Oxford University Press.

Higgs, M. 2023. "Leadership Narcissism, Ethics, and Strategic Change: Is It Time to Revisit Our Thinking About the Nature of Effective Leadership?" In *Organizational Change, Leadership and Ethics*, edited by R. Todnem By, B. Burnes, and M. Hughes, 177–97. New York: Routledge.

Maak, T., N. M. Pless, and F. Wohlgezogen. 2021. "The Fault Lines of Leadership: Lessons from the Global Covid-19 Crisis." *Journal of Change Management* 21 (1): 66–86.

Mackey, J. D., B. P. Ellen III, McAllister, C. P., and Alexander, K. C. 2021. "The Dark Side of Leadership: A Systematic Literature Review and Meta-analysis of Destructive Leadership Research." *Journal of Business Research* 132: 705–18.

Miao, C., R. H. Humphrey, S. Qian, and J. M. Pollack. 2019. "The Relationship Between Emotional Intelligence and the Dark Triad Personality Traits: A Meta-analytic Review." *Journal of Research in Personality* 78: 189–97.

Zeitoun, H., D. Nordberg, and F. Homberg. 2019. "The Dark and Bright Sides of Hubris: Conceptual Implications for Leadership and Governance Research." *Leadership* 15 (6): 647–72.

Research the topic of bright side/dark side leadership and provide a review of how this theory impacts emotional intelligence.

## Think About It

In the opening vignette, two members of the senior team are discussing this issue. Which person might you most identify with?

# REFERENCES

Dye, C. 2023. *Leadership in Healthcare: Essential Values and Skills,* 4th ed. Chicago: Health Administration Press.

Goleman, D. 2011a. *Leadership: The Power of Emotional Intelligence.* Florence, MA: More Than Sound.

———. 2005. *Emotional Intelligence: Why It Can Matter More Than IQ,* 10th ed. New York: Bantam Books.

———. 2000. *Working with Emotional Intelligence.* New York: Bantam Books.

# Part II

# COMPELLING VISION—
# THE SECOND CORNERSTONE

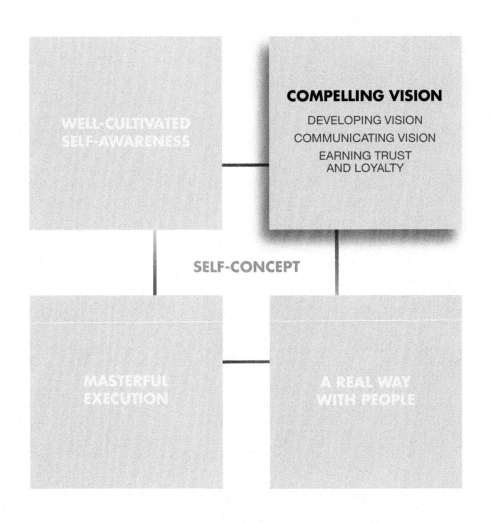

WELL-CULTIVATED
SELF-AWARENESS

**COMPELLING VISION**

DEVELOPING VISION
COMMUNICATING VISION
EARNING TRUST
AND LOYALTY

SELF-CONCEPT

MASTERFUL
EXECUTION

A REAL WAY
WITH PEOPLE

THE SECOND CORNERSTONE, Compelling Vision, involves the competencies that do the most to convince others that they should follow a particular leader. Built on the foundations of self-awareness and emotional intelligence, the Compelling Vision competencies—Developing Vision, Communicating Vision, and Earning Trust And Loyalty—are used to create a picture of the future that inspires others' hopes and aspirations, enough so that people will not only want to see this future realized, but will also want to personally support its pursuit through their own efforts.

"Vision without action is a daydream. Action without vision is a nightmare."

*Japanese proverb*

# CHAPTER THREE

# Competency 3: Developing Vision

**Crisis.** It was the wee hours of a weeknight, and Elizabeth Parris, CEO of St. Nicholas Health System, tossed and turned, replaying her board meeting from earlier that day. She had always enjoyed a good rapport with her board, but lately, the challenges the organization faced seemed to have become far more complicated, and her board was struggling to cope with the uncertain future. St. Nicholas had faced several major setbacks, mostly related to the main hospital in downtown Barkley. Located in a historic building, the main hospital cost more and more to keep up to code every year. The COVID crisis had hit the medical center especially hard, changing the culture and composition of the organization in ways senior leadership was still adjusting to. The inner city was also suffering from a severe economic slump, and competing with the other health systems in Barkley was becoming more difficult. There were growing complaints about physicians having too much power; decisions about healthcare capital equipment were driven almost entirely by their demands. Most of the employed physicians were at the main medical center, and those physician practices were bleeding money. Every day it seemed like Parris's attention was being divided into smaller and smaller chunks. She was getting dragged into operations challenges, and strategy was falling by the wayside. Parris was increasingly worried that the board was overfocusing on St. Nicholas's main hospital, leaving little time for thinking about the system as a whole, including the urgent need to prepare in earnest for value-based reimbursement and population health management.

**Complacency.** Meanwhile, Suburban West Hospital (SWH) was enjoying great financial success. Located in the fastest-growing area of greater

*(continued)*

*(continued from previous page)*

Barkley, SWH seemed unstoppable. SWH's CEO, Mary Moses, had made this solid community hospital even more efficient during her tenure. Profitability was high, turnover was low, staff were happy, and physicians were loyal and high quality.

Moses achieved her results by focusing almost exclusively on the inpatient side of SWH's business. While her inpatient focus persisted, the chances of its continuing success were diminishing. SWH had little competition in its western region, and Moses was constantly pushing for support to increase the number of beds in her hospital. Between this focus and Parris's attention being drawn toward the main hospital, the trend toward outpatient and non-acute care was not getting the attention it deserved, a reality that would eventually catch up with them both.

BOTH OF THESE SCENARIOS present opportunities for a leader to create and communicate a compelling vision, but they also pose formidable challenges to doing so. Parris's situation is perhaps more common in healthcare these days: waves of dramatic changes so numerous that they become hard to keep track of, let alone manage. Her challenge is to get people's attention away from the crises they individually face long enough to allow them to see a collective vision—a ray of hope showing what the organization could aspire to in the future. She also needs to get her board and others to focus on the unique changes occurring in the industry, changes unfamiliar to the traditional acute care enterprise that so many have grown up in.

The suburban hospital, on the other hand, may at first glance seem to be almost on autopilot. But while chaos is a more obvious obstacle to higher performance, complacency can be just as bad, if not worse. How do you motivate a group that is satisfied with the way things are to take their organization even further?

## WHAT IS VISION, AND WHY DOES IT MATTER?

In our experience, *vision* is one of the most sought-after competencies at the top levels of leadership. Vision can be defined most straightforwardly as the ability to create effective plans for your organization's future based on a clear understanding of trends, uncertainties, risks, and rewards. Some might call it the art of developing strategy. Highly effective leaders who have a strong vision will position their organizations to take advantage of the trends they perceive. For example, in healthcare, visionary leaders may anticipate new clinical and technological advances long before they are widespread and may commit their organizations to adopt them as they become available. They may see opportunities to get physicians more engaged with their organizations by connecting them through more cutting-edge practices. We contrast this with the "following the trends" herd mentality; exceptional leaders have the ability to identify the trends that make sense strategically and to adopt them early, before others copy them.

> **Developing Vision** means that you have a clear picture of the future, anticipate how the organization and its environment will be impacted by large-scale and local changes, can imagine the organization in the future and envision multiple potential scenarios or outcomes, have a wide perspective on trends, and can design competitive strategies and plans based on future opportunities.

Organizations that have visionary leaders tend to excel. They are usually first to market with new ideas and approaches to care; as a result, they often have higher profitability, which enables them to attract top-notch clinicians and, ultimately, better serve their communities.

## HOW HIGHLY EFFECTIVE LEADERS DEVELOP VISION

Although visioning is best thought of as an ongoing process, it has a definable sequence. The quality of vision first depends on a solid awareness and understanding of broad trends and their potential implications. From these, a vision gradually emerges, refined (but not limited) by critical thinking from the key people needed to pursue it and communicated to the people needed to implement it. Highly effective leaders use necessary skills to accomplish each of these elements of the visioning process.

### Maintaining an Awareness of Trends

Most senior leaders have learned how to keep up with important trends in healthcare. Frequently, they subscribe to a variety of trade journals, such as *Modern Healthcare* and *Healthcare Executive*, in addition to journals more specific to their functional areas. They may also hear about news updates from their various health administration listservs. These are good resources for keeping track of trends within healthcare, but they do not offer a complete picture of the major trends happening outside the industry that will affect healthcare. These publications also tend to be "preprocessed"—the conclusions have already been drawn for the reader.

Exceptional leaders are broad thinkers who dig deeper to better understand the emerging trends, even outside of healthcare. If asked what they are reading from outside the healthcare industry, good leaders may cite the occasional business publication. Visionary leaders, on the other hand, are more likely to mention multiple sources with compelling, though perhaps indirect, associations with their leadership and industry roles, such as biographies of successful leaders throughout history, analyses of broad economic trends (such as the effects of social and environmental policy on productivity), books on modern urban planning and development, articles on sustainable communities, or analyses of the rise and fall of ancient societies.

For some exceptional leaders, this pattern extends far beyond what they read. Imagine for a moment that you wanted to learn more about how nanotechnology may affect health services delivery in the future. If you were a typical leader, you might scour the healthcare trade journals to examine the implications others are drawing about likely outcomes. Or you might go further and scan nonhealthcare periodicals, such as *The Economist, The New Scientist,* or *Wired.* But if you were a truly visionary leader who sought to move your organization to the frontier, you could go as far as developing contacts and links well outside the field. Many leading scientists maintain lists of individuals who have requested updates on what is coming out of their labs. These lists contain not only other scientists but also industry leaders who simply want to stay informed about trends that could affect their businesses. Leaders may even reach out to venture capitalists who are on the forefront of developing innovations, to keep tabs on where funds are flowing.

### Understanding Risks, Rewards, and Uncertainties

Analyses to support strategic decision making are somewhat paradoxical. On one hand, a fact-based analysis is vital to sound judgment, offering leaders their only hope to develop at least a minimally objective perspective of what the future may hold. However, decisions always involve an emotional as well as a rational element; risk and uncertainty are always interpreted subjectively as well as objectively. Regardless of how well reasoned a course of action seems, resistance will come from the unfamiliarity the direction represents. On most matters, people would rather believe that change is unnecessary; an exceptional leader's vision is strong enough to allow people's trust in that leader to overcome this tendency.

### Communicating Vision

If the process is worked through effectively, the vision becomes the logical conclusion—the clear answer to the question raised by the analysis. There may be anxiety about how to get there, but there should be clarity about the appropriateness of the vision for the organization.

We discuss more about turning the vision into words and words into actions in Chapter 4. For now, we will leave it at the following key distinction: A good vision describes how the *organization* will be a better place because of the work of its people, but a breakthrough vision describes how the *world* will be a better place because of the work of the organization.

## WHEN DEVELOPING VISION IS NOT ALL IT COULD BE

We mentioned that strategic vision is one of the most important qualities boards look for in their senior hires. This competency, more than the others in this Cornerstone, tends to be the rare bird. In other words, there are far more senior leaders with excellent trust-building skills, outstanding communication skills, or both than there are strategic visionaries.

Part of the shortfall may be cognitive in nature; some elements of the visioning competency are hard to develop. However, less effective leaders may also make the following mistakes.

### Focusing Too Much on Tactical Operations

Many executives work long and hard hours day after day but seem to have no long-term impact on their organizations or communities. They become so mired in the tactical, routine matters that they do not have the time to develop and evaluate long-term strategies.

Leaders who lack vision are often relegated to putting out daily fires. One well-known CEO said, "The best leaders are those who have the ability to transcend the day-to-day and see out into the future. Those are the leaders who are going to shape needed change in our field." In some management circles, this ability is called being proactive rather than reactive.

For some leaders, promotion into a role that allows for broader and more long-range influence provides a welcome opportunity to think strategically. For others, however, the opportunity is either not taken or is not taken far enough. Sometimes the reason is discomfort or the feeling that reaching out is too much like sticking one's neck out. For other leaders, the capacity to think strategically has yet to be developed. Other leaders have the capacity to develop strategic vision but hold themselves back because of the comfort of their operation's focus, their lack of experience with the visioning process, or both. Healthcare tends to provide many opportunities to focus on day-to-day challenges if leaders decide to do so at the expense of building and communicating a compelling vision.

Those leaders who do manage to focus some time and energy on thinking about the future run the risk that their vision will remain nothing more than a set of ideas that are discussed from time to time during social conversation or perhaps just once in a true operational context. In other words, the vision may be presented but not meaningfully hardwired into operational meetings.

### Restricting Focus to Healthcare

Another way in which vision can fall short is if leaders focus their sights strictly on the business of their health systems. Within health administration, already a high-demand profession, there is a tendency to become isolated. The risk here is of losing sight of how healthcare is affected by broader trends, as well as how healthcare can impact well-being above and beyond the clinical service lines the organization relies on for revenue. Acute challenges—COVID and other health emergencies, staffing shortages, and financial setbacks, to name a few—risk further restricting leaders' field of vision to whatever feels most immediately pressing.

### Overreliance on External Advice

The sheer complexity of health administration creates a need for help in putting all the pieces together. Market summaries, consultant reports, and other sources can be immensely helpful, as long as leaders maintain a healthy skepticism. Questioning takes time, focus, and energy—it is tempting to let some things slide (analytic help is what you are paying for in the first place, right?).

A similar pattern we often see involves "following the leader," where a health system or group of health systems with prior success as early adopters become the de facto leaders for the broader industry. There is some psychological safety in deferring judgment to well-regarded, well-run health systems, and sometimes, maybe often, the strategy works. But it is rare for a leader to be described as exceptional if their main approach involves relying on other organizations to make sense of the future for them.

### Undervaluing Divergent Perspectives

Vision can also fall short if it is too tightly tied to a single leader—something that happens when leaders fail to engage their teams in refining, evolving, and challenging their organizational visions. For leaders who have enough power, peers and direct reports will go along with a vision they do not believe in just to stay on the leader's good side. If they are not encouraged to share their concerns or ideas about the future, the energy they bring to the effort will be borrowed energy, which is quickly used up and needs regular refills.

We can extend this example to other situations in which leaders resist challenges to their visions or resist the visioning process altogether. Some leaders view the visioning process as frivolous; they pride themselves on their abilities to solve problems in the moment or on pursuing opportunities in whatever form they may take. The approach may provide them with the most comfort, but it will not get the level of commitment from their needed collaborators that a shared vision will deliver. Jim Collins (2001) made this point by distinguishing "foxes" from "hedgehogs" in his seminal book *Good to Great*. In this book, the hedgehogs take a complex world and simplify it, while the foxes are scattered and try out many different strategies at the same time. Collins's book *Great by Choice* (Collins and Hansen 2011) expands on these concepts by describing leadership roles in creating the future they wish to see.

### When Being Visionary Is Not All It Could Be

When vision is lacking, it can look like any of the following:

- Focusing too much on tactical operations
  - Dealing with day-to-day fires crowds out long-range planning.
  - Long-term perspectives are not systematically integrated into regular operations.
- Restricting focus to healthcare
  - Social and professional networks and information sources are almost entirely within the healthcare industry.
  - Too little intellectual curiosity exists about broader trends or changes.
- Overreliance on external advice
  - The analytic work of others is accepted as-is, and conclusions are not adequately questioned.
  - The organization follows whatever the other health systems are doing, with inadequate analysis as to whether it is appropriate.
- Undervaluing divergent perspectives
  - Staff go along with a vision just because they want to stay on the leader's good side.
  - Concerns and ideas about the future are not discussed.

## MISUSE AND OVERUSE: HOW BEING VISIONARY CAN WORK AGAINST YOU

Without a doubt, leaders can focus too much on vision to the detriment of their organizations. When these downsides appear, they are often attributable to either an imbalance somewhere within the visioning process or overzealousness about visioning in and of itself.

### Balancing Poorly Between Planning and Operations

Leaders can also become so engaged with their vision that the day-to-day management of the enterprise does not get the attention it needs. A proper balance between long-term strategic focus and short-term tactics must be maintained. Problems often occur when leaders put too much emphasis on business development, strategic planning, and cutting deals. In the excitement of pushing new and exciting initiatives forward, operations may receive less focus, and the executives running operations may feel like second-class citizens. The imbalance can create a host of implementation problems as well. Planning executives may not develop the understanding of operations necessary to forge realistic plans. Conversely, operations executives may not have the influence they should have on the strategic planning process, resulting in less buy-in and engagement with its implementation.

### Focusing Too Much on the Process of Planning

Another sign of overzealous planning is a preference for process over outcome. Leaders with this pattern are overly eager to try out a variety of strategic planning approaches to "see where it takes us." Going through the planning process becomes the end goal in itself. This results in too much time spent on elaborate strategic planning retreats and a multitude of thick reports full of objectives, most of which are never achieved.

Another type of overzealous focus shows up in the use of data. Healthcare has more data sets available for analysis than almost any other industry; managers can be tempted to believe more is always better, such that analyses are pursued far beyond the point of diminishing returns. Executive teams can quickly fall into the bad habit of allowing analyses to unnecessarily slow down the execution of new initiatives or the implementation of needed changes.

### Underemphasizing Implementation

To paraphrase Thomas Edison, genius involves one part inspiration and 99 parts perspiration. Some leaders are so good at creating inspiring visions that they lose focus on how to make them happen. Even worse, they may come up with new visions before the old ones have had a chance to succeed or fail. When this happens, staff may lose interest and think "this too shall pass." Trust on both sides will suffer in the process. (See Chapter 4, "Communicating Vision," and Chapter 14, "Driving Results," for more tips on improving your implementation focus.)

---

**Misuse and Overuse: How Developing Vision Can Work Against You**

If a person overuses this competency, the following problems can result:

- Balancing poorly between planning and operations
  - Business development and strategic planning executives are elevated above the key operations people.
  - Day-to-day operations do not get the attention they need.
- Focusing too much on the process of planning
  - Technique is valued over substance.
  - Data are collected far beyond the point of diminishing returns.
  - Execution is unnecessarily slowed down.
- Underemphasizing implementation
  - New plans are created too frequently, and old plans are abandoned with inadequate (or inadequately communicated) rationales.
  - Colleagues develop attitudes of "waiting it out."

---

## HOW TO IMPROVE VISIONING

### Finding Role Models

If you are not in a C-level position, you may find useful guidance from senior leaders as well as from leaders within the business development and marketing departments of your organization. At higher levels, however, identifying good mentors for vision can be challenging, and you may need to look outside your own organization to find them. In thinking about who might have real strength in this area, ask yourself the following questions:

- ◆ Where are the innovations happening in healthcare right now?
- ◆ Where are the success stories?
- ◆ Where has a health system been taken from good to great?

You may need to develop relationships with consultants who are well traveled and well versed in new trends and ideas. Ongoing networking with healthcare peers outside your market can also be helpful.

### Additional Opportunities for Personal Development

An effective way to become more visionary is to make sure your horizons extend beyond the healthcare sector. Make sure you have opportunities for the outside world to reach you. Don't let healthcare dominate your social life and your reading list; set aside some time and focus specifically on trends outside of healthcare. Allocate time to interact with leaders from other industries. Finally, be certain that ample time is spent involved in community activities.

To hone your intuitions about how sector trends evolve, we recommend familiarizing yourself with some of the most influential theories and frameworks that have informed vision and strategy over the years. These include Everett Rogers's diffusion of innovation theory, Clay Christensen's disruptive innovation theory, and Michael Porter's five forces model (Christensen 2013; Porter 1998; Rogers, Singhal, and Quinlan 2019). Skill in long-term thinking can be developed through periodic exposure to individuals and organizations specializing in strategic foresight. Two of our favorites are the Future Today Institute and the nonprofit Institute for the Future, both of which offer a wealth of resources on their websites and YouTube channels. The Institute for the Future also offers courses and certifications in foresight, and the Future Today Institute's methods are described in the book *The Signals Are Talking* (Webb 2016). Healthcare-specific approaches to foresight development are also described in Garman's book *Healing Our Future* (Garman 2021).

Lastly, for a healthcare-specific look at strategy development, we recommend Walston's *Strategic Healthcare Management: Planning and Execution* (2023).

## SUMMARY

The capacity to develop vision, both individually and collaboratively, is a hallmark of exceptional leadership. You can improve this set of skills by learning useful frameworks, such as disruptive innovation theory, as well as applying them to key trends to see how they might change things. Most importantly, you also need to find your own unique point of view, which you can shape with the help of others, but you should not rely on them completely.

---

**Think About It**

Samantha Stoman, Dr. Maria Borman, and Dave Damron were at the Stomans' house one Saturday night when Dr. Borman said, "You two know that St. Nicholas is not going to go anywhere because we have no vision and no strategy. We just do not know where we are going. We are trying to do everything without any logical foundation. And on top of that, we do not have anyone at the senior table who can really shape a future vision."

Stoman disagreed, saying, "I just don't buy that. All we do is talk about vision and strategy. If we don't spend more time on running day-to-day operations in this new healthcare world, we will not stay ahead of the game. Everyone knows that if you do operations right, you will succeed in the market."

This is the classic "operations versus strategy" debate that organizational leaders often have. This balancing act can turn into a competition in which leaders who have more operational roles (like the chief nursing officer or chief operating officer) are pitted against those who have more strategic roles (like the chief planning officer or business development officer).

- One way that organizations balance managing daily operations with long-term strategic issues is to split their meetings. For example, a senior team may meet every Tuesday and focus only on tactics and immediate problems and then meet once a month to discuss and plan longer-term strategy. What are other ways that might help to keep a good balance between the two?
- There are several keys to becoming a more strategic thinker. They include being able to anticipate what will happen in the future, being able to interpret those trends, and getting others to see the changes that need to be made to prepare for that different future. If you are feeling overwhelmed by constant day-to-day operations challenges, what are some ways to ensure you have the time and focus to more fully develop this strategic side?

> **Think About It**
>
> In the recent St. Nicholas senior team meeting, the discussion on strategy (which was going in circles) was interrupted by Susan Edwards, VP of planning, who said:
>
> "Colleagues, Michael Porter is the master of strategy planning and visioning. He argues that to stay ahead of the competition, an organization must either offer lower prices or stand out for the quality of their services services—or maybe both. I think we need to face the fact that here at St. Nicholas, we are doing neither. We are the high-cost provider in the area, and while we do have some good quality indicators, we are not really offering anything unique."
>
> This comment sparked a heated argument.
>
> - Reflect on this short case example. Was Edwards right to bring up the topic of strategy and visioning?
> - If she wanted to take a more data-driven approach concerning St. Nicholas's cost- and market-differentiation position, what could she have done? How could that have changed the outcome?

## REFERENCES

Christensen, C. 2013. *The Innovator's Dilemma: When New Technologies Cause Great Firms to Fail.* Cambridge, MA: Harvard Business Review Press.

Collins, J. 2001. *Good to Great.* London: Random House Business Books.

Collins, J. C., and M. T. Hansen. 2011. *Great by Choice: Uncertainty, Chaos, and Luck: Why Some Thrive Despite Them All.* New York: Harper Business.

Garman, A. N. 2021. *Healing Our Future: Leadership for a Changing Health System.* Oakland, CA: Berrett-Koehler.

Porter, M. 1998. *Competitive Strategy: Techniques for Analyzing Industries and Competitors.* New York: Free Press.

Rogers, E. M., A. Singhal, and M. M. Quinlan. 2019. "Diffusion of Innovations." In *An Integrated Approach to Communication Theory and Research*, 3rd ed., edited by D. W. Stacks, M. B. Salwen, and K. C. Eichhorn, 432–48. New York: Routledge.

Walston, S. L. 2018. *Strategic Healthcare Management: Planning and Execution*, 2nd ed. Chicago: Health Administration Press.

Webb, A. 2016. *The Signals Are Talking: Why Today's Fringe Is Tomorrow's Mainstream.* New York: PublicAffairs.

# CHAPTER FOUR

# Competency 4: Communicating Vision

It was the end of an unusually long week, and Elizabeth Parris left the office feeling ecstatic. A year after facing a near-standoff with her board and several months after hiring her new executive vice president and chief operating officer, Miguel Jimenez, she had successfully led the creation of Vision 2040, the organization's long-term strategic plan. Vision 2040 included a $500 million makeover and expansion project, the establishment of a more distinct outpatient business unit, the takeover of the public health department for the region, and a comprehensive approach to population health management that was coordinated through the organization's health plan. It also involved partnering with two other health systems in two other large cities to form a network, allowing access to a much larger population base than just Barkley, as well as several new horizontal integration initiatives that could truly create the "health system of the future." This latter part of Vision 2040 was the hardest to explain. While the financial hurdles to fund this project were enormous, an even bigger challenge in Parris's mind was the crucial requirement that the entire physician and employee community understand what this network meant and be fully engaged in the change initiative.

Parris had discussed this challenge with her executive coach, who advised her to keep focused on linking changes to a systematic communications strategy. She started her weekend with the goal of developing a set of outlines that would wow the physicians and employees when she began her town hall meetings next month.

THIS VIGNETTE SHOWS the core of making vision happen. Leaders must engage various stakeholders to help them see the reason for change; leaders must, in essence, create a compelling call to action. To illustrate this point, consider this statement based on Greek history: When Pericles spoke, people said, "How well he speaks." But when Demosthenes spoke, they said, "Let us march."

In the previous chapter, we discussed what it means to develop vision. Creating and using vision as a tool for organizational change requires effective communication of that vision—turning a set of strategic and often complex concepts into a captivating story of where the organization is, where it will go, and how it is going to get there.

We call this competency *Communicating Vision* for several reasons. First, we want to distinguish it from the more general concept of communication, which can be almost as broad as leadership itself. In this chapter, we specifically address how highly effective leaders communicate vision, and how they create an environment where staff and physicians feel motivated to move with them toward that vision.

## WHAT IS COMMUNICATING VISION, AND WHY DOES IT MATTER?

*Communicating Vision* throughout any change process is essential to its success. At the same time, it is also incredibly challenging to effectively pull off. Most leaders routinely underestimate the amount of communication necessary to drive change efforts; as a result, many employees inevitably feel lost and confused by the change process, which can make them cling even more closely to their old but familiar habits.

> **Communicating Vision** means that you distill complex strategies into a compelling call to action, inspire and help others see a core reason for the organization to change, talk beyond the day-to-day tactical matters that face the organization, show confidence and optimism about the future state of the organization, and engage others to join in.

Effective leaders communicate not only about day-to-day issues but also about vision. In his book *Leading Change*, noted scholar John Kotter (2012) describes the level of vision-related communication in comparison to total workplace communication during a change effort. In his estimation, vision-related communication tends to comprise only about one-half of 1 percent of the communication people receive about their work. With this much competition, communication had *better* be captivating!

Spending time communicating future vision also helps ensure that everyone is on the same page. It aids in collaboration and enhances the coordination of work effort.

# HOW HIGHLY EFFECTIVE LEADERS
# COMMUNICATE VISION

Although there are as many communication styles as there are communicators, several qualities make any communication style stronger. Keep these in mind, and your communication will begin to reflect them.

## Communicating Clearly

Discussing clarity in vision communication may appear trite—after all, who would argue *against* communication clarity? However, in reality, few among us are as clear as we could be, as frequently as we could be, though most of us would like to think otherwise.

We can compare Communicating Vision to marketing. Think about the marketing slogans you have found most memorable. What did they have in common? Chances are they were straightforward, novel, even catchy—and without a single vague or unnecessary word. If they were really good, they stuck in your mind—you could not help but think of them. These same structural elements can be usefully applied to vision communication. You want these ideas to be compelling and to stick in people's minds.

## Communicating Widely

Effective leaders ensure that everyone who will be responsible for moving the vision forward hears it. They also use a wide variety of communication methods to describe vision so that the message fully permeates. This skill separates exceptional leaders from their well-intentioned but less-effective counterparts. Because communication can be labor intensive, shortcuts become tempting—placing a message in a corporate newsletter and considering the communication process finished, for example. This may make sense if all staff are required to read the newsletter *and* if the expectation is effectively monitored, but it is hard to justify otherwise.

Highly effective leaders will take the communication process even further. Beyond simply ensuring the message is heard, they will ensure that the message is *discussed*. For example, they might instruct managers to explicitly incorporate a discussion of the vision into their next staff meeting and then report back on what was discussed. Such cascading communication structures can go a long way in making sure key messages are reliably received.

## WHEN COMMUNICATING VISION IS NOT ALL IT COULD BE

When communication falls short of captivating, often one or more of the following may be the reason.

### Lacking Clarity, Focus, or Information

Clarity can suffer because of a number of problems. The communication may lack clarity because the vision itself lacks clarity. Alternatively, the communication may lack focus; it may contain too many elements for people to easily wrap their heads around. Still another problem stems from communicating too little information about the *how* of the vision. The further the vision is from the current state of affairs, the greater the need for some indication of the path the organization will take to get there. Without this path, staff may dismiss the vision out of hand—a risk made far more likely if there is recent history of abandoned visions.

### Lacking Meaning for the Audience

The challenge of making a broad organizational vision meaningful at department and sub-department levels is usually beyond the capabilities of any individual leader. Effective leaders know this and work with managers to develop local interpretations of how the efforts of a given division, department, or team will fit into this broader vision. Without this careful linkage, staff may only receive the corporate take on the vision and may have difficulty viewing their roles as part of that vision.

Another frequent problem is the articulation of a vision that does not clearly express how the vision affects everyone, and how everyone affects the vision. This risk exists any time a vision communication places special emphasis on a specific aspect of operations. Common examples include vision statements that draw special attention to the physicians, nurses, profitable service lines, or quality improvement initiatives. If poorly communicated, the vision will leave the counterparts (e.g., nonphysicians, non-nurses) feeling excluded.

### Communicating Infrequently

Although communication plans can (and should) be designed to be highly efficient, they are still typically time and resource intensive. Communications is a tempting place to cut corners, and so corners are often cut. The best prevention here is to arrange a review of all internal communications coming from the corporate level to ensure they make some mention of future plans. Think about it this way: Any time the vision of the future state of the organization is *not* mentioned, the status quo will take center stage.

---

### When Communicating Vision Is Not All It Could Be

Communication in the realm of strategic vision can fall short for any of the following reasons:

- Lacking clarity, focus, or information
  - A visual picture is not created, because it is either unclear or contains too many elements.
  - Lack of thought about the *how* makes the vision seem too far-fetched.
- Lacking meaning for the audience
  - The importance of individual roles is not adequately addressed.
- Communicating infrequently
  - The vision is rolled out and then rarely referred to again.

---

## MISUSE AND OVERUSE: HOW COMMUNICATING VISION CAN WORK AGAINST YOU

Overcommunication of the vision is not nearly as frequent as undercommunication. When communication fails, it is usually because of a problem with the communication itself rather than it being too frequent. The following patterns will cause your communication to be ineffective, regardless of frequency.

### Communicating Vision as an End Rather Than a Means

Occasionally, leaders may be accused of talking a great game and getting people excited about an idea or strategy that they are ultimately unable to implement. Leaders may routinely be caught up in the excitement of thinking (or dreaming) about what the future could be like, but the actions needed to make this future happen are conspicuously absent. The vision is thus discussed as a concept permanently divorced from the present day—a beautiful mirage across the wide chasm of inaction. The danger of this pattern is greatest in groups where no great sense of urgency has been cultivated to overcome the comfort of the status quo.

## Viewing Vision as the Program du Jour

Some leaders do not fully recognize both the power and the responsibility associated with setting and communicating organizational vision. For some, the vision is viewed more trivially, a slogan for the occasional staff pep rallies rather than a beacon by which to set direction. For others, particularly high-energy leaders who pride themselves for turning on a dime, the vision may change too rapidly over time, causing confusion and frustration among their staff. Leaders may try out so many different kinds of visions that staff and physicians may view them as just another gimmick program. Healthcare has been known for this, and leaders need to be cautious about falling into this trap.

## Communicating Too Specifically

Communications about vision can be too specific in a number of ways. Consider an organization that develops a vision with specific, objective goals (e.g., "We will gain 40 percent of the inpatient market share in the area," or "We will be the top provider of heart surgeries by market share in our market"). What if your organization achieves those types of measured goals? Your vision would dissolve, and you would need a new one.

Another example of communicating too specifically relates to timelines. Timelines are great for operational goals, but putting a vision on a timeline is often a mistake. Say you set "three years from now" as the time your vision will be achieved. You have just turned the vision into something that can be proved or disproved. People can start to judge early on whether they think the vision will be achieved; if it starts to look impossible, it may be abandoned prematurely. In short, it becomes an operational goal and loses some of its original power to unite and inspire.

> **Misuse and Overuse: How Communicating Vision Can Work Against You**
>
> When your communication is ineffective, regardless of frequency, one of the following is most likely the cause:
>
> - Communicating vision as an end rather than a means
>   - Communication is emphasized at the expense of implementation.
>   - Too much time is spent talking about doing instead of doing.
>
> *(continued)*

*(continued from previous page)*

- Viewing vision as the program du jour
  - Motivation building rather than direction setting is the primary goal.
  - Visions change too frequently and are thought of as gimmick programs.
- Communicating too specifically
  - Setting a timeline for the vision will eventually force the need to develop a new vision.
  - Vision becomes something that can be proved or disproved.

## HOW TO BETTER COMMUNICATE VISION

### Finding Role Models

The best way to find mentors in this area is to ask yourself, Who do I find most compelling to listen to? Who paints the most vivid, most exciting, and most believable pictures of the future? Once you have identified these individuals, take note of what they say, how they say it, and what really reaches you about their communication. These individuals need not be people you know personally—for example, politicians and religious leaders are some of the most powerful communicators. What is most important in this exercise is to develop the discipline of attending to the elements that make these communications really work.

Another approach you can take is to identify people (your peers and direct reports, for example) others seem to listen to the most. They need not be leaders you find particularly compelling; sometimes zeroing in on people who surprise you with their ability to captivate others can be useful. In these cases, try to learn what it is about this person's communication style that others find so intriguing and look for elements that you can adopt to your advantage.

### Additional Opportunities for Personal Development

The process of Communicating Vision in ways that facilitate change is well described in John Kotter's (2012) book *Leading Change*. Originally released in 2006, this book is widely regarded as a classic on this topic; we highly recommend it, as well as his more recent text: *CHANGE: How Organizations Achieve Hard-to-Imagine Results Despite Uncertain and Volatile Times* (Kotter, Akhtar, and Gupta 2021).

Understanding how change is experienced by others is crucial for communicating in ways that speak to the heart. For this we have found the writings of David Rock to be particularly insightful. Rock views leadership and organizational change through the lens of the neurosciences and uses these insights to explain organizational phenomena that are especially likely to trigger reward and threat responses. His books include *Quiet Leadership* (2006) and *Your Brain at Work* (2009).

If you are interested in fine-tuning your public speaking skills, there is no better method than practice followed immediately by candid feedback. Because this can often be very difficult to drum up in the workplace, consider a course with the local chapter of Toastmasters International (www.toastmasters.org). (If you have no local chapter, consider starting one.) The sole focus of this group is to improve the speaking skills of its members. We are told that the quality of the experience does differ depending on the chapter's membership; however, in general, leaders' and professional speakers' experiences with this organization have been favorable.

## SUMMARY

As important as vision is, it will not move an organization where it needs to go without systematic and compelling communication. In this chapter we described what effective vision communications can look like, as well as the ways in which these communications can miss the mark. Learning how to craft and systematically convey visionary communications will help you achieve exceptional leadership outcomes.

---

### Think About It

St. Nicholas just acquired Hummingbird Hospital, a rural facility located a two hours' drive from Barkley, which had once been a bustling place but lately has fallen on hard times. To provide Hummingbird Hospital with new leadership, Elizabeth Parris appointed Rosemary Ruiz. Rosemary had worked under Dave Damron, the senior business development officer at St. Nicholas, and had done all the research for this acquisition. She knew the challenges at Hummingbird and had a detailed plan of action she called The Hummingbird Vision. As her first activity two weeks after she arrived, she gave a more than 100-slide PowerPoint presentation to a combined meeting of the local board, the medical staff leadership, and her senior team at Hummingbird. Her slides were clear and concise. The presentation mapped out specific strategies and tactics for the next three years at Hummingbird.

*(continued)*

---

(continued from previous page)

The plan included 24 strategies and more than 250 tactics. She was proud that she had "covered everything" and felt that she had presented with great clarity. She knew that the next crucial step was to get the whole physician and employee community fully engaged in the plan and change initiatives.

What did Rosemary do wrong?

## Think About It

**Vision Statement One.** "Our vision is to be a health center of excellence and to provide the highest quality patient care at the lowest cost so that everyone in the communities we serve can benefit from our programs and services and our area will be recognized as a national leader for excellence and innovation in the delivery of healthcare, quality, and patient safety. We will be an employer of choice, providing a highly rewarding and enriching environment for our employees, physicians, and volunteers." (Fictitious vision statement but similar to those of many healthcare organizations.)

**Vision Statement Two.** "We are making cancer history." (Part of the vision statement from MD Anderson Cancer Center.)

- What are the pros and cons of each of these vision statements?
- Which vision do you think will be easier to communicate? Why?

## REFERENCES

Kotter, J. P. 2012. *Leading Change*. Cambridge, MA: Harvard Business Review Press.

Kotter, J. P., V. Akhtar, and G. Gupta. 2021. *CHANGE: How Organizations Achieve Hard-to-Imagine Results Despite Uncertain and Volatile Times*. Hoboken, NJ: Wiley.

Rock, D. 2006. *Quiet Leadership: Help People Think Better—Don't Tell Them What to Do*. New York: HarperCollins.

Rock, D. 2009. *Your Brain at Work: Strategies for Overcoming Distraction, Regaining Focus, and Working Smarter All Day Long*. New York: HarperCollins.

# CHAPTER FIVE

# Competency 5: Earning Trust And Loyalty

As Don Wilson began approaching retirement, he found he was having a hard time with it. He had been CEO of Academy Health, the large academic medical center in Barkley, for 15 years, during a time of abundant resources. Wilson had practiced as a general surgeon with the academic medical center for decades before moving into management. He had a lot of social capital throughout Academy Health; his wit, charm, and people skills had served him well for most of his tenure. Most importantly, early in his career as CEO, Wilson had been able to create and sustain very compelling strategic visions. One of his strategies involved developing a strong affiliation with St. Nicholas Health System, which allowed him to greatly expand his teaching hospital network without additional expenses. People were eager to work with him and follow him. Wilson's medical center had consistently achieved remarkable success. It recruited world-renowned physicians, grew a vast outreach program, and built up significant cash reserves.

But things were becoming more difficult. National policy changes were challenging Academy Health's operating model, and Wilson's vision for the future did not seem to be keeping up. Recruiting new talent to the organization was becoming more difficult, and turnover continued to be elevated. In public forums, he kept telling people that things were fine and getting better—a story the Barkley business papers regularly contradicted and many of his senior executives quietly questioned. The staff of the hospital continued to like him and wanted to believe him, but they were finding it harder and harder to do so. In just the past few years, the medical center had lost 10 percent of its market share, no longer had a

*(continued)*

*(continued from previous page)*

top-10 transplant program, and had lost several leading clinical researchers. Financial results were also shaky, with the organization needing to use cash reserves to cover operating losses. Wilson had also become more distant and communicated less and less with his direct reports. The warm and close relationships he had with many of the leading physicians also started to deteriorate. Working with his office door closed much more than usual, he also became isolated. The bottom line was that, despite his vision, Wilson had lost credibility with his followers.

---

THIS VIGNETTE ILLUSTRATES that having and articulating a vision is not enough to ensure that it is implemented successfully. A trust level with stakeholders must be established first and maintained throughout any change process.

Success in communicating vision depends a lot on the receptivity of the audience. Receptivity, in turn, depends heavily on trust. This chapter is about developing, cultivating, and, as necessary, repairing these relationships of trust.

## WHAT IS EARNING TRUST AND LOYALTY, AND WHY DOES IT MATTER?

People tend to be instinctively wary of those in leadership roles. The greater the distance between individuals and leaders, the more room there is for misunderstanding and the more likely the leaders may be mistrusted. *Earning Trust And Loyalty* is crucial for highly effective leadership; in many ways, it is the glue that holds work groups and organizations together. On the other hand, mistrust can create huge wastes of time and energy on activities that have nothing to do with the organization's mission.

**Earning Trust And Loyalty** means you are honest and straightforward, are willing to admit mistakes, are genuinely interested in the worries and hopes of others, show empathy and a general tendency to help others, consistently follow your promises with promised actions, maintain confidences and disclose information ethically and appropriately, and do your work in open, transparent ways.

## HOW HIGHLY EFFECTIVE LEADERS EARN TRUST AND LOYALTY

Given the natural tendency people have to be wary of those in power, leaders have an ongoing need to prove themselves trustworthy. However, leaders can easily earn trust points by simply being more accessible to staff. The more that leaders are seen as real, authentic people who are available to and concerned for the problems of their staff and colleagues, the harder it will be to view them with suspicion. Here are some ways that exceptional leaders earn their staff's trust.

### Being Accessible

Trust development is easier when leaders are open, honest, and share information freely. They build trust with others and share their feelings—even their fears and worries. The leaders people will trust the least are the ones who are cold and distant. Getting out of the executive suite frequently will enhance trust.

### Encouraging Openness

As a well-known CEO once said, "Trust grows over time—there are no shortcuts." Trust starts as leaders and followers get a sense that each other's actions are predictable. Trust then builds over time in cycles involving increasing familiarity and comfort with taking risks with each other. The evolution happens from both sides of the relationship; leaders take some personal risks when they reveal themselves, and staff take risks when they rely on their leaders.

Exceptional leaders care about their staff and will try to reduce the risks they face. They will actively cultivate an environment of high psychological safety, where people feel they can speak openly and honestly without fear of their comments coming back to haunt them. Leaders accomplish this not only by showing themselves to be open to feedback but also by thanking their staff for showing the courage to put their concerns on the table.

### Being Authentic

Authenticity is a critical component of trust. Many senior leaders talk frequently about engaging the hearts and minds of employees and physicians. To do that, they need to show who they are and what they stand for. This is the ultimate "walking the talk." Leaders who do this best embrace their own personal growth and then live their values by connecting authentically to their work.

The relationship between care and ability is another aspect of being authentic. Highly effective leaders care about their followers, and the followers know that their leaders have the skills and competence to do what is needed. Trust involves leaders who fulfill their promises; they have a high "action/word ratio." Staff, physicians, and other stakeholders want to know their leaders are not only willing but also *able* to do what they say they will.

When exceptional leaders realize that they are unable to keep a promise, they let people know right away. Whenever possible, they look for ways to make up for it, even if it is just a symbolic gesture to show that they take their promises seriously. Highly effective leaders know the worst response is to say nothing and hope no one notices. People usually do notice, and trust suffers even more.

## Modeling Behavior

Breakthrough leaders strive to set an example in all of their workplace interactions. If there are sacrifices to be made, they will step up first. If there are rewards to be given out, they will let others go first.

Being ready to pitch in is another way leaders show their character. By helping out in times of stress or crisis and doing tasks they normally would not do, leaders show their respect for the work their coworkers do. The implicit message is, "I wouldn't ask you to do anything I wouldn't be willing to do myself."

In fact, exceptional leaders are just as willing to pitch in with the tasks their coworkers hate the most as they are to pitch in where they can make the most difference.

## Turning Trust into Loyalty

Trust is best considered a necessary but not sufficient condition for loyalty. Trust becomes loyalty when followers experience the leader as supporting their own interests over a period of time. Exceptional leaders are capable of taking these individual interests and finding ways to bring them into alignment with the organization's goals. As in military parlance, the followers bind themselves to the course of action that is being taken.

## WHEN EARNING TRUST AND LOYALTY IS NOT ALL IT COULD BE

As we previously noted, most people are naturally wary of individuals in positions of authority. As such, no baseline of trust and loyalty is automatically granted with a particular leadership role. The opposite is usually more accurate: a person's baseline loyalty is to the role or the job rather than to the leader. Development of trust and loyalty will be impaired if a leader demonstrates any of the following.

### Being Unavailable

Some leaders are most comfortable staying in their offices. They may describe themselves as having an open-door policy but may send subtle signals that you had better have a good reason for interrupting them. Leaders who are described as difficult to approach usually have lower levels of trust from their staff.

Other leaders may engage their staff more regularly but still fail to convey a genuine concern about challenges they are facing. The difference between *having* and *showing* concern is important here: Most leaders have concern, but not all of them are adept at showing it. Some leaders find listening to their staff's complaints so discomforting that they feel compelled either to jump to an immediate fix or to push for a change of subject. While a change of subject has a more obvious effect, the fix approach also fails to convey a true sense of engagement; the unintended message staff may hear from the leader is, "How can I get this off my to-do list as quickly as possible?"

Still other leaders may show concern to their staff but will not stand up for them as much as they should. A leader might say, "I'll see what I can do" and then either not follow up or not circle back to staff to tell them what happened. In both cases, the result is the same: Staff will assume the leader did not care enough to do anything about their concerns.

### Lacking Follow-Through

Perhaps no more common barrier to trust building exists than a lack of follow-through. Lack of follow-through will often appear callous or even malicious, though this is rarely the intent. More often, the cause is an overwillingness to make promises without considering what it will take to make good on them. (In referring to trust building, one exceptional leader once told us, "Great leaders find it very easy to say no, and very hard to say yes.") Other leaders simply have not mastered their organizational skills to the point where they can keep track of what they told people they would do for them.

Of course, we all face situations where we have agreed to do something only to find out later we cannot honor that promise. In general, people can forgive such transgressions, assuming they do not become regular patterns. However, people are much less forgiving of leaders who do not accept personal responsibility for failing to live up to their commitments.

## Assigning Credit or Blame to the Wrong Person

Leaders chip away at trust and loyalty whenever they assign credit or blame to the wrong individuals. Leaders often do this with no willful intention whatsoever; they may simply be in the habit of describing the work of their group by saying "I" and may forget to acknowledge the team's contributions when they are in the room. Conversely, in the heat of the moment of learning about a failure on the part of team members, some leaders may be quick to harshly note individual accountabilities rather than to take the time to fully understand why the problems occurred, or they may fail to understand and acknowledge their own role in the problems.

In the moment, any one of these oversights may seem relatively benign. Over time, however, people get the message that there is a less certain payoff (and, in the case of blame, a greater risk) to the efforts they put forth on that leader's behalf. Typically, they will adjust their efforts accordingly.

## Failing to Lead by Example

We define leading by example according to two fundamental behaviors: (1) modeling the approach to work and the workplace that you request of others and (2) being willing to lend one's efforts to the work responsibilities of others.

Over the years, people have begun to interpret the phrase *leading by example* as though it were a description of a particular leadership style. In our view, leading by example is not a style but a practice. Leading by example means that the behavior of leaders corresponds with their statements. For example, autocratic leaders can lead by example; they may be autocratic, but their behavior reliably reflects this style. In similar fashion, participative leaders can lead by example by being participative on a consistent basis. The key is predictability; others must be able to rely on you. Leading by example is essential to highly effective leadership, regardless of the other aspects of the person's style. Indeed, in our review of leadership models, we were unable to identify any that appeared incompatible with leading by example.

Role modeling is fundamental not only to leadership but also to every facet of human relationships. We all are constantly attentive to the social cues of the people we interact with, and we are continuously modifying our behavior accordingly. If a person says one thing and does another, we are more likely to attend to what they did rather than what they said. (We will also be less likely to trust them in the future.) Leaders who do not remember this basic lesson in human nature will repeatedly undercut their effectiveness in building relationships of trust.

## Accountability at Too High Levels

As many healthcare organizations continue to grow larger, there is a tendency for authority levels to be centralized at higher levels, taking decision-making authority away from local settings. This can cause a lot of frustration for local staff who no longer feel that the leaders they know and see have any real authority.

---

### When Earning Trust And Loyalty Is Not All It Could Be

Leaders who do not build trust and loyalty to their full potential may have fallen short as a result of any of the following behaviors:

- Being unavailable
  - Leaders are not available to staff when they are needed and appear unconcerned about staff's challenges.
  - Leaders are unwilling to go to bat for staff.
- Lacking follow-through
  - Leaders lose track of what was promised to others or make promises that cannot be delivered.
  - Leaders do not acknowledge these as failures on their part; others are blamed or the failures are not acknowledged at all.
- Assigning credit or blame to the wrong person
  - The contributions of team members are not acknowledged.
  - Personal responsibility for decisions and actions is avoided.
- Failing to lead by example
  - Others are held to standards that the leader does not demonstrate.
  - Leaders are unwilling to go first into uncharted waters or to chip in when help is needed.

---

## MISUSE AND OVERUSE: HOW EARNING TRUST AND LOYALTY CAN WORK AGAINST YOU

We have seen a number of instances where leaders have overemphasized trust and loyalty to the eventual detriment of better performance. When this happens, one of the following patterns is usually present.

### Communicating Too Directly

On the one hand, open and candid communication is essential to maximizing performance. Without such dialogue, performance problems cannot be discovered and addressed. On the other hand, we all have a core self-concept that we guard jealously; we can only handle so much truth about ourselves at once. Leaders who fail to understand this are at risk for overcommunicating about performance deficits, which results in an environment that can feel harsh and punitive, and is simply not enjoyable to work in.

Candor must be tempered with considerations about how feedback will be received by an individual or group. A simple but often overlooked tip is to deliver criticism in one-on-one dialogue rather than in a group context. Another suggestion is to address interpersonal conflict by first acknowledging the value that the working relationship holds for you.

### Discouraging Dissenting Opinions

In some cases, open communication may be viewed as a challenge to loyalty. For example, when substantial organizational change efforts are implemented, such a premium can be put on being on board that dissenting opinions are actively discouraged. In these cases, employees may learn to keep their concerns to themselves for fear of being viewed as disloyal.

In other cases, leaders may be so successful in their compelling communications that employees become overly faithful. Employees may view the leader's actions in purely emotional rather than rational terms, so much so that groupthink sets in and they start to distrust their own independent judgment. Speaking up starts to feel like a failure on their part, and they begin to follow the leader's directives blindly.

## Overvaluing Loyalty

Some leaders may create a cult of personality around their roles such that loyalty is viewed as more important than the mission they were hired to support. Leaders may put too much emphasis on loyalty, valuing it more than other elements of job performance that may be more relevant to the organization's mission. Sometimes this is done by creating an "us versus them" mentality within a given group. Not surprisingly, such an approach will often do more to increase the leader's power base than it will to improve the organization; in the long run, the approach is hard to sustain at all.

A less harmful but still problematic issue involves leaders who try to foster loyalty within their teams by devaluing other groups within the organization. For example, support departments sometimes fall into a pattern of blaming the customer for service problems. Leaders who fail to challenge (or who may even encourage) the view that other departments are inferior in any way (e.g., less skilled, less professional) also indirectly create barriers to the development of useful cross-departmental working relationships as well as the resolution of challenges the departments may face in working with each other.

---

**Misuse and Overuse: How Earning Trust And Loyalty Can Work Against You**

The following can be symptoms of misuse or overuse of this competency:

- Communicating too directly
  - Frankness takes precedence over tact, diplomacy, and timing.
  - The leader fails to temper feedback.
- Discouraging dissenting opinions
  - Employees fear being viewed as disloyal and succumb to groupthink.
  - Critical thinking and dialogue are not actively encouraged.
  - Employees become overly faithful and begin to distrust their own judgment.
- Overvaluing loyalty
  - Loyalty is overvalued in comparison to other elements of job performance.
  - Loyalty to a leader or team is valued above loyalty to the organization's mission.
  - There is a distrust of people outside the department, group, or inner circle.

# HOW TO BETTER EARN TRUST AND LOYALTY

## Finding Role Models

Although loyalty could be measured in many ways, one of the most straightforward is employee retention. Within your organization, who has the best record of retaining staff? Have any new leaders at your organization brought a number of people with them? A human resources executive will likely know the answers to these questions and thus may have the names of some good potential role models. Top performers on employee engagement surveys are another great source.

Also consider any specific leaders whom you have trusted greatly. These may be good people to reconnect with or good experiences to reflect on. What was it exactly about their behavior that inspired that level of trust? What specifically might you do that will help others trust you to that same extent? Reflect also on leaders who recovered well from commitments they couldn't honor—in particular, how they managed these situations and the relationships they affected.

## Additional Opportunities for Personal Development

Getting an accurate read on the trust and loyalty people have in you can be difficult. In most cases, the only way to get at this may be to ask people, directly or indirectly, for this feedback. The direct approach involves finding an opportunity to talk with staff one-on-one to ask them about their experiences. Here are some model questions you might use as a starting point, depending on the specific nature of your relationship with the person you are meeting with.

◆ It's important to me that I follow through on my commitments. I try hard to do this, but I'm probably not perfect. Can you recall any specific times when I may have lost track of a commitment I made in the last year?
◆ I want you to feel comfortable talking to me about anything and know that I will respect your opinions. How well do you think I have done that? Are there any situations where you wish I had handled things differently?
◆ I want to be a good example for you and our team. But it's hard for me to know always how others perceive me. Can you give me some feedback on how I have been as a role model—in particular, any areas where I could improve?

A classic book on trust in leadership is Kouzes and Posner's (1993) *Credibility: How Leaders Gain and Lose It, Why People Demand It*. Chapter 2 of their book

("Credibility Makes a Difference") provides a compelling view of leadership from the follower's perspective. In Chapter 7 ("Serving a Purpose"), there is a useful section on losing and regaining credibility. The pre-eminent author and researcher on psychological safety is Amy Edmonson, whose book *The Fearless Organization* (2018) provides a wealth of wisdom on this topic. Bill George, former CEO of Medtronic and Harvard Business professor, has written two books, *Authentic Leadership—Rediscovering the Secrets to Creating Lasting Value* (2004) and *True North: Discover Your Authentic Leadership* (2007), with the overall theme that people trust you when you are genuine and authentic, and that this authenticity is a hallmark of exceptional leaders. Finally, Dye's (2023) book *Leadership in Healthcare: Essential Values and Skills* provides additional guidance on developing trust (Chapter 13, pages 215–30).

## SUMMARY

An exceptional leader's ability to develop and communicate vision is what gets others to follow them at first; the leader's ability to build and maintain trust is what keeps them following through the most challenging times. For most followers, loyalty is hard to earn and easy to lose. Exceptional leaders develop the competency to know where risks to trust are most likely to be; they work actively to protect trust and to fix it when it's damaged.

### Think About It

Human resources VP Jim Batten was talking with Barbara Buczinski, VP of patient care services, about building trust with staff. Buczinski stated, "It really is all about being yourself. I find that I have to spend a lot of time and help people get to know who I am and what drives me. In doing so, I think I will earn their trust."

Batten replied, "How true. And yet so many leaders seem to carefully orchestrate their actions and how they are seen. It is almost like a political campaign. You know that the people who are running for office are not really showing us their true selves."

- Debate the two sides of this issue. Should leaders be open and let followers see *everything*? Or should they be cautious in what is seen and what is known about them? In other words, are there situations where some withholding of information or even manipulation may be better?

> **Think About It**
>
> Human resources VP Jim Batten was talking one day about trust with CEO Elizabeth Parris. Parris commented, "I just don't think that you can measure trust. I know that people say you can't manage what you don't measure, but trust is one of those things that I don't see how you can measure."
>
> Batten replied, "Well, I think you can measure trust in two ways. The first is pretty simple. You ask if there is a trust relationship—and ask for a yes or no answer. In an employee engagement survey, we often include the item 'I trust my supervisor.' I also think that you can measure behaviors that come from trusting relationships. Again, if we do an employee engagement survey, we might include items like 'I trust what my supervisor tells me' or 'I can trust the information that I receive from senior management.'"
>
> Parris said, "I see what you mean. I just wish there was more science behind this topic."
>
> - Is there a scientific basis for trust? How might trust be measured and managed in an organization? Use your Internet search skills to examine these concepts.

## REFERENCES

Dye, C. 2023. *Leadership in Healthcare: Essential Values and Skills.* Chicago: Health Administration Press.

Edmondson, A. C. 2018. *The Fearless Organization: Creating Psychological Safety in the Workplace for Learning, Innovation, and Growth.* New York: John Wiley & Sons.

George, B. 2007. *True North: Discover Your Authentic Leadership.* San Francisco: Jossey-Bass.

———. 2004. *Authentic Leadership—Rediscovering the Secrets to Creating Lasting Value.* San Francisco: Jossey-Bass.

Kouzes, J. M., and B. Z. Posner. 1993. *Credibility: How Leaders Gain and Lose It, Why People Demand It.* San Francisco: Jossey-Bass.

# Part III

# A REAL WAY WITH PEOPLE— THE THIRD CORNERSTONE

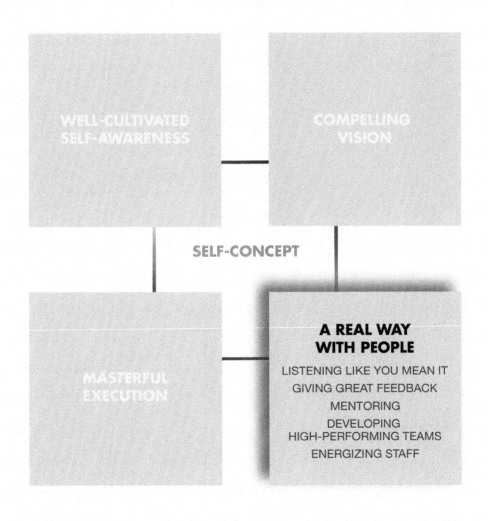

WELL-CULTIVATED
SELF-AWARENESS

COMPELLING
VISION

SELF-CONCEPT

MASTERFUL
EXECUTION

**A REAL WAY
WITH PEOPLE**

LISTENING LIKE YOU MEAN IT

GIVING GREAT FEEDBACK

MENTORING

DEVELOPING
HIGH-PERFORMING TEAMS

ENERGIZING STAFF

THE THIRD CORNERSTONE, A Real Way With People, involves the competencies most related to interpersonal effectiveness on a day-to-day basis. It includes competencies that build staff engagement ("Listening Like You Mean It" and "Energizing Staff") as well as their skills ("Giving Great Feedback," "Mentoring," and "Developing High-Performing Teams"). As Kaitlin Madden (2011) writes, "Relationship building is the most fundamental element of leadership. Establishing strong relationships with people enables them to trust and respect you, in turn giving them a reason to follow your lead."

"Relational skills are the most important abilities in leadership."

*John C. Maxwell (2005)*

# CHAPTER SIX

# Competency 6: Listening Like You Mean It

Liam Pak, St. Nicholas's head of marketing and public relations, checks her notes as she waits for Emily Gohara to finish another meeting. She has been waiting for almost 20 minutes but does not mind too much; she knows Gohara is very busy with other priorities, and she appreciates the opportunity to talk to her. Pak has been under pressure to create a comprehensive marketing communications plan, and she will need Gohara's backing for it.

Meanwhile, Gohara is meeting with her controller and the external auditor. The news is not good: Several new projects went over budget and will likely push the health system into the red this month. Inpatient admissions were also down, and losses in the employed practices were higher than expected. Emily will need to report these issues to the board later this week. At best, she will hear "I told you so." And she would rather not imagine the worst-case scenario.

Gohara comes out of the meeting and sees Pak waiting. She has had a rough day, but she does not want to cancel on Pak again. Pak follows her into her office and excitedly starts outlining her ambitious marketing plan. A less-seasoned executive, she jumps right to her ideas for flashy social media ads and event sponsorships without first building her business case. Gohara only hears what sounds like another huge money pit opening up in front of her. She has already made up her mind to reject the proposal, but she lets Pak keep talking out of politeness and exhaustion. Her silence soon turns to seething as Pak continues her image-focused presentation; Pak, thinking Gohara is losing interest, picks up her pace. Pak wraps up her pitch with, "I'm getting the sense that the timing isn't the best for this. Yes?"

"Yes," says Gohara, relieved that Pak arrived at the conclusion herself.

This vignette describes a typical conversation between two leaders in healthcare: different perspectives clashing awkwardly in an inadequately planned, poorly executed meeting. We can feel the frustration and disappointment on both sides, and we can probably relate to the experiences of one or both people.

Throughout the conversation, each had chances to interact differently that would have increased learning, enhanced mutual understanding, and improved the outcomes. These chances were missed for lack of better listening skills.

## WHAT IS LISTENING LIKE YOU MEAN IT, AND WHY DOES IT MATTER?

*Listening Like You Mean It* distinguishes true active listening from all other forms. Many people think they are good listeners, but we all know there is a difference between really trying to understand someone versus simply waiting for your turn to talk. Listening, and showing that you are listening, are skills that most of us can improve. As a leader, it is worth your while to do so; it will boost the trust people have in you and improve your ability to lead them effectively, especially during times of significant uncertainty and change.

> **Listening Like You Mean It** means you maintain a calm, approachable demeanor; you are seen as warm, gracious, and welcoming; you are patient, open-minded, and willing to hear people out; you get to the real meaning behind the words people say (i.e., you get to the point); you keep in touch through formal and informal channels; and you build strong rapport over time.

Active listening makes a leader more effective in several key ways. Perhaps most importantly, listening helps you better understand the goals, priorities, and views of the people you work with. This understanding equips you to have more helpful and meaningful conversations about the work you do together, which can also lead people to trust you more deeply.

Listening can also help you to be a more effective change agent. With a better understanding of your peers, direct reports, and superiors, you will have an easier time understanding how people feel about their work as well as how they think organizational changes may affect them. When you propose changes, you will be better able to anticipate fears and concerns and address them proactively. This capacity to solve problems makes these leaders better at creating and sustaining high-energy organizations.

# HOW HIGHLY EFFECTIVE LEADERS LISTEN LIKE THEY MEAN IT

Great listeners grasp a great deal of meaning from what a speaker says. But they also get a lot from who the speaker is. Exceptional leaders understand the motivations behind the message and appreciate the speaker's unique point of view.

## Understanding the Message

Beyond the surface content, great listeners will also understand the *why* behind the message—what has led the speaker to their statement, presentation, or request. They will feel the speaker's emotions, and they will perceive the level of agreement or disagreement in the ongoing conversation.

As you improve your listening skills, keep in mind that every message is crafted by a person who is trying to get a set of needs met—maybe their own, the team's, or the patient's. These speakers are expressing needs and revealing something about themselves, hoping that the listener will understand them better.

## Showing Respect for the Messenger

What if you do not agree with the message? Effective listeners will still show they value and respect the thoughts, opinions, and ideas of speakers. When they disagree, they will still recognize that the speaker's perspective is valid and make sure the speaker feels heard. Instead of saying the speaker is wrong, effective listeners will view the disagreement as a difference in opinion or perspective: something to be explored in a way that both parties gain a better understanding of each other.

# WHEN LISTENING LIKE YOU MEAN IT IS NOT ALL IT COULD BE

Leaders often vary widely in their listening effectiveness depending on the circumstances at hand. The following are some of the ways listening can fall short of being effective, and why.

### Listening Inattentively

Inattentive listening can come from different causes. For example, some leaders like to talk to people throughout the day; others prefer working alone. Leaders who like to work alone (sometimes called introverts) can have more trouble with inattentive listening. They may give off signals that they do not want to be disturbed, or they may seem impatient when people do talk to them.

Another type of inattentiveness can arise from not having dependable communication channels. Leaders who do not have regular meetings with their staff (or who often cancel them); who do not reliably answer voicemails, e-mails, or texts; or who answer them in ways that show they did not really read and understand the message can send the same implicit (albeit unintended) message to others: Your communications are not that important to me.

Mobile phones and other communications devices have made the problem of inattentive listening much worse. Some leaders find it hard to set these devices aside when they are with others. The message people get is that their needs are not worthy of the leader's full attention. Inattentive listening habits are also a greater risk in virtual meetings, in which the temptation to split attention can be especially high.

### Hearing Selectively

*Hearing selectively* means tuning out information the listener disagrees with. We all do this sometimes, and need to; leaders do not have the capacity to work through every disagreement they have. But this also works against us in two important ways: (1) it can prevent us from taking in useful new information, and (2) it can stop us from recognizing the legitimacy of divergent perspectives. Taking the time to understand *why* a staff member does not agree with you can be an important part of building and maintaining the working relationship. People are usually less upset about being disagreed with than being ignored.

### Being Impatient

Impatience is a pervasive barrier to effective listening. Almost all leaders in healthcare work under extraordinary time pressures, and listening can sometimes feel like an unproductive use of time. The ever-present temptation is to find ways to "listen more efficiently." Efficiency can be virtuous, but it is often pursued in the wrong ways.

In situations of acute time pressure, effective leaders will tell a speaker how much time they have available so the speaker can manage that time wisely. The less effective approach is to try to reach a speaker's conclusion before the speaker is finished talking. This might involve finishing the speaker's sentences or, even worse, assuming you have the "gist" of it and simply cutting the comments off and taking your own turn. In some uncomfortable dialogues, or those in which the leader cannot productively respond in the moment, she may even change the subject without warning.

## Being Emotionally Volatile

Emotional volatility goes by a number of names: "short fuse" and "hair trigger" come to mind. It represents a basic failure of listening in that the leader's emotions are overtaking her ability to objectively hear what the speaker is saying.

The consequences of being volatile can be severe. At a minimum, it decreases people's trust to the point that they may actively hide bad news from the leader to avoid being scolded. At worst, it will cause people to withdraw from the working relationship altogether.

## Providing Time Rather Than Attention

Some leaders master the art of "listening without listening." They do all the right things to ensure their peers and direct reports have adequate access to them, and they do not rush people or cut them off. But the listening is ultimately a façade; silence is provided for politeness's sake, with all mental energy wandering elsewhere or formulating rebuttals rather than considering what the speaker has to say.

---

**When Listening Like You Mean It Is Not All It Could Be**

In leadership roles, listening can fall short for any of the following reasons:

- Listening inattentively
  - Direct reports are given the impression that their communications are bothersome intrusions.
  - Few or no routine settings are provided in which listening can take place.
  - The listener is attending to his devices rather than giving others his full attention.

*(continued)*

---

*(continued from previous page)*

- Hearing selectively
  - Divergent opinions are ignored.
  - Time is spent formulating counterarguments rather than listening.
- Being impatient
  - The listener jumps to erroneous conclusions and cuts people off prematurely.
  - The listener changes the subject rather than concluding it.
- Being emotionally volatile
  - The listener reacts with visible anger, disgust, or disappointment.
- Providing time rather than attention
  - The listener is effective at taking turns but substitutes silence for genuine listening.
  - The listener focuses on formulating rebuttals rather than on taking in what is being said.

## MISUSE AND OVERUSE: HOW LISTENING LIKE YOU MEAN IT CAN WORK AGAINST YOU

It is difficult to conceive of leaders getting themselves into trouble for listening too much. Indeed, former US President Calvin Coolidge was famously quoted as saying, "No man ever listened himself out of a job." In our experience, if leaders are viewed as overdoing it on listening, it is usually because they are engaging in one or more of the following.

### Taking Too Passive an Approach to Listening

Some leaders do not take enough control of the listening process. A common example is a meeting where the organizers provide too little structure, allowing some people to take over the conversation and/or steer it in their own direction. Leaders who are too afraid of causing conflict may also fall into this trap. They may allow others to air their views but won't challenge them publicly, even if they disagree. In the end, these leaders will do what they want to do anyway, regardless of the feedback they receive, leaving others confused and frustrated.

## Using Listening to Avoid Action

When leaders have to make tough choices, listening can sometimes become a stall tactic. Getting input from stakeholders is an important step in many difficult decisions, but it can also be overdone. If you have ever been stuck in an endless survey process (i.e., a survey that only leads to more surveys), then you are familiar with this dynamic.

---

**Misuse and Overuse: How Listening Like You Mean It Can Work Against You**

Listening is rarely viewed as an overused skill. However, perceived overuse is usually a symptom of one of the following problems:

- Taking too passive an approach to listening
  - People are allowed to take the podium without regard to time or efficiency, particularly in meetings.
  - Points of disagreement are not expressed or explored.
- Using listening to avoid action
  - The leader listens too acutely when a decision must be made (and may not listen enough at other times).
  - Requests for additional input, opinions, and discussion are used as excuses to delay needed action.

---

# HOW TO IMPROVE AT LISTENING LIKE YOU MEAN IT

## Finding Role Models

Where do you find good listening mentors—people who can help you hone your listening skills? One approach is to look for people who are professionally trained in listening, such as counselors, therapists, and chaplains. However, while these professionals may be terrific listeners, they may not be as practiced at balancing listening against the other time constraints managers regularly face. People who are likely to be good at balancing attention against time pressures include executives in human resources management, marketing and communications, community relations, and philanthropy and development. These roles often involve the need to carefully attend to agendas that may or may not be compelling or personally relevant, and that they may personally disagree with, and often under considerable associated time constraints.

## Additional Opportunities for Personal Development

We recommend to all readers, no matter how seasoned, that they seriously consider working on their listening skills. Our experiences and those of others who provided input for this chapter suggest most of us have more room for improvement in this area than we may believe and will see more payoff from improving these skills than we may realize.

As with many of the skills discussed in this book, the best approach to improving your listening skills involves a small amount of education and large amounts of practice with feedback.

### Seek Out Feedback

Feedback is essential for improving listening skills. None of us are always good or bad listeners. We may do better or worse depending on factors like the topic, audience, and time of day. Also, because we never intend to listen poorly, it can be hard to pinpoint when we are listening well or not.

Trusted colleagues can help you with this. If someone tells you that they feel like you do not listen to them, ask them to give you specific examples. Start by looking back, but then ask them to also help you identify examples going forward.

If a colleague agrees to give you this feedback, promise yourself to work extra hard to use it. If they have genuinely caught you at a listening low point, thank them for their help. If there are other circumstances that prevent you from listening better, at least take the time to explain this: "I understand that you didn't get to finish telling me your concerns. Unfortunately, the meeting agenda was starting to run late, and I felt we had to move on to give enough time to the other items."

### Develop a Clear, Active Listening Posture

Displaying active listening involves more than silence—body language and eye contact also play a substantial role. If you have ever seen someone roll their eyes after hearing something, then you know what bad listening looks like; other signs include checking the time, sighing loudly, looking away, or looking at your phone or computer screen. Body language associated with effective listening includes facing the person who is talking, sitting up straight, maintaining good eye contact, nodding in acknowledgment or reacting to key points the speaker is making, and taking notes.

### Summarize

Summarizing is a particularly useful technique in situations where your own opinions disagree strongly with someone else's. In these situations, challenge yourself to summarize the speaker's comments back to him: "If I understand you correctly, you think you are more qualified for this project than I am because you have prior experience with their department's VP, and I do not. Is that correct?" Challenging yourself to take this step serves several goals. First, and most importantly, it forces you to listen to what the other person is saying at a deep enough level that you are able to represent it back. Second, it helps you decentralize from your own perspective long enough to gain a glimpse of the speaker's perspective. Third, if you still disagree with the speaker, he is less likely to believe it is because of a lack of understanding.

Summarizing can also be helpful in less heated dialogues. You can think of them as checkpoints that provide you with the opportunity to be sure you and others are still proceeding with a common understanding.

### Ask Probing Questions

Probing questions are follow-up questions designed to elicit a deeper understanding of a subject. One style of probing—requesting specifics—focuses on clarifying the message: "You said employees are upset about this change. How many employees are we talking about? How upset are they? Do they want to resign? Do they feel betrayed or merely inconvenienced? How would you compare their reactions to the premium increase (or other example)—stronger, weaker, or about the same?" A time-based probe can help clarify whether an issue seems to be a flare-up versus an ongoing trend that may be building steam: "How long has this been going on? How consistent has the trend been?"

### Monitor Your Emotions

Strong emotional reactions can quickly derail good listening practices. This can play out in several common ways.

- *Shock.* You might react with shock when you find news or ideas difficult to believe. In these situations, it is important to guard against the tendency to dismiss the information or to react too strongly to it. A good way to handle this reaction is to put it on the table in a nonthreatening way: "This comes as a surprise to me. I may need a few minutes to take this in."
- *Anger or disgust.* Reactions of anger and disgust can happen when you believe someone is thinking or acting incompetently or in a way that is not in the best interests of your department or organization. In these situations, there is often a need to convey an important learning point or to foster a better understanding between yourself and the other person; however, this need may be competing with an instinctive feeling of being threatened and

a commensurate reflex to strike back. A more moderate, and typically more effective, approach is to use questions instead of attacks: "Can you help me understand how this would positively affect our department?" or "How would this resolve the problem?"

- *Elation.* We can all come up with examples of when our negative feelings toward someone else interfered with our ability to attend to their communication. The same is true about positive emotions. If you find yourself getting overly excited about an idea, you may find your own internal thought process triggering at such a fast pace that you lose the thread of what is being said.

- *Boredom.* A reaction of boredom most often comes from judging the communication to be irrelevant, unimportant, or not delivered efficiently (e.g., unnecessary or overly elaborated details). Sometimes, particularly if the speaker is anxious, both the communicator and the listener will be well served by some assistance in framing the message: "Let me see if I understand the heart of the matter here." Other times, however, the meta-communication the speaker may need to hear is, "I want to feel you value my opinion and will take the time to hear me out." In these cases, the challenge is more internal: Find the anchors to keep yourself appropriately and mentally engaged in the dialogue. Balancing your focus between the content of the message and the personal meaning behind the content can be a useful approach.

### Schedule Time with Smaller Groups

Large group meetings, while effective for many purposes, do limit participants' comfort in disclosing points of disagreement. You can facilitate the flow of feedback by finding occasions to meet with smaller groups of staff. Smaller group meetings also allow you more opportunities to build individual relationships of trust.

### Find Opportunities for One-on-One Conversation

Just as small group meetings can provide a higher quality of feedback over large groups, so too can one-on-one communication over small groups. Think for a moment about the people you rely on most in your organization. Do you have opportunities to talk to each of them one-on-one once in a while? If you do not, you should consider creating these opportunities from time to time. Talking with someone individually gives you a unique opportunity to reflect not just on the work you do with this person but also on the quality of your working relationship. It is important to note that this practice has become even more important with the proliferation of virtual meetings.

### Visit Teams on Their Turf

Highly effective listening means going beyond a "my door is open" policy to a "let me knock on your door" policy. While staff appreciate responsiveness to their concerns, there are few actions that demonstrate concern more concretely than planned and purposeful visits to worksites.

### Focus Closely on Virtual Meetings

Highly effective listening is more challenging when the participants are not in the same room. You can improve your virtual meetings by following some simple tips: keep your camera on, look at the camera as if you are making eye contact, ensure you are in a quiet environment or mute yourself when you are not speaking, and make sure everyone is given the chance to share their thoughts. Some leaders also follow up with a phone call to make sure everything is clear after a virtual meeting.

### Mind Your Limits

Despite your best efforts, at times you will not be as effective a listener as you would like to be. Fatigue can be a barrier to effective listening—for example, at the end of a hard day or week, or after difficult conversations or disappointments. Another key barrier is role conflict—someone coming to talk with you about a concern at a time when your mind is firmly pointed elsewhere, or when you need to be preparing for your next meeting.

How you handle those situations depends partly on your ability to overcome your fatigue or distraction, as well as on how fatigued you are. On the one hand, concentration, like other skills, improves with practice—if you push yourself to listen through your fatigue, you will continue to get better at it. For this reason, taking the time to listen can sometimes be better than putting a conversation off.

However, there may be times when you are too tired or distracted to have any hope of listening effectively. In these situations, efforts to overcome your fatigue will not pay off, and diplomatically delaying the conversation is the better move. You can do so by first acknowledging the importance of what the speaker has to say before requesting a postponement: "I can see this is an important concern to you, and it deserves my full attention. However, right now I won't be able to give you the attention you deserve. I will be too distracted by this meeting coming up later today. I'd like to find a time when I can give you my undivided attention on this matter. What does tomorrow morning look like for you?"

Given how important listening is to interpersonal effectiveness, there are also numerous books that provide an in-depth treatment on this topic. Two excellent reference books that go into greater detail on listening practices are physician Mark Goulston's (2009) book *Just Listen: Discover the Secret to Getting Through to Absolutely Anyone* and Edgar Schein's (2013) *Humble Inquiry*.

## SUMMARY

There are few more powerful tools for building staff engagement than giving employees the sense that their leader hears and understands where they are coming from. Exceptional leaders are particularly adept at sending this message to the people they work with through their body language and actions in the context of listening.

### Think About It

Dr. Linda McKenzie had become one of the top surgeons in Barkley by the time she turned 45. She graduated from a top-tier medical school, completed a world-class residency, and had been selected for one of the top fellowship programs in the country. She was smart, hardworking, and talented, and loved taking on the most challenging cases with the toughest attendings. She was widely viewed as a natural leader: confident, decisive, and driven. She had a rapid climb up in surgery, ultimately becoming vice chair of the department. Everyone expected her to become the first female chair of surgery at St. Nicholas Hospital. Yet the more position power and influence she gained within the organization, the more assertive (some would say aggressive) she became. It reached the point where, according to a number of the residents and nurses, "Linda was no longer able to manage her own arrogance." Her conversations became lectures, and her team meetings became a forum for her to belittle others. She did not really change who she was; she just became a more extreme version. She still was one of the top surgeons in the country, and her referral base continued to grow. But with all this success, there was a cost. She ignored social cues. She didn't get it when her team sat there quietly as she droned on. Slowly but surely, Dr. McKenzie lost trust and respect among her team and some of her peers. She became so convinced that she was always right that she turned others off. People no longer sought her out or wanted to work with her. She started losing valued and experienced nurses, and some residents began gravitating to other surgeons. She got into petty fights with other executives over resources and direction. Each argument ended with others saying something along the lines of, "You seem to be certain that you're right," and Dr. McKenzie responding, "That's because I am." She was shocked, then, when the chair and Dr. James, the CMO, told her she was out of the running for the chair position. In fact, Dr. James suggested that she consider another hospital in which to practice. Although the communication surprised her, they had tried to warn her several times before, but she never really heard them. She thought her achievements made her untouchable.

*(continued)*

*(continued from previous page)*

- How do factors like expertise, power, or status affect people's ability to listen?
- How might you help Dr. McKenzie to change her style?

## Think About It

Go back to the Introduction of this book and review the section on self-concept (pages xxx–xxxiii). In what ways might having a negative self-concept harm listening? How can having a more a positive self-concept boost your listening skills?

## REFERENCES

Goulston, M. 2009. *Just Listen: Discover the Secret to Getting Through to Absolutely Anyone.* New York: AMACOM.

Madden, K. 2011. "What Makes a Good Leader at Work?" CareerBuilder. Accessed December 22, 2023. http://web.archive.org/web/20150424002118/www.careerbuilder.com/Article/CB-2062-Leadership-Management-What-makes-a-good-leader-at-work.

Maxwell, J. C. 2005. *Developing the Leaders Around You: How to Help Others Reach Their Full Potential.* Nashville: Thomas Nelson.

Schein, E. 2013. *Humble Inquiry: The Gentle Art of Asking Instead of Telling.* New York: Berrett-Koehler.

# CHAPTER SEVEN

# Competency 7: Giving Great Feedback

It is 11:20 a.m., and the nursing leadership team is waiting for Stockard Smith to arrive for their weekly meeting that was supposed to begin 20 minutes ago. Smith had become the interim VP of patient care services and chief nursing officer (CNO) a few months ago, after the previous CNO, Barbara Buczinski, began experiencing health problems. Although it is unlikely that Buczinski will return, St. Nicholas has not started looking for a permanent replacement yet.

Several years earlier, Buczinski and the nursing leaders had committed to be on time for their meetings, so they would always start and end on time. The leadership team cannot start without Smith, so they use the time however they can—checking in with their units, checking their phones, or pulling each other out into the hall for conversations. When Smith finally arrives, she looks quite frustrated. She stomps in, sits down, lets out a loud sigh, and says, "Okay, let's go."

It's obvious to everyone that Smith is struggling to learn this new role and still do her other work, but she is doing pretty well overall. The rest of the team knows this, so no one wants to say anything to her about being late.

The meeting continues, but time runs out before the last item on the agenda—an action item from Rick Kramer, the director of surgery, about the new quality program that he wants to start next week. Patti Juniper, the nurse manager in the emergency department, realizes there will not be enough time to address it and suggests tabling it until next week. Kramer, who is now furious, turns to Smith and says, "This is ridiculous. I want you to remember we didn't get to this because you couldn't be bothered to come to this meeting when you were supposed to. If we have any sentinel events this week, I hope you feel personally responsible!" (For the record, Smith's response to Kramer's outburst was even less polite.)

THIS VIGNETTE ILLUSTRATES several exchanges in which feedback could have been helpful but was not nearly as effective as it could have been. Smith's lateness was inconveniencing the nursing team and making them less productive. But the team was reluctant to talk to Smith about it, partly because they felt sympathy for the challenges she faced in her new role. Smith didn't even know about the punctuality rule, because no one had told her about it when she joined the group. When someone finally told her about the rule a few days after the meeting, it was in a rude way. Smith did not take it seriously, and the problem led to another unproductive argument.

However, this team can hardly be described as dysfunctional. They are doing good work for the hospital, and Smith is starting to master her new role. But with better ways of giving and receiving feedback, Smith could learn faster, and the team could make decisions even more efficiently.

## WHAT IS GIVING GREAT FEEDBACK, AND WHY DOES IT MATTER?

*Giving Great Feedback* is, at its essence, sharing information about performance in the best ways to help people improve. For our purposes, we are referring to interpersonal feedback, which is feedback that is transmitted from one individual to another, and by "help," we mean that the feedback makes them want to do better and shows them how.

> **Giving Great Feedback** means you set clear expectations, bring up important issues in a way that helps others hear them, are open to dealing with difficult topics and sources of conflict, address problems and difficult people directly and honestly, give timely criticism when needed, and give feedback messages that are clear and unambiguous.

If you have ever taken a course on human resources or leadership skills, you have probably learned some rules of thumb about delivering feedback. Some helpful and familiar guidelines are to give feedback as soon as possible after the event, to describe what you saw objectively, to suggest a specific way to improve, and to end on a positive note. These are all good tips for feedback, but they are less helpful for thinking through the relationship context in which the feedback happens. Feedback messages *always* happen within the context of a relationship. We choose who we want to give feedback to and when, based on what we know about the person and how we think they will react. The receiver's reactions, in turn, will depend on their self-concept and expectations about us. If leaders fail to recognize and attend to these relationship factors when they give feedback, the feedback may still work—but it won't be as powerful and useful as it could be.

## HOW HIGHLY EFFECTIVE LEADERS GIVE GREAT FEEDBACK

Leaders with exceptional feedback skills are better at attending to contextual factors. Whenever they are considering giving feedback, they start by checking their own motives through a process like the following.

### Defining the Real Issue

Highly effective leaders know that the core issue and best target for feedback may not reflect the problem as initially presented. Too often, busy leaders are not clear when they define problems. They may avoid saying what they mean or use vague words. In contrast, highly effective leaders zoom in on the real issues and focus on the true concerns by using more specific and direct language. For example, let's go back to our vignette, where Kramer yelled at Smith for being late. If Kramer had taken more time to think about why he was angry, he might have better understood the complexity of the situation. Maybe he resented being last on the agenda, which he thought meant that Smith did not care enough about starting the new quality program. Or maybe Kramer had already kept quiet about Smith's lateness in several prior meetings, and he was now reacting to the whole pattern more than to the single event. By not recognizing either of these possibilities, Kramer's feedback is probably way too harsh for Smith's immediate offense.

### Evaluating the Issue

Exceptional leaders ask themselves if the *benefit* of addressing the issue is likely to be worth the *cost*. One book on leadership development featured a section called "Feedback: Give It Often." We disagree with this premise. Highly effective leaders assess the value or benefit of addressing an issue before talking to the person involved. They often let things go because they are not that important in the big picture. As a wise CEO once told one of us, "You have to decide if the juice is worth the squeeze." This decision is not as easy as it may seem because it can be very subjective.

In the vignette, some of the nursing team members might have chosen to ignore the lateness issue because they were afraid that pushing Smith too hard might make her harder to work with. Some may have wondered if she might be given the role permanently since no search process had been started. Some may not have cared that much about the meetings starting late. If these were real concerns, it might make sense to have supported Smith quietly instead of giving her constructive feedback. (In reality, the likelihood that Smith would resign over this feedback is probably very low.) On the other hand, leaders can sometimes see behaviors as more serious than they really are. Such a leader might react to a typo in an e-mail and a careless patient safety violation with the same harsh tone.

### Setting the Stage

Once a decision has been made to deliver feedback, highly effective leaders will make sure they give adequate thought to setting the stage for delivery. If the climate of the discussion is safe, there is a much better chance the receivers will be able to accept the feedback without getting overly defensive, and then productively use it to improve their performance. If the leader is particularly upset, she may decide to delay the conversation rather than risk failing to deliver the feedback in a measured way.

### Balancing Feedback

Highly effective leaders make sure the people they work with receive an appropriate balance of positive and constructive feedback. Some go as far as to mentally pencil in a small chunk of time during the workday to develop and deliver positive feedback to their staff. People appreciate receiving positive feedback, which is perhaps reason enough to pursue this practice, but positive feedback also serves another purpose: It helps staff have greater resilience to the constructive feedback they receive. If a person feels like he is generally doing okay, he will usually feel less of a sense of personal vulnerability when he receives constructive feedback and will be more able to hear and productively use the feedback he receives.

## WHEN GIVING FEEDBACK IS NOT ALL IT COULD BE

Problems with the delivery of feedback can stem from motivation or from the need for better methods. Here are some common reasons feedback can fall short.

## Being Reluctant to Critique

Some leaders view critiques as punitive measures and will avoid them until they feel they have no other option. This bias can be compounded by the recognition that many healthcare staff work extraordinarily long hours and under considerable pressure—what kind of monster would needlessly add pain and suffering to the mix?

In reality, critiques are needlessly painful only if they are delivered poorly or too infrequently. The latter is a lesson often associated with the wait-and-see approach (i.e., holding off on giving feedback in the hope that the performance problem will self-correct). When the problem persists, a leader may be on the hook not only for confronting the problem but also for explaining the sudden interest in a problem that has persisted for so long.

## Hesitating to Praise

At least as frequent a problem is hesitating to praise. Leadership roles tend to focus on fixing things, and it is easy to forget to bring attention to what is going well. Most leaders will acknowledge extraordinary performance, but the praise is frequently expected in such situations and so has less emotional impact on the recipient than receiving praise for more routine successes.

## Structuring Feedback Poorly

Feedback can also fall short if it is not well delivered. If the focus is too narrow, it may not be taken seriously by the recipient; if too wide, it can come across as an attack. If it is too vague, the recipient will leave feeling puzzled, or worse, helpless, about how to improve. Another important consideration is the amount of emotional force behind the message. As the saying goes, "Leaders cast long shadows"; what feels like a slap on the wrist in delivery can come across like a bullet in receipt. Conversely, leaders who find themselves in great pain when delivering critiques may overly sugarcoat a message and then feel frustrated when the recipient does not seem concerned about the problem performance.

## Giving Judgmental Feedback

Sometimes focusing a feedback message just on behavior is difficult, particularly when the behavior is either part of an ongoing pattern or seems so common-sense that it is hard to believe the person would not know better. However, going any deeper than the observed behavior can quickly render a feedback message less effective; it creates a level of defensiveness that becomes a potent distraction from the feedback itself. Exceptional leaders are certain to describe the situation factually, refrain from expressing opinions or value judgments, and focus on the actual behavior and consequences (i.e., keep focused on the *what* of the situation); on the other hand, less effective leaders tend to create a debate about the *why*.

**When Giving Feedback Is Not All It Could Be**

In leadership roles, listening can fall short for any of the following reasons:

- Being reluctant to critique
  - Critiques are viewed as punishments and not delivered until someone "really deserves it."
  - There is a bias toward the wait-and-see approach for performance problems.
- Hesitating to praise
  - Leaders fail to provide positive feedback as a routine part of work.
  - Leaders are reluctant to deliver praise except in unusual circumstances.
- Structuring feedback poorly
  - Critiques are too focused on the individual rather than on the problem behavior or performance.
  - Feedback is delivered with too much or too little force or is too vague.
- Giving judgmental feedback
  - Critiques are focused on the *why* of the behavior rather than the *what*.
  - The feedback recipient's defensiveness distracts him from hearing the feedback.

## MISUSE AND OVERUSE: HOW GIVING FEEDBACK CAN WORK AGAINST YOU

For leaders who are described as giving too much feedback, often one or more of the following patterns is present.

## Giving Feedback Too Quickly

Some leaders have too much of a hair trigger when it comes to delivering feedback. Leaders who do not stop to ask themselves, "Is this an issue worth addressing?" fall into this category. In a similar vein, leaders can be too quick to jump to action after hearing about problems from a third party. If leaders do not first inquire about the "offender's" side of the story, they set themselves up for a lot of defensiveness from the feedback receiver.

## Delivering Feedback Too Frequently

It is possible to give feedback too often. This can happen when leaders have unrealistic expectations about performance improvement. Some skills and behaviors, particularly the more complex and ingrained ones, take more effort to change than we may realize. The best antidote is to set mutually agreed-on goals and timelines for performance improvement and to limit constructive feedback on the focal issue during the interim periods. For some leaders, the sense of loss of control associated with backing off for a while is too much to bear. If this is the case, the leader's need for excessive control may be the real issue that should be addressed.

## Giving Imbalanced Feedback

Sometimes when leaders are described as providing too much feedback, the real concern is an imbalance between positive and negative feedback. Positive feedback often helps staff to be more resilient to critiques; conversely, if they are not receiving positive feedback, the critiques sting all the more. Of course, the imbalance can also happen on the positive side; some leaders indeed overuse the "strokes" to the point where they come across as perfunctory or gratuitous. If this is the case, it may suggest some general problems with the leader's ability to read her direct reports.

### Misuse and Overuse: How Giving Feedback Can Work Against You

Leaders are sometimes described as giving too much feedback. Typically, that will look like one or more of the following:

*(continued)*

(continued from previous page)

- Giving feedback too quickly
  - Attention is drawn toward unimportant performance problems.
  - Feedback is based on hearsay alone.
- Delivering feedback too frequently
  - The leader has unrealistic expectations about the velocity of performance improvement.
  - Feedback is used as an excuse for micromanagement.
- Giving imbalanced feedback
  - Constructive feedback is overemphasized, and positive feedback is lacking.
  - Critiques are delivered with too strong a tone or emphasis.

## HOW TO IMPROVE AT GIVING FEEDBACK

### Finding Role Models

Because so much of the most transformative feedback happens one-on-one rather than in public, identifying good mentors can be difficult. The best approach may be peer nomination: Ask people whom they would identify as particularly good at providing feedback. Another approach is to ask a senior human resources executive for his recommendations; he should have both the mental framework for such an assessment and the broad knowledge of leaders in your organization from which to make informed suggestions.

### Additional Opportunities for Personal Development

The best way to learn more skillful feedback approaches is to practice and to get feedback yourself. Often the best place to start is with someone you already feel you have a solid working relationship with. Enlist this person's help in crafting effective feedback dialogues. You might also ask them to role-play with you any particularly challenging feedback sessions you need to have with others.

For managing the delivery of constructive feedback in the context of your relationship with others, we recommend two books, *Crucial Conversations* (2011) and *Crucial Accountability* (2013), by Kerry Patterson and colleagues. These books provide structured approaches to some of the trickiest kinds of conversations, as well as walk-through examples from which to learn.

If you think you need to provide more positive feedback in addition to your critiques, try setting aside five minutes per day for this specific task. You might add this as a note in your daily calendar. At first this exercise may feel forced, but over time you should find it easier to identify positive things your staff have done and find opportunities to express your appreciation.

## SUMMARY

Delivering feedback in the right ways and at the right times makes a big difference in improving performance over time, which is why leaders who are particularly skillful at it tend to be viewed as exceptional. Practicing feedback using structured approaches may feel awkward at first, but it can quickly improve your effectiveness at this crucial skill. Finding the right balance of positive and constructive feedback, as well as when to deliver each, takes even more practice, but its mastery can be even more rewarding in terms of overall effectiveness.

### Think About It

According to research done by the *Journal of Consumer Research* and reported in the *New York Times* (Tugend 2013), "As people gain expertise, feedback serves a different purpose. When people are just beginning a venture, they may not have much confidence, and they need encouragement. But experts' commitment 'is more secure than novices, and their focus is on their progress.'"

This means that giving feedback is far more complex than many leaders think.

- Based on your own experiences receiving feedback, do you agree with this description?
- What are some memorable examples of feedback you've gotten, positive or otherwise?

### Think About It

Revisit the opening vignette at the beginning of this chapter in which the new chief nursing officer, Stockard Smith, dealt with the feedback situation.

- If you were Smith's executive coach and you had been sitting in this meeting, how would you counsel her? What other underlying problems might be going on in this scenario?

# REFERENCES

Patterson, K., J. Grenny, and R. McMillan. 2013. *Crucial Accountability: Tools for Resolving Violated Expectations, Broken Commitments, and Bad Behavior*, 2nd ed. New York: McGraw-Hill.

Patterson, K., J. Grenny, R. McMillan, and A. Switzler. 2011. *Crucial Conversations: Tools for Talking When Stakes Are High*, 2nd ed. New York: McGraw-Hill.

Tugend, A. 2013. "You've Been Doing a Fantastic Job. Just One Thing." Published April 5. www.nytimes.com/2013/04/06/your-money/how-to-give-effective-feedback-both-positive-and-negative.html?pagewanted=all&_r=0.

# CHAPTER EIGHT

# Competency 8: Mentoring

Although Mary Moses had just started as the chief administrative officer (CAO) of Suburban West Hospital, part of the St. Nicholas Health System, she was already well aware of the challenges she would have to overcome in the next few years. Suburban West had been very successful, but many of its department heads had been in their positions a long time and had grown too comfortable with the steady financial situation. Some were good at dealing with people but not as good at managing finances. Others were good at budgeting and revenue management but failed to invest in their leaders' development, to the detriment of their staff. There were also a host of individual challenges: one department head always hired outsiders and never promoted from within, another could not hold on to people, and still another seemed to spend more time in grievance hearings than with his staff.

The previous CAO had been more of a public figure—a visible presence in the community but scarcely available to his staff. He took a hands-off approach to management: "Do well, and I'll leave you alone; do poorly, and you're out of here." Moses knew she would need to do things differently.

IN THIS VIGNETTE, Moses realizes that some of her new staff are underperforming at least in part because they lack certain skills. Moses has the advantage of being new; she doesn't need to change any old expectations or habits. She also faces a number of challenges: She may not have enough time to mentor everyone who could benefit from more guidance, and she may not have all the skills her staff need to learn. Beyond these basic concerns are more complex ones: How hard should she push people? Who should she be more lenient with? How long should she give them to improve? And how can she ensure mentoring is strengthening, not weakening, her working relationships? Exceptional leaders often stand out from good leaders by how well they recognize and address these questions.

## WHAT IS MENTORING, AND WHY DOES IT MATTER?

For our purposes, *Mentoring* comprises all actions leaders take to support the long-term growth of their staff. Of particular concern are the career goals these individuals have. Do they feel they are progressing in their jobs and careers? Can they increase their responsibilities, either in their current roles or in new ones? Do they feel free to explore different opportunities within or outside the organization?

> **Mentoring** means you invest time to understand your staff's career aspirations, work with them to create engaging mentoring plans, help them develop their skills, support career development in a nonpossessive way (e.g., encouraging staff to move up and out if important for their advancement), find stretch assignments and other opportunities that help them learn new skills, and model professional development by improving your own skills.

We emphasize the relationship and the goals rather than the methods because activities will vary depending on the staff's needs and the leader's ability to personally meet those needs.

Going back to the vignette, Moses's analysis of her staff's performance issues leads her to conclude that mentoring is needed. However, in our experience, exceptional leaders *always* provide mentoring, not just in situations that clearly need it. This is true regardless of the overall performance level of the department or organization; in fact, mentoring is more likely to happen in teams that are already high performing—it may be how they got that way in the first place.

## HOW HIGHLY EFFECTIVE LEADERS MENTOR

In our experience, the following qualities are hallmarks of mentorship in highly effective leaders.

## Taking a Comprehensive Approach

The most effective mentors focus attention on *all* of their direct reports. Returning to the vignette that started this chapter, Moses recognizes the need to mentor this group of leaders but appears to be in some danger of falling into a common trap: focusing on the "problem children." The departments in the red are likely to be the ones she herself will be under scrutiny for, so a bias toward attending to these groups is understandable. But what about the departments that are performing well? In addition to fixing problems, a highly effective mentor will also seek ways to make good departments great and to turn great departments into world-class operations.

## Building on Relationships

For you to be a highly effective mentor, your direct reports must come to believe their individual interests will be well served by listening to you. The first step in this process is developing a clear understanding of your direct reports' interests and goals. Mentoring will be most powerful when it focuses on individuals' needs as well as the needs of the organization.

Highly effective leaders meet routinely with each of their direct reports to explore career goals. Once they gain an understanding of how individuals would like to see their jobs, careers, and areas of accountability over the next several years, they can then discuss areas for improvement, simultaneously looking for ways by which these improvements can also serve the individual's goals.

## Emphasizing Clear, Consistent Follow-Through

As our emphasis on the relationship suggests, high-performance mentoring requires a long-term commitment to the process. In addition to starting strong, exceptional leaders robustly build the mentoring process into their workflow. Many of these leaders have regularly scheduled meetings with their direct reports to focus on mentoring; the meetings may not be frequent, but they are held consistently.

## Participating in Staff Development

In a high-performance approach to staff development, the leader will actively work with staff on skill development. For example, if an off-site educational program is called for, the leader will have some involvement in helping the staff select an appropriate one. When the program is complete, the leader will find time to discuss what was learned with the staff. Forethought will also be given to opportunities in which the new skills could be practiced on the job, so that these opportunities for application and reinforcement of learning are taken.

### Encouraging Growth

Exceptional leaders recognize that higher-performing staff are also more employable elsewhere, but that does not stop them from developing their staff. They understand that the value of being viewed as a powerful mentor exceeds the cost of replacing staff when they outgrow their roles. How can this be? Consider the references coming from previous employees. A job with a strong mentor is described as a valuable learning opportunity—one that helped them prepare for the even better position they now hold. A job with a weak mentor is described as a dead end—one that the former staff members "escaped" to accept their new position.

## WHEN MENTORING IS NOT ALL IT COULD BE

In several common situations, mentoring is not as effective as it might be. The ones we have encountered most frequently include the following.

### Undervaluing Mentoring

If leaders do not view mentoring as an essential part of their roles, chances are it will fall by the wayside. For some leaders, the driving force is left too much in the hands of their staff; they mentor the direct reports who make a point of demanding it, and they are far less attentive to everyone else. The typical result is that the vocal high performers continue to develop their skills, the quiet high performers get frustrated about being passed over, the low performers are ignored until they become serious problems, and the B players never get any better. Some leaders do not even make the initial investment in learning their staff's career goals—or, if they do, they fail to remember them or at least write them down somewhere accessible.

Another way mentoring can fall short is if leaders view mentorship as about supporting training rather than about the relationship. We see this in leaders whose automatic reactions to performance improvement needs are to send staff to an off-site conference, workshop, or class. While these approaches can be very helpful in improving knowledge, they usually do little to develop skills and even less to ensure that skills transfer successfully to the staff's workplace.

## Undervaluing Staff Development

Some leaders take a more fatalistic "you either have it or you don't" view of skill development. These leaders may not have well-developed abilities to track performance improvement over time, or they may take an overly informal approach to this process. As a result, these leaders tend to think performance levels are more static than they really are.

For some leaders, this tendency shows up as a bias toward replacing people rather than mentoring them. In senior-level positions in particular, many organizations show a bias toward hiring outside talent rather than developing it from within.

## Being Too Possessive

Some leaders are overly possessive of their staff. These leaders may actively avoid mentoring staff out of fear that they will outgrow their positions and leave. Other leaders create barriers to their staff working on some developmental projects out of fear that other departments will poach them. They may mistakenly believe that if they don't develop their team members, those members are more likely to stay put; in reality, their higher-performing staff in particular are more likely to leave if they don't feel that they are developing in their job.

## Lacking Mentoring Skills

Mentoring can also fall short because of a lack of skills in the mentoring process itself. Some of these skills relate back to our discussion of feedback in Chapter 7. Others relate to the leader's ability to recognize the naturally occurring opportunities for direct reports to develop skills.

Let us consider the latter point in more depth. Think about how you decide who does what in your own department or organization. Chances are, most work goes to the individuals you believe will do the best job, because of either past experiences or relevant skills. Indeed, our industry's approach to human resources is essentially designed to ensure that this is the case. With this in mind, it becomes easier to see how mentoring involves some unnatural approaches to work, at least on occasion. From the mentoring perspective, the question is not always "Who will be most *successful* at this task?" but rather "Who stands to *learn* the most from working on this task?"

---

### When Mentoring Is Not All It Could Be

Mentoring can fall short of optimal for any of the following reasons:

- Undervaluing mentoring
  - Professional and career development is viewed as the responsibility of the individual.
  - Staff's career goals are not tracked.
  - The bias is toward event-driven development (e.g., sending staff to workshops).
- Undervaluing staff development
  - The leader takes a short-term view of her staff.
  - The bias is toward buying rather than making talent.
- Being too possessive
  - The leader is overly concerned about staff outgrowing positions or being poached by other departments or organizations.
- Lacking mentoring skills
  - The leader lacks a clear sense of how mentoring works and what his role in mentoring should be.
  - On-the-job opportunities to develop staff's skills are not identified or methodically pursued.

---

## MISUSE AND OVERUSE: HOW MENTORING CAN WORK AGAINST YOU

If mentoring was taken to the logical extreme, we would no longer have a place of productive work. Instead, we would have a place of education. Of course, an organization can stay in business only if the economic contributions of staff exceed the size of their paychecks, so the learning aspects of a job can be taken only so far. The ideal balance finds the sweet spot that maximizes both organizational performance and individual development. But when this balance either leans too far toward mentoring or is not well executed, the following pitfalls might be seen.

## Miscommunicating Developmental Decisions

Developing highly effective mentoring relationships requires regular communication, and sometimes not just with the individual receiving the mentoring. Direct reports are often quick to view learning opportunities, even developmental assignments, as being doled out unfairly. Developmental decisions often make good sense, but their rationale is often not well communicated to staff. In these situations, sometimes the best remedy is simply to better articulate how these decisions are made, attending in particular to any skill development needs that a staff member may feel are not receiving appropriate attention. However, leaders should also avoid dismissing concerns about fairness too quickly; uneven attention to developmental needs is a reality in many leadership teams.

## Overemphasizing Star Performers

When it comes to mentoring, star performers represent a mixed blessing. On the positive side, they tend to yield the highest returns on the time their leaders invest in them. But for this reason, they also tend to receive more of the leaders' focus to the detriment of other staff. Some leaders have a misguided notion that focusing attention on the stars will inspire the now-jealous B players to try harder so they can also reap their rewards. While this tactic may work for some direct reports, others may become less motivated, and their efforts may actually decline.

## Failing to Address Performance Problems

The one area in which some leaders face a genuine risk of overdoing mentoring is in working with staff who are chronically underperforming in their roles. In some cases, the cost of mentoring someone into a role definitely exceeds the return. Sometimes the problem stems from escalating commitment: Leaders may start to view the considerable time they spent building the staff's skills as a sunk cost that they need to recoup; giving up on a staff member's ability to learn a given skill set begins to feel like a personal failure on the leader's part. For other leaders, the problem may stem from discomfort in addressing performance problems and/or transitioning poor performers out of roles that are beyond their capabilities. A leader who overidentifies with her staff or who over personalizes her role is at particular risk for this vulnerability.

**Misuse and Overuse: How Mentoring Others Can Work Against You**

A focus on mentoring can work against a leader in any of the following ways:

- Miscommunicating developmental decisions
  - The rationale for mentoring is not well explained or justified to the team.
  - The leader is viewed as playing favorites.
- Overemphasizing star performers
  - Development opportunities are too imbalanced toward star performers.
  - Other team members receive little or no mentoring and become demoralized.
- Failing to address performance problems
  - People are given too much time and too many opportunities to improve.
  - The leader fails to recognize when termination or redeployment should be pursued.

## HOW TO BECOME A BETTER MENTOR

### Finding Role Models

We have described mentoring as a complex, multifaceted aspect of the leader–direct report relationship; as such, the most appropriate people to help you develop your skills will depend on the specific skills for which you have the greatest need.

In general, the best mentors are leaders who have helped many direct reports get promoted. If your organization has a more formal mentoring program (e.g., a program that pairs up junior managers with senior leaders who are not in their direct chain of command), you might find some particularly good mentors there. You can ask the person who runs the program for suggestions.

For help in learning the mechanics of the mentoring process, you can look for leaders who are also educators. Examples include department chairs who regularly work with post-docs (especially if they have a good track record of placing them), executives who work with administrative fellows (if they get good feedback), or senior clinicians who have reputations as outstanding preceptors. Mentoring is also the stock-in-trade of many executive coaches; they not only use these skills in their own work, but also teach them to other leaders.

## Additional Opportunities for Personal Development

Mentoring is a skill that develops only with practice. If you do not currently have direct reports, look for other ways you can help people develop their skills. For example, working with interns (paid or unpaid) can be an excellent way to practice and to learn. You can also take on leadership roles in community organizations and mentor there. If your organization has any formal mentoring programs, ask how you can get involved.

You can also find mentoring opportunities at local professional education events, especially the ones that have shorter lunch or dinner sessions. These events are frequently attended by younger professionals who are looking for career advice and guidance. Visiting with them over dinner or during receptions can provide good opportunities to share your insights and ideas.

We encourage you to visit the American College of Healthcare Executives (ACHE) website (www.ache.org) for more resources on mentoring. ACHE has an online mentorship program called the Leadership Mentoring Network. You can use it to find a mentor or to become one yourself. You can also connect with your local ACHE chapter or the ACHE Regent in your area. If you want to learn more about coaching, a good book to start with is *Coaching for Performance* by John Whitmore (2002). In this technique-focused book, Whitmore adapts sports coaching approaches for use in the workplace.

If you want to work on your relationships with poor performers, we recommend *Crucial Confrontations* by Patterson and colleagues (2005). This book teaches you how to address performance issues in a positive and effective way, even in the most challenging situations.

## SUMMARY

In recent years especially, the considerable pressure to do more with less has led to fewer managers doing the same or more work. It also means there are more new leaders needing guidance from fewer experienced leaders. This means that mentoring junior staff is harder but also more important than ever. If you feel like mentoring is taking too much of your time, we urge you to remember how much you benefited from the mentors you had in your early career, and let these memories inspire you to pay it forward.

## Think About It

Develop a business case for a mentoring program in an organization. Answer the following questions:

1. How will mentoring be defined? How will the program's success be measured? How is mentoring different from coaching?
2. Should mentors come from inside the organization or outside?
3. Will mentors be paid any stipend or bonus for their service?
4. Should any individual be eligible to receive mentorship?
5. What training should mentors receive?
6. How often should mentors meet with their mentees?
7. Should the mentoring program be separate from the organizational succession plan?
8. Should the mentorship program be run by human resources or by an outside expert? Should an individual be empowered to intervene if problems surface between mentors and mentees?
9. Should the mentoring program be built into the leadership development program? The high-potential leadership program?

## Think About It

Elizabeth Parris held this conversation with human resources VP Jim Batten: "Jim, we really do not have much of a succession plan for either our senior leaders or our middle managers. I think this is a serious weakness. At minimum, I think we need to start setting up our potential leaders with some senior-level mentoring. Come to the senior team meeting in the next couple of months and present a plan of action that the group can discuss."

Assume you are the consultant helping Batten develop this plan. Identify some key action steps and milestones for implementing a mentoring program at St. Nicholas, as well as any issues or concerns to keep in mind along the way. (For more resources on succession planning, see chapter 17.)

## REFERENCES

Patterson, K., J. Grenny, R. McMillan, and A. Switzler. 2005. *Crucial Confrontations: Tools for Resolving Broken Promises, Violated Expectations, and Bad Behavior.* New York: McGraw-Hill.

Whitmore, J. 2002. *Coaching for Performance: Growing People, Performance, and Purpose.* London: Nicholas Brealey Publishing.

# CHAPTER NINE

# Competency 9: Developing
# High-Performing Teams

As the newly promoted chief administrative officer (CAO) at
Suburban West Hospital, Mary Moses had the chance to reshape
the hospital's leadership team to better serve the organization's
needs. With a lot of support from the system, she hired several new middle
managers within her first 18 months, all of whom were excellent. She now
felt the team was ready to achieve the system's ambitious goals to grow the
organization, build two more outpatient sites, open an urgent care center,
build a new outpatient surgery center, open a new seven-story multispecialty
building, and become one of the system's models for the future.

But things changed quickly when the new team started having serious
problems. Every new project seemed to end in a bitter and divisive conflict.
Initiatives involving major changes inevitably pitted the veteran members of
the leadership group against the "new kids on the block," and new program
initiatives turned new members against each other. Discussions about
strategic direction felt like tense negotiations. As a result, everything was
taking much longer than it should.

Moses wanted to respect the autonomy of each group member, but she
was getting fed up with their constant, unproductive conflicts. She decided
to talk to them about her frustrations at the end of the next meeting. When
the time came, she made an impassioned speech about how the vision for
Suburban West, which they all agreed on, was now at risk because the group
could not figure out how to work together.

The speech did quiet the meetings down. But the conflicts continued,
just outside the meeting room. As more time passed, Moses sensed the

*(continued)*

*(continued from previous page)*

members of the team becoming stiffer and more formal with each other. She tried to bring up the issue again for discussion. When she did, everyone agreed the group was not making progress as fast as they needed to, but no one seemed to have any good ideas for how they could work better together.

THE SITUATION DESCRIBED in this vignette highlights several dynamics that often happen in senior leadership groups. All members of the group have an understanding of the organization's goals—the greater good—which conflict from time to time with their individual roles as advocates for their department's goals. This tension leads to the formation of allegiances, both opportunistic and long-term, as leaders find common interests and opportunities to "horse trade" to marshal support. The dimension of history also exists, in which memorable and regrettable transactions from the past become filters through which the contemporary challenges these leaders grapple with are viewed.

We can encapsulate this enormous complexity in the deceptively simple concept of teamwork.

## WHAT IS DEVELOPING HIGH-PERFORMING TEAMS, AND WHY DOES IT MATTER?

For our purposes, we define a *team* as a group of leaders who share common goals and must depend on each other for success. This definition is flexible enough to include different types of leadership groups, even if they do not meet the strict definition of teams. Our focus is not on creating the perfect team, but rather on maximizing productivity within the team in whatever form it takes, and on examining how exceptional leaders use their teams to their fullest potential.

**Developing High-Performing Teams** means you select executives who collaborate well, actively support the concept of teaming, foster open and constructive dialogue on important issues, motivate and reward team members for working together, limit the political maneuvering that happens outside the team, celebrate successes together, and cope as a group with setbacks and disappointments.

# HOW HIGHLY EFFECTIVE LEADERS DEVELOP TEAMS

Building a highly effective team requires leaders to pursue five essential activities:

1. Get the best people for team roles.
2. Align them with a shared vision and collective goals.
3. Build trust among team members (as discussed in Chapter 5).
4. Strengthen the bonds between team members.
5. Support team members in resolving the inevitable conflicts arising from group interactions.

With these five activities in mind, we have observed that the following competencies often distinguish the highest performing leaders.

## Getting the Best People for Team Roles

In his book *Good to Great*, Jim Collins (2001) explains why it is crucial to "get the right people on the bus." To achieve this goal, leaders must have a solid focus on hiring team players. Effective leaders are careful in their hiring practices; they try to develop a deep and critical understanding of candidates and are willing to spend the time needed to make the best possible hiring decisions.

What sets apart exceptional leaders in this category? They focus on hiring as a continuous process. These leaders constantly think about attracting and retaining talent, and they regularly look for good people before they even need them. They build strong networks of professional contacts, and they keep those networks active throughout their careers. They stay in touch with the high performers they have worked with before; those people become prime recruiting sources in the future. If these contacts are not interested in a specific role, they will still be able to provide valuable references. These leaders also monitor the succession planning processes going on within their organizations, looking for people with high potential whom they may need in the future.

## Building a Sense of "We"

In senior leadership teams, collective goals can be tricky to manage. Leaders need to set them and make sure they are followed, but they also have to balance them with individual accountability. There is also a natural tension between supporting the executive team and representing one's own staff that needs to be balanced carefully.

The best leaders understand these tensions and will find effective ways to help the group keep an optimal balance. Tools that can be very effective in enhancing a team focus include team goal setting and team-based reward systems; a balanced scorecard can also help ensure that the team goals do not overshadow individual accountabilities.

### Developing Cohesiveness

Attending to team effectiveness also means attending to the cohesiveness of the team. Techniques that can help to build team cohesiveness include the following:

- *Increasing the frequency of interaction.* The more teams interact, both formally and informally and both on and off the job, the more opportunities members have to know each other as people and the more cohesive they can become.
- *Providing opportunities to discuss group goals, and how they can be best achieved.* Providing incentive compensation goals that are tied to group efforts can also help focus the team toward greater cohesiveness.
- *Developing a healthy sense of competition against other teams.* To the extent that individuals can be rallied around a common "enemy," even if that enemy exists mostly in fun, cohesiveness is likely to increase.

### Working Through Conflicts

Every team has conflicts. Carson Dye (2023) wrote in *Leadership in Healthcare: Essential Values and Skills* that many healthcare CEOs try to stifle conflict among their senior teams. Exceptional leaders, in contrast, learn to expect conflict and will lead their teams to develop rules of engagement that guide them in their debates and deliberations.

To minimize harm in conflict, highly effective leaders work hard to:

- ensure there is fairness in resource allocation among team members,
- minimize the growth of smaller intragroup cliques (often by keeping the group size small in the first place),
- keep personal reactions out of the bounds of the conflict,
- ensure team members have minimal role ambiguity, and
- ensure team discussions take place within the confines of the team.

## WHEN DEVELOPING HIGH-PERFORMING TEAMS IS NOT ALL IT COULD BE

Team development falls short in a number of ways. The most common are outlined as follows.

### Using the Team for the Wrong Reasons

If teams are used for the wrong reasons, they will not yield the benefits normally attributed to teamwork. Leaders may fail to use the power of the many and may not see the value that can come from group discussion and problem solving. Instead, they may use teams solely for show-and-tell–type meetings, where group members merely report on their individual activities. Another less effective approach is to use teams as congregations, with an expectation that members rally unquestioningly around the leader's decisions rather than provide healthy skepticism and skillful contribution.

### Maintaining Too Much Control

Teams will not reach their full potential if leaders are unwilling to cede enough control to allow members the chance to weigh in on issues and ask questions. Some leaders place too much emphasis on ensuring that meetings proceed smoothly and without debate. Without these critical opportunities for input and dialogue, decisions are inevitably less thought out and tend to have less overall buy-in from the team.

### Overemphasizing Individual Roles

One of the greatest barriers to fully developing teams is viewing team members more as individual contributors and less as team contributors. If leaders place primary emphasis on achievements that are individually oriented, then team members will respond in kind. This can also happen when there is little setting of team goals or incentives for achieving these goals. Superior teams are constantly focused on both team development and team performance.

## Underemphasizing Team Development

Although most senior leaders have had at least some exposure to team-building efforts, too often the approach is event-driven; rarely does it involve methodically implementing lessons learned into the regular team meeting settings. Although team-building exercises can be informative, they will not build a team for you or even improve team performance.[1] These types of interventions are helpful only to the extent that they are woven meaningfully into an effective, ongoing commitment to team development.

If teams have no routine way to discuss processes and decisions, they will have little chance to grow and develop as a group.

## Treating Others Unequally

For teams to work effectively, they need to perceive a level playing field for all members. Maintaining equitable treatment requires active work on the part of the leader; a natural tendency often exists to create an in-group/out-group within the team, particularly when leaders work more closely with some members than with others. Power imbalances within the team can also be a source of conflict; if they are allowed to continue unchallenged, they can create significant barriers to smooth team functioning.

---

### When Developing High-Performing Teams Is Not All It Could Be

Team development can fall short for any of the following reasons:

- Using the team for the wrong reasons
  - Team meetings are only "show and tell."
  - Team members are expected to confirm support rather than provide healthy skepticism.
- Maintaining too much control
  - Meetings do not allow creative input on ideas and problem solutions.
  - Disagreement and conflict are not allowed to surface.
- Overemphasizing individual roles
  - Staff are regarded as individual contributors.
  - There is too little setting of team goals or incentive for achieving team goals.

*(continued)*

---

*(continued from previous page)*

- Underemphasizing team development
  - Team building is too event-driven (e.g., too much reliance on Myers-Briggs assessments or other facilitated team-building exercises).
  - No regular forum exists in which team processes can be discussed.
- Treating others unequally
  - The tendency exists to create an in-group/out-group within the team.
  - Some staff receive clear preferential treatment without clear justification.
  - Power imbalances within the team are allowed to continue unchallenged.

## MISUSE AND OVERUSE: HOW DEVELOPING TEAMS CAN WORK AGAINST YOU

While many executive groups can benefit from a more team-oriented approach, the risk of misuse and overuse also exists. This risk can show up as any of the following problems.

### Using Teams to Avoid Decision Making

The team approach can be misused to avoid making decisions or to avoid accountability for them. For example, a decision that would be best handled unilaterally by the CEO may instead be discussed for weeks on end. Team protocols can also evolve a rigidity that ends up precluding timely decision making. We have seen team structures limit themselves by historical policy; a fast decision might be avoided for no better reason than overemphasizing protocol or simply thinking it feels too rushed.

### Creating a "Country Club" Team

A particularly dysfunctional example of team overuse involves the attempt to create a "country club" environment—one in which security and comfort of team members become the primary objectives. While the working environment should not be uncomfortable, too much stability creates a stale culture. Highly effective teams, in contrast, will frequently challenge the status quo and will always be on the lookout for how they might improve.

### Overemphasizing the Need to Keep the Peace

Placing too much emphasis on teams can discourage healthy tension and disagreements that arise over different points of view. To keep the peace, less effective leaders may actively discourage healthy competition among team members. They will try to place too much attention on treating everyone the same rather than acknowledging diversity in efforts, ideas, and abilities. Conflicts often present opportunities for improvement; avoiding conflicts rather than addressing them just to maintain harmony will significantly impair team performance over time.

### Overemphasizing the Team

Sometimes leaders act as though the team is everything. Their constant references to the team take precedence over ensuring both individual accountability and a clear understanding of roles within the team. A lack of individual accountability often becomes a barrier to addressing individual performance problems and is thus another source of productivity loss.

---

**Misuse and Overuse: How Developing Teams Can Work Against You**

- Using teams to avoid decision making
  - Situations that call for individual leadership are overdiscussed.
  - Decisions are delayed unnecessarily because of protocol.
- Creating a "country club" team
  - Team member happiness is overvalued.
  - Security and stability are overemphasized.
- Overemphasizing the need to keep the peace
  - Healthy competition among team members is actively discouraged.
  - Too much attention is paid to treating everyone the same rather than acknowledging diversity in efforts and abilities.
- Overemphasizing the team
  - The team lacks individual accountabilities and clear roles.

---

## GETTING BETTER AT DEVELOPING HIGH-PERFORMING TEAMS

Most of us do not enter our professional careers with a refined set of team development skills. Team leadership, like teams themselves, evolves to higher levels of performance through a combination of skill development, practice, and open, candid dialogue about opportunities for improvement.

### Finding Role Models

Role models for high-performing team development are best found by joining and participating in a number of teams and task forces. Many organizations use temporary task forces to address problems and tackle projects. Participating in these can provide many opportunities to learn both the helpful and harmful approaches to team development.

Many operations executives are adept at forming and sustaining effective teams. They often need to accomplish multiple actions by pulling together a diverse group of contributors. Medical services corps leaders who run the hospitals and clinics for our armed forces also tend to be talented in developing and using teams.

Joining boards or other outside groups in the community can provide opportunities to study effective team performance. Participation in church or synagogue leadership teams can give you insights, in particular, into managing volunteers and using persuasion in team management.

### Additional Opportunities for Personal Development

There are many team development books on the market. Some of the better ones are listed at the end of this chapter. Many of these books take a theoretical or mechanical approach, which can make for difficult reading. One noteworthy exception is Patrick Lencioni's (2002) highly readable *The Five Dysfunctions of a Team*. Lencioni also suggests, as we do, that trust is a critical foundation for superior team performance. Another is General Stanley McChrystal's *Team of Teams* (2015). Lastly, there is an excellent review of the science of improving teamwork by Christina Lacerenza and colleagues in *American Psychologist* (2018).

## SUMMARY

The work of healthcare leaders is increasingly team-based. We expect this trend to continue and quite possibly intensify alongside the increasing focus on population health and value-based care. When there is a lot of time pressure to get through an agenda, carving out the time to reflect and improve team process can be particularly hard. But in our observations of exceptional leaders, that time is well worth it.

## Think About It

Many organizations use team-building exercises and programs, often at a retreat away from the workplace. Some of these exercises can be controversial because they may disrespect or invade team members' dignity or privacy. Activities that involve physical or athletic games may make some people uncomfortable. Peer pressure and feeling the need to conform can create resentment. Some individuals feel team-building exercises have little to do with what they do in their jobs the other 364 days of the year.

- Identify at least three approaches to team building, and weigh each against the others in terms of how relevant and useful you think they would be for a specific team.
- Talk to one or more friends or colleagues about their experiences with team-building exercises. Ask for their honest opinions about how helpful the exercises were and in what ways.

## Think About It

Building teams involves several complex challenges. The first is that many teams are brought together only based on functional skills (CEO, COO, CFO, CNO, and so on). These individuals play these formal technical roles because of their expertise and position title. Because of this, the impact that the personality has in individuals playing informal roles (e.g., people who act as idea generator, the conscience, the devil's advocate, the caretaker, the comedian, and so on) is often overlooked. Moreover, the role that individual values play in team functioning creates a complex set of dynamics. Lastly, there is no universally recognized way to measure team effectiveness.

- Research the effect of individual factors (e.g., values, personality, diversity) on team effectiveness. What seems to make the biggest difference?
- Develop several methods to improve team effectiveness through a deeper understanding of individual factors.

## NOTE

1. A meta-analytic review of 72 controlled team interventions found positive and significant medium-sized effects on both teamwork and team

performance. See McEwan D., G. R. Ruissen, M. A. Eys, B. D. Zumbo, and M. R. Beauchamp. 2017. "The Effectiveness of Teamwork Training on Teamwork Behaviors and Team Performance: A Systematic Review and Meta-Analysis of Controlled Interventions." *PLoS One* 12 (1): e0169604.

## REFERENCES

Collins, J. 2001. *Good to Great: Why Some Companies Make the Leap . . . and Others Don't.* New York: Harper Business.

Dye, C. 2023. *Leadership in Healthcare: Essential Values and Skills.* Chicago: Health Administration Press.

Lacerenza, C. N., S. L. Marlow, S. I. Tannenbaum, and E. Salas. 2018. "Team Development Interventions: Evidence-Based Approaches for Improving Teamwork." *American Psychologist* 73 (4): 517.

Lencioni, P. 2002. *The Five Dysfunctions of a Team: A Leadership Fable.* San Francisco: Jossey-Bass.

McChrystal, G. S., T. Collins, D. Silverman, and C. Fussell. 2015. *Team of Teams: New Rules of Engagement for a Complex World.* New York: Penguin.

McEwan, D., G. R. Ruissen, M. A. Eys, B. D. Zumbo, and M. R. Beauchamp. 2017. "The Effectiveness of Teamwork Training on Teamwork Behaviors and Team Performance: A Systematic Review and Meta-analysis of Controlled Interventions." *PloS one* 12 (1): e0169604.

# CHAPTER TEN

# Competency 10: Energizing Staff

After another disappointing drop in patient satisfaction scores, Barbara Buczinski decided she needed to back off from driving her improvement initiatives to spend some time learning how other hospitals were getting it right. Her organization's patient satisfaction survey vendor offered to connect her with a high-performing health system in Jacksbury, a market similar to hers. Buczinski called Marcia Lahey, the vice president of quality at the other health system, who graciously offered to host Buczinski for an on-site visit.

On the train ride there, Buczinski found herself thinking of all the ways this other organization must be different from hers; for starters, they probably did not have the same labor shortages or union problems. Surely, they did not have the same financial pressures. They were probably serving wealthier communities, too.

But what she saw in the other organization nearly made her jaw drop.

The health system she visited was actually much worse off than hers in many ways. Its pay structure was below market, its facilities were much older than hers, and the payer mix was even more challenging than what St. Nicholas worked with. Yet the clinical staff seemed happy, the customer service scripts were followed consistently, and the patients clearly felt they were well cared for. And if the physicians there had complaints about the electronic health record, they were not nearly as vocal about it.

At the end of her visit, she met with Marcia Lahey. Buczinski had just one question on her mind: "How on earth do you do it?" Lahey's answer seemed very simple: The team worked together to find meaningful goals, they communicated progress widely and consistently, and they used both

*(continued)*

*(continued from previous page)*

success and failure to drive more progress. Lahey was quick to add that their organization indeed had many of the same challenges Buczinski described, but the group had become good at keeping their individual needs separate from the group's goals. She also acknowledged that the team had grown through their shared experience of the COVID-19 pandemic. The period was as difficult there as in the rest of the country, but the team's collaborative focus allowed them to successfully implement innovative operational processes to increase their clinical capacity when needed, and almost all team members were still there, a testament to their commitment to the organization.

THIS VIGNETTE CONTRASTS two hospitals in terms of the energy level of their staff. Although staff motivation may not explain all the differences in performance outcomes, it could be playing a key, though indirect, role. By making sure that staff keep a positive outlook on their work, Lahey is also increasing the chance that they would be open to try new approaches, give people the benefit of the doubt, and cope with disappointments.

In Cornerstone 2, we looked at how leaders can most effectively communicate their vision to get people excited about their participation. We also discussed the importance of ongoing communication, and how hard this can be to do consistently. In this chapter, we build on this theme, looking at how exceptional leaders seek not just commitment but *high-energy commitment* from the people they rely on. Developing and sustaining a high-energy workplace may be one of the most difficult tasks healthcare leaders face. Success in this area often sets apart the truly great leaders from the good leaders.

## WHAT IS ENERGIZING STAFF, AND WHY DOES IT MATTER?

We describe *Energizing Staff* as the activities leaders do to boost the motivation in the people they work with. Motivation, in turn, can be defined as the amount of effort an individual wants to put into their work. In healthcare, energizing staff often means helping people stay in touch with the service orientation that brought them to the field in the first place and helping them see how their efforts are making a difference for others.

**Energizing Staff** means you set a personal example of good work ethic and motivation; talk and act with enthusiasm and optimism about the future; enjoy taking on new challenges; do your work with energy, passion, and drive to succeed; help others recognize the importance of their work and find it enjoyable; and have a goal-oriented, ambitious, and determined working style that resonates with others.

Leaders have more of an effect on staff motivation than they may realize; it is therefore an area that distinguishes high-performing leaders from average performers, and the highest performers from the good ones. Indeed, the extent to which leaders inspire their staff has well-documented positive effects on job performance, as well as their mental health (Montano, Schleu, and Hüffmeier 2023).

## HOW HIGHLY EFFECTIVE LEADERS ENERGIZE STAFF

The most energizing leaders have usually mastered the following aspects of the process.

### Understanding Individual Goals and Priorities

Exceptional leaders carefully adapt their approaches to differences in individual needs. They realize that what motivates one individual can be irrelevant or even demotivating to another. A common example is public recognition; some individuals like being singled out and publicly praised for their accomplishments, while others avoid the spotlight and feel embarrassed or ashamed if it is thrust on them. Another example relates to the relative value of extra-role experiences—the opportunity to present about a successful change initiative during a professional association's evening meeting may be much more rewarding for a single, career-minded up-and-comer than for a seasoned, family-oriented manager.

### Celebrating and Sharing Successes

Highly effective leaders work to ensure that both individuals and the teams supporting them are appropriately recognized for their achievements. They use the energy that comes naturally from successes by tapping into it and sharing it with their staff.

The value of recognizing staff may seem obvious; in reality, it rarely happens as often as it should, for many reasons. For one, health administration tends to involve constant, unexpected change; the crisis of the afternoon quickly draws attention away from the success of the morning. For another, the managerial role tends to frame accomplishments as basic expectations of the job; it becomes very easy to view these achievements as just what you are paid to do. Strong leaders avoid this temptation and make sure that recognition and celebration are a regular part of the workplace.

### Having a Sense of Humor

Given the business of healthcare, the risk of becoming—and staying—very serious at all times is constant. Certainly, some aspects of the job are not suitable for light-heartedness (e.g., poor patient experiences or clinical outcomes, hard but necessary job changes); however, too much seriousness can itself drain staff's energy levels.

Many leaders are described as having a good sense of humor. What sets exceptional leaders apart is not so much how fun or funny they are, but rather their ability to use lightheartedness to their strategic advantage. Humor can be a powerful device for breaking through unproductive tension; it can also help people find the distance they need from a problem to make more objective decisions and can enhance creative thinking about challenges a team may be facing.

Beyond humor, highly effective leaders strive to make their workplaces enjoyable. They want their staff to be eager to come to work; they take a serious interest both in the concerns staff have about the workplace and in the ideas they offer about making the workplace more fun.

## WHEN ENERGIZING STAFF IS NOT ALL IT COULD BE

When staff are not enthusiastic, engaged, and motivated, they are also not performing at their best. When this happens, the leader may be contributing to the problem in the following ways.

### Undervaluing Motivation

Some leaders think that motivation is not their responsibility. They believe that people come to work for money or career advancement, nothing more. As a result, they don't give much feedback, recognition, or encouragement to their staff. They don't realize how much they can influence their staff's energy and motivation levels.

This is a mistake. While it's true that each person has their own level of motivation, the work environment matters—a lot. And the leader is the one who sets the tone and culture of the work environment.

## Underdeveloping Motivational Skills

Some leaders do care about motivating their staff but may not know how to do it well. They might be low-energy or introverted themselves, and expressing enthusiasm or excitement may not come very naturally. They might also have a limited repertoire of motivational techniques, which get overused.

High-performing leaders who are introverted or have lower energy can overcome these barriers by learning from others who are good at motivating people. They can also delegate some of the motivational tasks to people who have more energy and enthusiasm.

## Tolerating Cynicism

Nothing kills energy faster than cynicism. High-performing leaders will not tolerate cynicism and will address it promptly and respectfully. They will challenge the cynical person to offer constructive solutions or alternatives and will also reinforce the positive aspects of the team and their work.

Lower performing leaders will let cynical comments go, out of either discomfort with confrontation or a lack of skill in tactfully addressing them. They may justify their inaction by telling themselves, "Everyone is entitled to their opinion," or by convincing themselves the comments are not a big deal—"Everyone knows he's a cynic. No one will listen to him." In our experience, neither rationale is particularly accurate or helpful to the team's functioning. In the most serious cases, the leaders may not recognize the cynicism because they themselves have grown cynical; in these cases, unless leaders confront their own cynicism, little hope exists of raising the enthusiasm of the team.

### When Energizing Staff Is Not All It Could Be

Leaders can misuse or misapply energizing, in any of the following ways:

- Undervaluing motivation
  - Leaders do not view energizing staff as an important part of their job responsibilities.
  - Leaders fail to understand or appreciate how they can influence others' energy and motivation levels.
- Underdeveloping motivational skills
  - Leaders take a one-size-fits-all approach to motivating staff.
  - Leaders may be too introverted or too low-energy themselves.

*(continued)*

*(continued from previous page)*

- Tolerating cynicism
  - Cynical behavior among staff is allowed to go unchallenged.
  - Leaders may be cynical about their own roles.

## MISUSE AND OVERUSE: HOW ENERGIZING STAFF CAN WORK AGAINST YOU

Leaders can misuse and also overuse their emphasis on energizing. Rather than creating energy, they end up creating discomfort; the result is usually a net loss of productivity. This can occur because of any of the following.

### Having Too Much Energy

Many successful leaders have unusually high energy levels—a great asset for enduring the long and stressful days they must frequently endure. However, if your energy level is too far above your direct reports', they can be left feeling worn out rather than energized. You need to match your energy level with your team's and give them space and time to recharge. You also need to make sure that your performance goals are realistic and relevant, not arbitrary or self-serving.

### Being Too Excitable

Some leaders focus too much on energizing their team and not enough on delivering results. They might set easy goals that don't challenge their team enough. They might celebrate every achievement, no matter how small or expected, and the inevitability of the successes may make these celebrations seem hollow for staff. This can lead to a team feeling bored, complacent, or cynical. Celebrations that become routine quickly lose their motivating power, as does the proliferation of recognition awards. The first award is always the most powerful; adding more awards decreases their overall impact. Any celebrations of a repeating nature (e.g., employee of the month) should be monitored carefully and discontinued when they reach the point of diminishing returns.

**Misuse and Overuse: How Energizing Staff Can Work Against You**

If a leader is viewed as overdoing it on energizing, it could suggest any of the following problems:

- Having too much energy
  - Enthusiasm crosses the line to grandiosity.
  - Reaching the bar is underemphasized and setting the bar higher is overemphasized.
- Being too excitable
  - Expectations are set so low that success is certain, yet still celebrated.
  - Staff feel obligated to go along with too many perfunctory celebrations.

## ENERGIZING STAFF POST-COVID

The COVID-19 pandemic has been a huge challenge for the healthcare sector and all who work in it. For almost three years, healthcare providers faced unprecedented demands, risks, and pressures. They had to deal with patient volumes, high acuity and mortality, and sociopolitical issues that sometimes made them feel unappreciated or even attacked for their heroic efforts.

In light of these factors, healthcare leaders need to recognize the toll that the pandemic has taken on their staff and make their engagement a top priority. Caregivers may still love their work and find it meaningful, but they may also be exhausted, burned out, or traumatized by what they have gone through. They need to know that their leaders care about them as people, not just as employees.

To create a truly energized team in a post-COVID environment, leaders need to be visible, engage with their staff and get to know them personally, provide on-the-spot recognition for work well done, and express thankfulness to those who choose to come to work every day in the organization. Because of the impact to employees' lives both inside and outside of the work environment as a result of COVID-19, access to resources that support emotional and mental well-being have become one of the primary motivating factors to ongoing engagement and motivation (De Kock et al. 2021). Leaders must be mindful of this fundamental need and engage their teams in a thoughtful dialogue about work conditions, encourage personal wellness and a work–life balance, and be able to connect employees with available programs (employee assistance programs, spiritual care, etc.) that may help them begin to recover from the emotional toll the pandemic has had. By taking a personal interest in the well-being of your employees, you can help to create a group that is not only energized about their work, but also more invested in the organization.

## WHAT TO DO TO BETTER ENERGIZE STAFF

### Finding Good Mentors

Particularly good mentors for energizing staff can be found in teams and organizations where high loyalty and significant resource constraints coexist. Leaders of thriving volunteer organizations fit this description well; success in these positions is particularly dependent on skill in helping volunteers put in effort to further the organization's social mission. Successful entrepreneurs can be another example. Many entrepreneurs, particularly in the early stages of their companies, have little in the way of material reward to provide their staff; the currency they do have is the hopes and dreams people have about their future success.

### Additional Opportunities for Personal Development

There is no shortage of writings about staff engagement, which is further testament to its fundamental importance to leadership. Here are some writings that we and our colleagues have found particularly helpful. An article that is popular among chief medical officers is Steve Brewer's (2022) "Using Adaptive Leadership to Engage, Empower and Energize." Jim Haudan's (2008) book *The Art of Engagement* provides additional useful approaches to energizing staff across a variety of industries. And the article by Cross and Dillon (2023), *The Microstress Effect: How Little Things Pile Up and Create Big Problems—And What to Do About It*, provides excellent suggestions.

In the area of well-being, Tait Shanafelt, Jon Ripp, Lisolette Dyrbye, and colleagues have produced some very thoughtful and evidence-based descriptions of effective systems-based approaches. Our colleague Katherine Meese has also been pursuing pioneering work in applying the principles of positive psychology to workplace flourishing. Key citations for all authors are available in the references section at the end of this chapter.

## SUMMARY

No matter how important an organization's work and mission is, staff will face ebbs and flows of their energy in response to the personal and organizational challenges they face. These changes have become much more intense since COVID-19. Exceptional leaders are aware of how their staff are feeling and what they need to stay motivated and engaged. The strategies suggested in this chapter can help you in developing your own approach to energizing your staff while still keeping true to your own personal style.

---

### Think About It

Healthcare organizations typically are very process oriented. However, process and arduous use of policies and procedures reduce the energy and enthusiasm that staff have about their work and their level of engagement in the workplace.

- How might leaders best balance process with outcomes?

---

### Think About It

Alfie Kohn (author of *Punished by Rewards*, 1999) contends that money is not always a motivator. He suggests that "rewards are most damaging to interest when the task is already intrinsically motivating" (Brandt 1995).

- Research some of Kohn's thoughts and premises.
- How might his ideas conflict with some of the ideas presented in this chapter?
- How might these apparently conflicting perspectives be reconciled?

---

## REFERENCES

Brandt, R. 1995. "Punished by Rewards? A Conversation with Alfie Kohn." www .alfiekohn.org/teaching/pdf/Punished%20by%20Rewards.pdf.

Brewer, S. 2022. "Using Adaptive Leadership to Engage, Empower and Energize." Medical Group Management Association. Published June 20. http://mgma.com /articles/using-adaptive-leadership-to-engage-empower-and-energize.

Cross, R., and K. Dillon. 2023. *The Microstress Effect: How Little Things Pile Up and Create Big Problems—And What to Do About It*. Brighton, MA: Harvard Business Review Press.

De Kock, J., H. Latham, S. Leslie, M. Grindle, S. Munoz, L. Ellis, R. Polson, and C. O'Malley. 2021. "A Rapid Review of the Impact of COVID-19 on the Mental Health of Healthcare Workers: Implications for Supporting Psychological Well-being." *BMC Public Health* 21 (1): 1–18.

Dyrbye, L. 2023. "Taking Action Against Burnout: Organizations Moving Forward with Impact." *Joint Commission Journal on Quality and Patient Safety*. https://doi.org/10.1016/j.jcjq.2023.07.008.

Dyrbye, L., B. Major-Elechi, J. T. Hays, C. H. Fraser, S. J. Buskirk, and C. P. West. 2020. "Relationship Between Organizational Leadership and Health Care Employee Burnout and Satisfaction." *Mayo Clinic Proceedings* 95 (4): 698–708.

Haudan, J. 2008. *The Art of Engagement: Bridging the Gap Between People and Possibilities*. New York: McGraw-Hill.

Kohn, A. 1999. *Punished by Rewards: The Trouble with Gold Stars, Incentive Plans, A's, Praise, and Other Bribes*. Boston: Houghton-Mifflin.

Meese, K. A., and A. Garman. 2021. "Moving Beyond Burnout Towards Physician Flourishing." In *Enhanced Physician Engagement: Volume 1—Motivating and Leading at a Higher Level*, edited by Carson Dye, 243–62. Chicago: Health Administration Press.

Montano, D., J. E. Schleu, and J. Hüffmeier. 2023. "A Meta-analysis of the Relative Contribution of Leadership Styles to Followers' Mental Health." *Journal of Leadership & Organizational Studies* 30: 90–107.

Ripp, J., and T. Shanafelt. 2020. "The Health Care Chief Wellness Officer: What the Role Is and Is Not." *Academic Medicine* 95 (9): 1354–58.

Shanafelt, T., D. Larson, B. Bohman, R. Roberts, M. Trockel, E. Weinlander, J. Springer, H. Wang, S. Stolz, and D. Murphy. "Organization-wide Approaches to Foster Effective Unit-Level Efforts to Improve Clinician Well-being." *Mayo Clinic Proceedings* 98 (1): 163–80.

Shanafelt, T., and J. H. Noseworthy. 2017. "Executive Leadership and Physician Well-being: Nine Organizational Strategies to Promote Engagement and Reduce Burnout." *Mayo Clinic Proceedings* 92 (1): 129–46.

# Part IV

# MASTERFUL EXECUTION—THE FOURTH CORNERSTONE

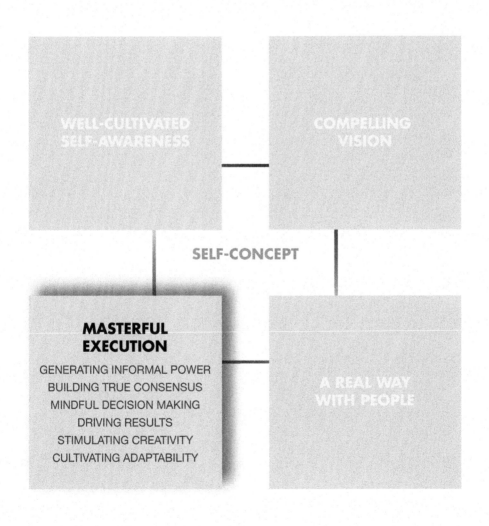

WELL-CULTIVATED
SELF-AWARENESS

COMPELLING
VISION

SELF-CONCEPT

**MASTERFUL
EXECUTION**

GENERATING INFORMAL POWER
BUILDING TRUE CONSENSUS
MINDFUL DECISION MAKING
DRIVING RESULTS
STIMULATING CREATIVITY
CULTIVATING ADAPTABILITY

A REAL WAY
WITH PEOPLE

THE FOURTH AND final Cornerstone, Masterful Execution, involves the competencies most related to the day-to-day work of leadership. It includes competencies that emphasize using the goodwill within working relationships ("Generating Informal Power") and finding common ground on which to move forward ("Building True Consensus"). It also includes optimally balancing information and intuition in charting the path forward ("Mindful Decision Making"), ensuring people are appropriately challenged to maximize their performance ("Driving Results"), and helping people expand their capacity to innovate and look beyond conventional solutions ("Stimulating Creativity" and "Cultivating Adaptability").

# CHAPTER ELEVEN

# Competency 11: Generating Informal Power

From the chime on her phone, Elizabeth Parris knew that her executive in charge of the employed physician group, Dr. Maria Borman, would soon finish her meeting with Dr. Bruce Red. Parris was at an impasse with Dr. Red on some key aspects of the new strategic plan, and she wanted to avoid a confrontation on the matter.

The previous meeting between Dr. Borman and Dr. Red had been disappointing; Dr. Red had raised many issues that Dr. Borman could not address. This time, Borman had done her homework and prepared a solid case for the proposed changes. She had researched every question Dr. Red had asked before and prepared for a number of others he might bring up. But after an hour with Dr. Red, which felt like an eternity, she felt the negotiations had actually gone backward several steps.

A few minutes later, Dr. Borman called Parris to update her on the situation. She listened for a while, then cut her off.

"Maria, how's your relationship with Dr. Randy Carl?"

"The chair of surgery? Fine, why?"

"What I mean is, do you have a positive 'bank account' with him?"

Dr. Borman thought a moment and said, "I guess so. We helped him out a lot when his surgery center ran into trouble. We set up a good co-management agreement, helped him hire new docs, and gave him prime space in our new building."

Parris smiled. "We may need to cash in a favor."

Dr. Borman was doubtful about the idea but followed Parris's lead. She set up a lunch meeting with Dr. Carl to see if he could help convince Dr. Red

*(continued)*

*(continued from previous page)*

to change his mind. Dr. Carl not only agreed to back them up, but he also said he was glad to be able to repay his "debt."

Sure enough, by the end of the week, Dr. Red e-mailed Parris and Dr. Borman saying he thought maybe he had been too stubborn with them. He agreed to support some of the most critical requests, although he still insisted on some other (relatively trivial) changes. Dr. Borman breathed a sigh of relief. She also made a mental note about the relationship between Dr. Carl and Dr. Red for future use.

THIS VIGNETTE ILLUSTRATES a common reality in every organization: Getting things done often requires more than rules and logic; it requires knowledge of how specific people relate to one another and the ability to creatively apply that knowledge. The more complex the initiative, the more these informal relationships are likely to matter. Success in building and using these networks is another way that the highest performing leaders often stand out from their peers.

## WHAT IS GENERATING INFORMAL POWER, AND WHY DOES IT MATTER?

*Informal power* is the ability to influence others without resorting to formal authority (i.e., without saying "Do it because I'm the boss").

**Generating Informal Power** means you understand how power and influence work in organizations; develop compelling arguments or perspectives based on knowing people's priorities; develop and maintain useful networks up, down, and across the organization; build a reputation as a go-to person; and effectively shape others' thoughts and opinions, both directly and indirectly.

Formal power lets leaders directly influence their direct reports and may also let some leaders (e.g., compliance officers) influence people by appealing to a set of agreed-upon rules. Informal power covers everything outside of that official structure and is usually where most power resides.

The classic research of French and Raven (1959) identified six fundamental sources of power, each with more or less association with formal authority:

1. *Legitimate power* comes from the position a person has and the officially recognized authority that comes with that position.
2. *Coercive power* comes from the threat of punishment. (This type of power tends to be viewed most negatively when it is part of leadership.)
3. *Reward power* comes from the ability to provide benefits or rewards (e.g., money, recognition, promotions).
4. *Expert power* comes from knowledge or special expertise.
5. *Referent power* comes from the respect or admiration that someone has for someone else.
6. *Information power* comes from having access to valued information or data (e.g., serving on a committee where important updates are received and/or decisions are made).

Both kinds of power—formal and informal—are related to the ability to gain access to and activate cooperation, support, information, resources, money, and opportunities within the organization.

## HOW HIGHLY EFFECTIVE LEADERS GENERATE INFORMAL POWER

Exceptional leaders tend to use the following approaches to generating informal power.

### Approaching Power Strategically

Highly effective leaders are selective about whom they build informal power relationships with. They look for the people who are most likely to be helpful to them in the future. For example, a high-performing leader will usually seek out the most skilled person or people in each department as their contacts rather than assume the department head is the best person to know.

This does not mean that great leaders will only work with the top performers in any department; they are not scheming and manipulative in their relationship building. However, when it comes to the proactive steps they take to build their networks, high-performing leaders know the value of prioritizing their efforts, and they will focus on where the talent is and where the opportunities for relationship development are richest.

### Being Efficient with Power

Although the idea of having a relationship "bank account" with people is widely recognized, the counting of favors and support is not very precise. Some kinds of support are more valuable than others, and some require more effort than others. The best leaders learn how to build these relationships with an eye for efficiency.

Some of the most efficient approaches to informal power involve a leader's ability to influence someone's decisions on behalf of someone else, as in the case of Dr. Borman influencing Dr. Red through the help of Dr. Carl. The brokering of support, especially when the costs to the leader are low, can yield substantial returns in informal power.

### Returning Favors

Paying back favors is as important as requesting them in the first place. Exceptional leaders recognize the debt they have to others for their support and are happy to repay it. Interpersonal relationships usually involve some quid pro quo, or exchange process. One well-known leader has called this process "interpersonal economics."

## WHEN GENERATING INFORMAL POWER IS NOT ALL IT COULD BE

Leaders who do not have informal power bases may have one or more of the following problems.

### Undervaluing Informal Power

Some leaders, even in more senior leadership roles, are not comfortable with the idea of doing anything outside of formally recognized policies and hierarchies. Leaders may care a lot about fairness and due process—and in many cases, official channels are the best ones to follow. However, the view can also be taken too far, to the point where *any* informal action is seen as unethical or sneaky.

A less extreme view held by some leaders is that politics is a normal part of organizational life; leaders put up with politics but do not see it as a personally useful tool. In the process, they are missing important opportunities to be more effective in achieving their goals.

## Involving the Wrong People in Networks

Leaders who do take their informal networks seriously may still fall short if they do not invest their efforts in the right people. Some leaders do not give enough thought to why they are building a network in terms of what it should do for them. Or, some leaders focus too much on quantity and not enough on quality; as a result, their network is too spread out, and the return on their efforts declines. Finally, leaders may focus too much on the formal power positions (e.g., department heads), which may or may not always be the best power sources or the most efficient networks to keep.

## Using Ineffective Approaches

Some leaders are not as good as others at network building. For example, a more strategic networker will recognize the kinds of contacts or networks they may need before they actually need them. Many leaders will instead build their networks only when the needs come up. Examples include making contacts in the philanthropy department only *after* deciding to start a fundraising campaign, or finding a contact in employee relations *after* an employee discipline problem comes up. Although this approach can work fine for most leaders, we would not call it highly effective; because well-tended connections tend to grow stronger over time, leaders are usually better off if they develop networks proactively.

In addition to falling short on early identification, informal power will also be weaker if leaders are not as skillful in their relationship development efforts. For example, some leaders focus too much of their energy on the social aspects of their relationships. They may make a point of attending office parties and responding to social media posts, thinking this is helping them build effective working relationships. In developing an effective informal network, the message you want to send is "I am helpful to know." By focusing solely on the social side of the relationship, you only send the message "I am your friend." When it comes to generating informal power, a year's worth of dutiful attendance at office social events is nothing in comparison to a single, well-timed assist with a difficult workplace challenge.

Another way in which leaders' network-building efforts can go wrong is if they do not recognize and honor the need for reciprocity. This may seem obvious; indeed, in our experience, the failure is rarely intentional. We again go back to the topic of trust building: Good leaders may do well enough that they can be forgiven for the occasional oversight; great leaders strive to avoid the oversights in the first place.

Lastly, leaders must recognize that people differ in their general orientation toward reciprocity. While most people within healthcare want to help others, some try to get what they can out of their relationships with little thought to giving back whatever support they have received. These relationships must be managed especially carefully, so the leaders' support is not coming at the expense of their own goals.

---

### When Generating Informal Power Is Not All It Could Be

If informal power does not reach its full potential, the cause can be any of the following:

- Undervaluing informal power
  - Informal power is viewed as unethical or underhanded.
  - Politics are tolerated but not proactively used to the organization's benefit.
- Involving the wrong people in networks
  - Leaders do not effectively prioritize relationships to develop.
  - Formal power structures are overly relied on.
- Using ineffective approaches
  - Leaders do not develop networks in advance of needing them.
  - Leaders fail to reciprocate assistance or fall short in follow-through.
  - Leaders don't hold others accountable for reciprocity.

---

## MISUSE AND OVERUSE: HOW GENERATING INFORMAL POWER CAN WORK AGAINST YOU

Some leaders spend much more time and energy on getting informal power than is needed to support their role. Below are some common patterns.

### Focusing Too Much on Personal Agenda

Leaders who are very good at building relationships may be tempted to use their networks to support decisions that are more for their own benefit than for the organization's. In some extreme cases, a leader's job security may depend mainly on who they know. In other cases, leaders have used their informal networks to rebel against senior leadership.

Any time leaders try to build informal power based on personal agendas rather than organizational goals, they can end up with badly imbalanced networks. These leaders may find themselves in the know about key decisions and actions that affect them, but they will have much less useful power bases for ensuring effective performance in their roles.

## Overvaluing Relationship Building

For leaders who really like the relationship-building parts of their roles, this process can become the end rather than the means. Earlier, we mentioned the problem of focusing too much on the nonwork parts of relationship building. We are not suggesting that attending office social functions is a bad practice, only that it can be overdone. Whether it is fair or not, creating the impression that one always has time for social events can be viewed as slacking or self-aggrandizing by peers and direct reports: "She's off schmoozing again." The attention paid to networking can also take away too much attention from other important parts of the job. Effective leaders pay attention to the norms of their peers about how often they go to social events and how much time they spend at them. They also tend to plan more strategically for the opportunities these events provide to efficiently catch up with people they may not see regularly.

## Playing Power Politics

Leaders who go too far along this spectrum of relationship building may find themselves involved in power politics. They start to see the workplace as a competitive arena with winners and losers. Their political activities become a way to stand out and get noticed. The development of relationships and the ability to cash in favors become too central to their work.

---

### Misuse and Overuse: How Generating Informal Power Can Work Against You

Informal power can decrease a leader's effectiveness if the following occur:

- Focusing too much on personal agenda
  - Relationships are developed to preserve one's position rather than support the organization.
  - Network development emphasizes being in the loop over supporting organizational goals.

*(continued)*

---

*(continued from previous page)*

- Overvaluing relationship building
  - Nonwork (social) aspects of relationship development are overemphasized.
  - Network development comes at the expense of other essential aspects of the leader's role.
- Playing power politics
  - Politics becomes a game in which the goal is to be noticed.
  - Relationships are viewed from a win–lose perspective.

## HOW TO IMPROVE ON GENERATING INFORMAL POWER

### Finding Role Models

Informal power generation tends to be an intentional activity, and as such, people who are particularly good at it can often articulate how they approach developing these relationships. Finding these people can be a little tricky, however. By definition, the people most skilled with informal power are the individuals in the organization whose power is far higher than would be expected by virtue of their formal job title. However, informal power often tends to be a quiet art. The most effective leaders will not bring attention to their informal power, except when it is necessary to do so. However, there are some telling indicators, including the following characteristics:

- *Faster or more varied career trajectories.* Leaders who are better at generating informal power tend to be promoted more quickly than their peers. Also, for leaders who have worked in a number of different organizations (or in consulting firms), generating informal power is more of a survival skill.
- *Cross-departmental roles.* Leaders whose success most depends on organization-wide or cross-organizational collaboration also tend to have well-honed informal power skills. This is especially true for roles with neither legal/policy stipulations nor strong senior-level endorsements to fall back on. These people must truly exercise influence without authority to be successful.

### Additional Opportunities for Personal Development

If you are interested in learning more about how to develop informal power, a classic text on this topic is Cohen and Bradford's (2005) *Influence Without Authority*. This book provides excellent formulas to help you evaluate your assumptions, consider the interests and needs of others, and negotiate mutually beneficial exchanges to achieve your goals. Thematically, their book emphasizes the principle of building relationships by assuming everyone is a potential ally. For a more modern examination of the role helping others tends to play in one's own success, we recommend *Give and Take* by Adam Grant (2013). Chapter 7, "Chump Change," is particularly helpful in considering approaches to working with people who have trouble understanding the importance of reciprocity in their working relationships.

Because informal power is such a mainstay of organizational behavior research, almost any college-level textbook on organizational behavior will provide useful material. A favorite of ours is Henry Mintzberg's (1983) classic, *Power in and Around Organizations*.

If thinking strategically about informal power is new to you, we recommend trying out some of the formal tools that are available for assessing and diagnosing influence networks. The tools can be helpful in quantifying and visualizing what your networks look like, including areas that may be providing relatively lower or higher payoffs and areas in need of further development. *The Hidden Power of Social Networks* (Cross and Parker 2004) is a particularly good practitioner-oriented text that contains many tools for assessing social networks. Cross's follow-up book, *Beyond Collaboration Overload* (2021), offers many useful approaches to successfully managing social networks without becoming overwhelmed.

## SUMMARY

The dynamics of informal power and politics are realities in all organizations. Trying to ignore them or minimize their impact is not always a good use of energy. Exceptional leaders are skillful at capitalizing on these realities to support their organization's goals as much as possible. By understanding how decisions are really made, and by whom, as well as who the most helpful resources across the organization are, leaders will find themselves much more capable in their roles.

**Think About It**

The phrase *office politics* describes how individuals try to boost their personal power within an organization.

- What are some of the ways that leaders can reduce the negative effects of this phenomenon?

**Think About It**

Most successful leaders build many networks or alliances. Yet many negatives can also come out of alliances. Some alliances are not as powerful as others. Some seem to be dominated by individuals who are not that respected. Other alliances are tied only to the control of finances and can rapidly fall apart if the budgets get tight. And often individuals find that they are doing more favors for people than they get back.

- What are some steps that can be taken to manage alliances so that benefits are maximized and drawbacks are minimized?

## REFERENCES

Cohen, A. R., and D. L. Bradford. 2005. *Influence Without Authority*, 2nd ed. New York: John Wiley & Sons.

Cross, R. 2021. *Beyond Collaboration Overload: How to Work Smarter, Get Ahead, and Restore Your Well-Being*. Boston: Harvard Business Review Press.

Cross, R., and A. Parker. 2004. *The Hidden Power of Social Networks: Understanding How Work Really Gets Done in Organizations*. Boston: Harvard Business School Publishing.

French, J. P., and B. Raven. 1959. "The Bases of Social Power." In *Studies in Social Power*, edited by D. Cartwright, 150–67. New York: Institute for Social Research.

Grant, A. 2013. *Give and Take: A Revolutionary Approach to Success*. New York: Viking Adult.

Mintzberg, H. 1983. *Power in and Around Organizations*. Englewood Cliffs, NJ: Prentice Hall.

# CHAPTER TWELVE

# Competency 12: Building True Consensus

**Scenario A.** Alicia Zielinski was frustrated. As the new CEO of one of St. Nicholas Health System's rural hospitals, she had spent the past 15 months rebuilding her executive team. The group had been working together for five months now, and although each executive had outstanding qualifications, decision making on key strategic initiatives was hardly any better. Zielinski valued input from her executive team members and did not want to just listen to them and then make the final decision. She had hoped that by forming this team, they would make many decisions together by consensus. She wanted to benefit from the collective knowledge of the team and use the group discussion process to improve the quality of their decisions. But each member seemed stuck in their own functional area. Discussions regularly drifted into a focus on turf issues and attempts to clarify their own roles.

**Scenario B.** Randall Repito, president of the St. Nicholas Health Plan, was overseeing his first budget process at the insurance company. He had given his leadership group a lot of freedom, but the last three iterations of the budget had landed at bigger and bigger losses. The mandate to show at least a 2 percent profit on operations had been clear from the start. Repito called the leadership council together for a meeting in his office on Friday afternoon. He stated, "Folks, our goal could not be clearer: We need a budget that shows a 2 percent profit on operations. You have spent the past week revising the budget, and each time the loss gets worse. I meet with the system CEO next Tuesday and then have the board meeting next Thursday night.

I suggest you come in tomorrow and use the weekend to finish the budget. If I don't have a budget that shows a 2 percent profit by Monday morning, I will find other executives who will reach their targets."

THESE SCENARIOS DESCRIBE just two examples of how well-meaning executive teams can fail to work together toward the best outcomes. There are no obvious problem performers, just problem processes. In our last chapter, we discussed the importance of stockpiling informal power as well as the methods that seem to work most effectively for doing so. This chapter is about using that power, along with other negotiating skills, to help people move toward consensus. In the process, we investigate how groups can better work together in collective decision making.

## WHAT IS BUILDING TRUE CONSENSUS, AND WHY DOES IT MATTER?

*Consensus* means general agreement or harmony. *Building True Consensus* involves using group decision making and other methods to ensure a critical level of general agreement is reached and maintained about both the decision at hand and the consensus-building process itself.

> **Building True Consensus** means you present issues in ways that make them clear from different perspectives, separate the issues from the people representing them, skillfully use group decision methods (e.g., Nominal Group Technique), make sure that quieter group members are included in discussions, find shared values and common adversaries, facilitate discussions rather than direct them, and make sure the consensus-building process itself is seen as fair and appropriate.

Most decisions that leaders make do not have equal outcomes for everyone who is affected. As such, leaders rarely have the chance to develop initiatives or find solutions that everyone likes equally. The art of consensus building involves developing the levels of support needed to move initiatives forward without making some individuals feel left out, slighted, or otherwise powerless to affect the organization—or making other individuals feel too powerful. Consensus building can be a lot of work, requiring careful planning to ensure it involves the right amount of time and attention. Spend too much time on it, and you have too little time for other parts of your role. Spend too little, and your initiatives will not get the long-term support they need for success.

# HOW HIGHLY EFFECTIVE LEADERS BUILD CONSENSUS

Leaders who are skilled at building consensus have the following traits in common.

## Knowing When to Count Votes and When to Weigh Them

Not every decision made within an organization requires consensus. Exceptional leaders understand this and will convey this to their leadership teams. They also let their teams know in advance how their input will or will not affect the ultimate decision. Sometimes, they will seek their team's input but will reserve the right to make the final decision. Other times, they will inform their leadership groups that the decision will be a purely democratic process. Still other times, they will ask the group to actively participate in a consensus process to move toward a decision that will involve a synthesis of the viewpoints of the entire group.

When consensus is called for, effective leaders ensure the following factors each receive appropriate attention:

- *Balance.* This means finding the right level of agreement for a given decision or initiative. The best consensus builders do not try to get everyone on board, but instead try to get enough support to move forward. They will keep building consensus until they reach that point, and they will stop trying to convince others after that.
- *Efficiency.* Building consensus can take a lot of time and energy. Exceptional leaders know how to make the process work efficiently. For example, they can tell when a battle is winnable and and when it is not; however, even for battles that can be won, they learn to tell when the effort will be worth it and when it will not be.
- *Technique.* Besides deciding whom to work on and whom to give up on, the most effective consensus builders have a good number of strategies to address the *how*. They tailor their approach to each person's goals and priorities, both related to the decision at hand and also to each individual's need for power and social standing among their peers. The most effective consensus builders make it easy to say yes—for example, by finding ways for people who disagree to change their minds without losing face.

The process of building consensus is not just asking for everyone's opinions and then taking a vote on the final decision. That approach might leave some people feeling ignored or overlooked, and it could lead to suboptimal decisions.

While voting is a quantitative process involving a count, consensus building is a qualitative process that integrates diverse needs and perspectives. It does not mean everyone will think the final decision is the best one, but everyone should feel their views were heard and considered.

## WHEN BUILDING TRUE CONSENSUS IS NOT ALL IT COULD BE

True consensus building is more art than science; no one gets it right all the time. However, there are some common barriers that can impair a leader's overall results.

### Using a Command-and-Control Approach

Some leaders lean too heavily on their formal authority in making decisions that affect others. As a result, they lack an understanding or appreciation for consensus building. Some of these leaders will stifle consensus-building efforts because they do not view them as valuable. Others believe using consensus building will legitimize others' disagreements with them, diminishing their own power along the way. The command-and-control style is becoming less and less accepted; most people want the opportunity to question and even challenge authority and will not tolerate having their input stifled.

### Approaching Consensus Unevenly

Even leaders who understand the importance of consensus building can get themselves into trouble by failing to maintain a clear focus on their goals for the process. Some leaders find it particularly challenging to face vocal opposition; as a result, they tend to give in disproportionately according to how loudly a dissenter complains rather than considering how central the dissenter's role is or how powerful his influence may (or may not) be. Leaders do not need to give in many times before their colleagues recognize this weakness and begin to use it as a tool when it suits them.

Some leaders only seek consensus from those most likely to provide it. These leaders have a bias toward approval seeking rather than support seeking; they may have an easier time getting initiatives started, but these initiatives will move forward with less support, which is often reflected in the lower quality or speed of their eventual results.

### Lacking Sensitivity to Interpersonal Process

For some leaders, the consensus-building process itself is the greatest bottleneck. This can be caused by a lack of experience with consensus building, a lack of knowledge about the players and their histories, or occasionally a more basic lack of understanding of interpersonal process. At times, leaders may not want to offend a team member by pushing for a decision. There may also be occasions when certain individuals within a team may have certain sensitivities to specific issues (e.g., the chief financial officer and the budget; the chief nursing officer and nurse staffing) and the team leader does not allow discussions related to these topics to be managed by the group.

---

**When Consensus Building Is Not What It Could Be**

- Using a command-and-control approach
  - Leaders do not recognize the value of consensus in building long-term support.
  - Leaders view others as obliged to go along with decisions because it's their job.
- Approaching consensus unevenly
  - Too much ground is given to the most vocal individuals.
  - Getting approval is emphasized over getting support.
- Lacking sensitivity to interpersonal process
  - Leaders lack experience with the consensus-building process.
  - Leaders lack a clear understanding of the needs and priorities of the people involved.

---

## MISUSE AND OVERUSE: HOW BUILDING CONSENSUS CAN WORK AGAINST YOU

Many leaders overuse or misuse consensus building. In our experience, the following patterns are usually to blame.

## Being Biased Toward Universal Agreement

Whenever leaders are described as overdoing consensus building, it is usually because they place too much emphasis on getting everyone to agree. For most initiatives of any complexity, universal agreement is an impossible goal; still, some leaders press on pursuing it, wasting time and energy to push as closely as they can to all-inclusive buy-in. Along the way, they may too quickly redesign plans in a misguided effort to capture additional votes, leading to unnecessary and inefficient cycles of reworking and diminishing returns.

## Building Unnecessary Consensus

Even leaders without a universal agreement bias may overuse consensus building. For example, at times leaders face decisions that will negatively affect *all* stakeholders—decisions that no one is likely to support but that still must be made for the good of the organization. To seek consensus on such a decision is unproductive at best and, at worst, will lead to much effort and time being spent on a hopeless cause. Other leaders overuse consensus building in working with their direct reports.

For some leaders, the real issue is their discomfort in saying no to their staff. Rather than taking a harder line, they resort to pleading; as a result, staff are extended an inappropriate amount of power in their roles. Although leading through inspiration and encouragement is often best, staff still need to respect the formal authority of the leader's role.

---

**Misuse and Overuse: How Building Consensus Can Work Against You**

- Being biased toward universal agreement
  - Too much effort is devoted to getting every person on board.
  - Leaders are too quick to redesign plans to accommodate disagreeable individuals.
- Building unnecessary consensus
  - Consensus is sought when it is not needed or helpful.
  - Consensus is sought even when a decision outcome is already clear.

---

# HOW TO ENHANCE CONSENSUS BUILDING

## Finding Role Models

Several common organizational roles require highly skilled consensus builders and therefore tend to have good role models for this competency. Internal consultants, particularly those with stellar reputations for getting things done, are often good choices. Strategic planning consultants are often quite adept at consensus building, as are Six Sigma and Lean Management specialists. Training and education managers are also often well versed in consensus-building tools, and they may also have some experience in teaching these skills to others.

## Additional Opportunities for Personal Development

One of the best ways to enhance skills in this area is to volunteer to lead a strategic planning or other group process in a community not-for-profit organization, association, church, or synagogue. Members in these settings often hold passionate views and feel far less need to express agreement (particularly if their jobs are not at stake).

Given that consensus building is both widely recognized as important but also difficult to master, many workshops and books are available to support skill development. Among our favorites is *Decisive: How to Make Better Choices in Life and Work* by Chip and Dan Heath (2013).

Effective consensus building also involves the use of group process techniques. Readers are encouraged to learn more about the many resources that teach the following techniques:

- Nominal Group Technique
- Brainstorming
- Force field analysis
- Affinity mapping
- Fishbone diagrams
- Scenario sketching

These techniques are used so widely that information and instruction on many of these techniques can be easily found through an Internet search.

## SUMMARY

Building True Consensus is difficult to master and distinguishes exceptional leaders for at least two reasons. First, when people agree on a common goal, they will work harder to achieve it. Second, when people feel that their opinions matter, they will show greater support for decisions even if they do not agree with them. Therefore, getting better at building true consensus is a worthwhile goal for any leader.

### Think About It

The vignette that started this chapter described some group dynamics in the senior team at St. Nicholas. Elizabeth Parris used a hands-off leadership style and did not pay much attention to how consensus developed. Usually she let three of her senior VPs—Dr. Howard James, Samantha Stoman, and Dave Damron—make the important decisions. Over time, the rest of the team stopped participating in the strategic discussions and instead deferred to these three.

However, as as the pace of changes in the healthcare industry accelerated, St. Nicholas needed a more robust and forward-looking approach to direction-setting. Parris's regional executive vice president, Duhal Malinka, took her to lunch one day and said, "Liz, you know I respect you a lot. But I have to tell you something that I think is hurting our ability to compete. I don't think you realize it, but you have given practically all the authority to shape strategy to Dr. James, Stoman, and Damron. And while I think they are all good leaders, none of them are strategic thinkers. Howard is stuck in the old model of hospital-based care and knows almost nothing about primary care. Samantha is a traditional finance person who focuses too much on acute care revenues. And Dave's only focus has been acquiring more primary care practices. The fact is, we have no one with any depth on population health and managing care across the continuum. Frankly, we are still acting like adding more inpatient beds is our only strategy. And the real problem is that our decision-making processes are not really based on consensus."

Parris listened intently to Malinka and, after a pause, responded, "Duhal, I agree with you completely. This has been bothering me for a while now. But I don't know how to fix it."

- If you were Malinka, what would you suggest to Parris about how she can improve her senior team's ability to build a more consensus-oriented approach to strategy development? Think about the St. Nicholas senior leadership team or another team you are familiar with that needs to make rapid decisions.

## Think About It

Many healthcare organizations have adopted such strict consensus-type processes into their decision making that they often seem paralyzed, unable to make timely decisions when needed. This often happens when multiple meetings and discussions have to take place over a period of time. Compounding these challenges are the electronic communications tools that too often replace face-to-face meetings, causing frustration for many leaders.

- Write a set of guidelines for decision making that you think could support consensus without allow it to become frozen ("analysis paralysis").

## REFERENCE

Heath, C., and D. Heath. 2013. *Decisive: How to Make Better Choices in Life and Work*. New York: Crown Business.

# CHAPTER THIRTEEN

# Competency 13: Mindful Decision Making

Judy Flores, the president of the St. Nicholas Ambulatory Services Corporation, was still a bit annoyed as she walked back to her office after the staff meeting. She had just spent most of the meeting reversing some new policies and procedures about unscheduled absences and overtime that she had approved just weeks before. The changes were made in the first place because Kim Brown, one of her managers, had told her that the old system was unfair to the working moms in her department. Brown had convinced Flores that the changes would not affect the budget and that everyone in the division would be happy with them.

Shortly after Flores approved the changes, she learned that the other two managers strongly opposed them. They argued that the changes would make it harder to deal with staff who had attendance issues, and that the overtime policy, which was already being abused, would be even worse under the new rules.

The whole thing reminded Flores about the workshop she had attended a year or so ago on decision making. The instructor had recommended keeping a journal of important decisions to help her notice patterns in her judgments and avoid "selective memory." In light of her recent experiences, she decided to give journaling another try.

She searched for the decision journal file from the workshop and opened it. She was shocked to see what she had written in her last entry, about ten months ago. It ended with this analysis, in two points:

"(1) I am very sensitive about work–life balance, and my staff know it. I need to be more skeptical when they say this is the reason they want

*(continued)*

*(continued from previous page)*

something. (2) If someone tells me 'all my staff agree' about something, I need to double check whether that's really true." She chuckled as she thought about copying and pasting those two points to the end of today's entry.

---

THIS VIGNETTE HIGHLIGHTS three key aspects of leadership decision making. First, it shows how decision-making biases can affect everyday actions over time. Second, it shows that decision making is a very complex but patterned process, much of which happens without us fully thinking about it. Third, the result is something we can probably all relate to: having to learn the same lesson over and over again to change a habit.

In this chapter, we take a closer look at executive decision making. Becoming more mindful of your decision making takes deliberate effort, but it pays off in improved decision-making habits and higher decision quality.

## WHAT IS MINDFUL DECISION MAKING, AND WHY DOES IT MATTER?

**Mindful Decision Making** means you are aware of the approach you take to making decisions; base your decisions on a good balance of ethics, values, goals, facts, alternatives, and judgments; use decision tools (such as force-field analysis, cost–benefit analysis, decision trees, and paired comparisons analysis) effectively and at appropriate times; and can realistically assess true importance and urgency.

Some people view decision-making capabilities as relatively fixed and think some leaders are just better at making decisions than others. Although the quality of leaders' decisions does depend partly on intelligence and experience, it also depends a lot on the intentional approaches they use for decision-making. That aspect of decision making involves skills that leaders can learn and improve.

## HOW HIGHLY EFFECTIVE LEADERS MAKE DECISIONS

Highly effective decision makers pay particular attention to the following aspects of their decisions.

## Assessing the True Urgency

At the senior executive level, many decisions are described as urgent and in need of immediate action. Effective decision makers will know when a decision really needs immediate action and when it does not. If a decision is urgent, mindful decision makers can act with the information they have and live with the results. For decisions that are not urgent, these leaders might still act quickly, but only after considering whether the decision quality could improve with more time, analysis, and/or input.

## Choosing the Best Approach

There is no one best way to make all decisions. The first step for effective decision makers is to decide how they will decide. They will ask themselves questions like these:

- Who will be affected by this decision?
- How much say, if any, should these people (groups) have in the decision-making process?
- What are the most important things I need to know to make a good decision?

The answers to these questions will then influence how they make the decision—who gets involved and how, how much time they spend on the process, how much consensus is needed (see Chapter 12), and when to make the decision.

## Analyzing the Decision

Analysis means gathering information, identifying possible courses of action, and weighing the pros and cons of each. Highly effective analyzers use a systematic but not overly detailed approach to their analyses. Because looking at everything can take a lot of time and resources, often it is better to look at just enough. In many cases, spending more time to get more data or continue pondering a planned course of action can lead to failure. In healthcare, making decisions without complete information is a required skill. Leaders who can use their experience, judgment, and others' trust tend to be the most efficient decision makers.

### Using Good Judgment

The quality of a leader's judgment is determined by how well she uses her experience and information to make a decision. Two qualities in particular tend to distinguish the judgment of exceptionally skillful decision makers. First, they choose from a broader array of options. In other words, a highly effective decision maker will see more options, including new and different ones. Second, they are better at explaining *how* they came to a particular decision, which we will discuss next.

### Acting with Consistency and Integrity

Exceptional decision makers are often described as acting with consistency and integrity. Both of these qualities relate to transparency; these leaders tend to be better at explaining and, when needed, justifying their decisions. When doing this, their goal is not to argue that they are always right; instead, it is to demonstrate that their *process* is thoughtful, balanced, and fair. Here, the trust-building competencies we discussed in Chapter 5 are particularly relevant. Leaders who are viewed as great decision makers will also be seen as trustworthy: "I know that whatever she decides will be in the best interest of the patients we serve."

## WHEN MAKING DECISIONS IS NOT ALL IT COULD BE

Most leaders have good decision-making skills and habits. People would not call them bad decision makers; however, they would not call them amazing decision makers either. Some of these leaders could be outstanding decision makers, but one or more of the following barriers holds them back.

### Being Too Scared of Making a Bad Decision

For some leaders, the key challenge is their fear of making a wrong decision. We have to put this in the right context: All leaders make mistakes, and from what we have seen, most leaders know this. But they differ in how comfortable they are with being wrong. Some can admit it, easily and without apology; others try whatever they can to avoid looking like they made a mistake. These leaders might lose sight of which decisions are important and which are not. Decisions involving greater uncertainty and ambiguity will be especially hard for them.

## Not Willing to Take Risks

Some leaders do not consider options that are different or unusual. This is common in healthcare; many managers were drawn to this career path in part for its apparent stability.

An overfocus on risk avoidance can show up in several steps of the decision-making process. During the brainstorming phase, when the goal is to come up with a breadth of options, leaders might not lead by example with creative options. They might also step in early to rule out particularly creative or innovative ideas. This can be as subtle as chuckling at someone for being "way out there" with a suggestion; the message staff will get is "I'm not willing to consider anything new or bold."

In the later steps of decision making, this can show up again in how much risk leaders are willing to take and how much change they will tolerate. They might prefer to go slow and give themselves a lot of room to back out later if they want to.

## Lacking Good Decision-Making Methods

A leader's decision-making process may itself have problems in several ways. One common example is reliability—the consistency of the process as others see it. Even if leaders are methodical in their decisions, they may overlook the need to explain their approach to others. If coworkers do not understand the process behind the decisions, they may view the decision making as confusing or haphazard.

For some leaders, the decision-making process itself is lacking; for example, they may regularly fumble one or more of the fundamental steps. For some, the most challenging steps involve assessing how a decision will affect key stakeholders. While the results of complex decisions are often not fully predictable ahead of time, some leaders are less effective than others at thinking through and managing these effects. These leaders may not reach out to stakeholders for their input into the decision-making process at times when that input would improve the quality of the decisions as well as the buy-in.

Framing is another step that causes problems for some leaders. Framing involves coming up with clear and useful ways to describe the problem and the options available for addressing it. Leaders who are exceptionally good with details can sometimes feel overwhelmed by this step; they might see a decision as a problem to be carefully solved, when a "good enough" decision is what is needed.

The analysis step can be another stumbling point. For example, some leaders rely too much on past experiences to guide their judgments. Giving up what has worked in the past can be hard, especially if it is still working fine now. The best decision makers regularly challenge themselves and their coworkers to consider new options, recognizing that although a past decision may still be a good option, it may not continue to be the best option.

## MISUSE AND OVERUSE: HOW DECISION MAKING CAN WORK AGAINST YOU

Even leaders with well-honed decision-making skills may not be exceptional decision makers if they focus their time and energy on the wrong things. Here are some common ways that good decision makers prevent themselves from getting better results.

### Making Decisions Just to Make Them

Earlier, we made a case for good-enough decision making. But while some leaders get into trouble overanalyzing decisions, others don't analyze them enough. These same leaders might be proud of how fast they can make decisions and might not see how their quick judgments create the need to rework plans later.

Often this problem is related to a leader's discomfort with having decisions in their inbox for too long. Leaders in this category would do well to improve their ability to deal with uncertainty as well as their comfort in taking more time to make decisions when it makes sense.

## Overanalyzing Decisions

Some leaders are too cautious when making decisions, using more time or resources than the decision needs. Common patterns include tabling decisions without a good reason, adding analysis steps that do not clearly provide more useful information, and asking for additional opinions from people who have already given input. The pattern can annoy peers and direct reports; worse, it often will not make the decisions better, and may make them worse.

This pattern can be symptomatic of a basic discomfort with making and taking responsibility for decisions. Trying to get more input all the time might suggest that the leader is trying to dodge accountability by crafting decisions as "what they asked for." Leaders who are overly fearful of being wrong sometimes display this pattern.

## Overconfidence

Some leaders are too confident in their own decision-making skills. For these leaders, the quality of their decisions might suffer because they skip steps in the process. For example, they might not seek out "devil's advocate" opinions that would help them clarify and sharpen their reasoning. When they do get dissenting opinions, they may dismiss them too quickly without taking the time to understand their concerns. (Even if the quality of the decision at hand does not suffer from missing this step, buy-in surely will.) A related issue is selective memory, a tendency to forget about or downplay decision-making patterns that have caused trouble in the past.

**Misuse and Overuse: How Decision Making Can Work Against You**

- Making decisions just to make them
  - Decisions are rapid but lack sufficient analysis.
  - Input is not sought, or it is sought but not attended to.
- Overanalyzing decisions
  - Redundant steps in analyzing options are taken (e.g., multiple sources of the same information or multiple surveys addressing very similar questions).
  - The leader seeks more input than is necessary.

*(continued)*

*(continued from previous page)*

- Overconfidence
  - The devil's advocate step in making decisions is skipped.
  - Leaders fail to see the importance of others' contrary perspectives.

## HOW TO IMPROVE MINDFUL DECISION MAKING

### Finding Role Models

To find good role models of Mindful Decision Making, look for leaders who are successful in positions requiring both high-quantity and high-quality decisions. Roles like chief operating officer and executive vice president come to mind, as well as leaders who oversee many different service lines or departments. Executives in strategic planning roles tend to be very good at using analysis in decision-making, and efficiently collecting input from key stakeholders. (For more tips on getting agreement for your decisions, see Chapter 12.)

### Additional Opportunities for Personal Development

If you have never formally tracked or evaluated the decision making that you or your team does, we recommend trying this for a while. Adding a quick lessons-learned step into your decision-making process can be very helpful for uncovering the patterns in your approaches and finding ways to improve them over time.

Leaders who are too risk averse or afraid of being wrong can usually benefit from spending time on understanding and facing these fears. Often the fears come from unrealistic assumptions about what will happen: "If I'm wrong about this decision, I'll surely lose my job." Checking these assumptions against reality can be very helpful in overcoming this overly cautious pattern.

There are many books that focus on improving decision making. In our experience, serious books on this topic are not quick reads. They can take a lot of time to slog through, and using their suggestions takes a lot of discipline. For those motivated to do so, we have several recommendations.

An excellent book on developing your intuitive decision-making skills is Gary Klein's (2003) *Intuition at Work*. The focus of this book is on using experience to inform decisions and using the results of past decisions to inform future ones. You might think of it as continuous quality improvement for your decision making.

A more in-depth treatment of decision making, but still with a practical, how-to focus, is J. Edward Russo and Paul Shoemaker's (2002) *Winning Decisions*. It is a more engaging read than *Intuition at Work*, and it covers a wider range of applications (including much more material on group decision making), though the topics are covered in less depth.

For more specific healthcare application and a more quantitative focus, we recommend the popular *Evaluation and Decision Making for Health Services* by James Veney and Arnold Kaluzny (2005).

Finally, a lot of research in recent years has come from the field of behavioral economics, offering many useful perspectives on how people make decisions, the common biases that these approaches often have, and strategies for keeping these biases in check. Several popular books have made many of these concepts much more accessible, including Daniel Kahneman's (2013) *Thinking, Fast and Slow*, and Dan Ariely's (2010) *Predictably Irrational*. Kahneman's follow-up book, *Noise: A Flaw in Human Judgment* (2021), provides practical recommendations for leaders and teams to more successfully manage many of these biases.

## SUMMARY

Decision making is central to most leaders' roles, yet many leaders spend little time systematically reflecting on how they make decisions. Developing a mindful approach to decisions can help you improve your decision quality over time, by revealing the biases and blind spots we all have but few of us take the time to identify.

### Think About It

Ralph Warren was a self-confident and decisive CEO. He spent the first ten years of his career working for Crimson Judge, a legendary CEO who had been in charge at his hospital for more than 30 years. Warren served first as a vice president and then COO under this superstar. After 20 years of serving as CEO of three other community hospitals, he took a new position in a large and complex academic medical center with a strong research focus and a parent university of international renown. Warren believed that his decisiveness was his greatest strength as a leader. He felt he had modeled his style after Judge's, and this had served him well. If asked what his decision-making style was, Warren would summarize it in four key points: "First, I have faced every possible situation that a CEO can encounter in the field. I have seen it all. Second, decisions are like math to me—there is

*(continued)*

*(continued from previous page)*

always a clear-cut solution. Third, I think that acting fast and with courage shows the organization that they can trust me and my vision. And finally, I simply don't believe in mistakes; sure, I may make course corrections along the way, but nothing major."

- Clearly Ralph Warren can articulate his decision-making philosophy. What might be wrong with it? How might Warren encounter problems in his new job?

## Think About It

A great deal of decision making takes place in a group setting. This requires expert communications skills. One of the suggested steps in the book *Crucial Conversations* (Patterson et al. 2013) is to "State Your Path"—in other words, disclose your own personal point of view and conclusions, and create an atmosphere that helps others feel secure telling their stories as well.

- Research the topic of "rules of engagement" in group interaction and detail how these can help the conversations described in the *Crucial Conversations* approach.

## REFERENCES

Ariely, D. 2010. *Predictably Irrational: The Hidden Forces That Shape Our Decisions.* New York: Harper Perennial.

Kahneman, D. 2013. *Thinking, Fast and Slow.* New York: Farrar, Straus and Giroux.

Kahneman, D., O. Sibony, and C. R. Sunstein. 2021. *Noise: A Flaw in Human Judgment.* New York: Little, Brown & Company.

Klein, G. 2003. *Intuition at Work: Why Developing Your Gut Instincts Will Make You Better at What You Do.* New York: Doubleday Business.

Patterson, K., J. Grenny, R. McMillan, and A. Switzler. 2013. *Crucial Conversations: Tools for Talking When Stakes Are High*, 2nd ed. New York: McGraw-Hill.

Russo, J. E., and P. J. H. Shoemaker. 2002. *Winning Decisions: Getting It Right the First Time.* New York: Crown Business.

Veney, J. E., and A. D. Kaluzny. 2005. *Evaluation and Decision Making for Health Services*, 3rd ed. Frederick, MD: Beard Books.

# CHAPTER FOURTEEN

# Competency 14: Driving Results

Bill Sutor, the new vice president of support and facility services, wanted to get to know his new team better. He asked each of his direct reports to send him a summary of their achievements and goals for the past and coming year. This was not something they had historically prepared, but the previous SVP had given them the heads-up that Sutor would expecting these reports, so most of the staff had prepared them in advance.

As Sutor reviewed each the report, he saw that everyone was meeting or exceeding their performance targets. Collectively, the departments were the most efficiently run they had been in their history. Each had set some realistic and achievable goals for the next year, aiming for some gradual improvement without concern that direct reports would dismiss the goals as impossible to reach. The report from the plant facilities department seemed to be a particularly strong success story, with substantial progress made on staff absenteeism and turnover. The employee development department also described substantial improvements, including doubling the amount of training provided to employees without adding any new trainers—cutting the cost of training in half.

All this would seem like good news. Yet when Sutor emerged from his office, he looked very serious. He called George Boucher, the administrative director of plant facilities, into his office.

"Let me start by first thanking you for preparing this annual report, particularly on such short notice," Sutor said. "It gave me a good idea of what your department is good at, and what it needs to work on. Now then, we're going to need to revise your goals moving forward . . ."

Among the many dynamics this vignette suggests is an apparent gap between Sutor's expectations and those of his direct reports. On the surface, each of the departments seems to be doing well. But from Sutor's experience in prior roles, he believes they could be doing even better. He decides to make higher performance a top priority, capitalizing on the natural tension and uncertainty created whenever a new leader comes in.

This chapter is about how leaders can help their staff and departments achieve more. Leaders who are good at this have mastered a set of skills that we call *Driving Results*.

## WHAT IS DRIVING RESULTS, AND WHY DOES IT MATTER?

*Driving Results* describes all activities leaders engage in to define, monitor, and ensure high performance from themselves and their staff. It is also a set of habits that help ensure goals are clarified and reinforced, progress is regularly discussed, and accomplishments are acknowledged and can be used to redefine expectations.

> **Driving Results** means you inspire people toward greater commitment to a vision, challenge them to raise their standards and goals, keep them focused on achieving goals, give them honest and constructive feedback, take quick action to fix any problems, act with urgency and initiative, and proactively work through any obstacles that might hinder performance.

The habits of Driving Results are essential for high-performance leadership; they are often the difference between teams that go above and beyond and teams that merely meet their targets. No team can do everything perfectly; when leaders know what to look for and when to intervene, they can address problems earlier on, achieving higher levels of success down the road.

## HOW HIGHLY EFFECTIVE LEADERS DRIVE RESULTS

When it comes to Driving Results, exceptional leaders can be distinguished by the following characteristics.

## Looking for Process Improvement Opportunities

The strongest leaders tend to recognize process improvement opportunities that their peers do not see. This may stem in part from greater experience with process improvement; however, it also seems to reflect a greater tendency to *look* for these opportunities. Process improvement is more a general orientation for this group than a tool to be brought out for use on identified problems.

## Staying Focused

In addition to their ability to spot process improvement opportunities, exceptional leaders also tend to keep themselves and others continuously focused on process improvement. They can readily bring any conversation back to the ultimate goals (e.g., efficiency, quality, bottom line).

## Keeping Organized

These leaders also have a knack for keeping track of agendas and milestones that their peers may allow to fall through the cracks. Some leaders accomplish this by keeping excellent notes or using project management tools; others methodically delegate record-keeping. Both end up in the same place—with more reliable monitoring.

## Having Boundless Energy

Being described as dependable and productive is one thing; being described as unstoppable is quite another. Exceptional leaders are often described in this way: Once they set their mind to something, it will either happen or it was not meant to be—period. On a day-to-day basis, these leaders tend to see every barrier as temporary, and they look to move around them as efficiently as possible. When the barriers are more indirect, these leaders will proactively surface them so they can be addressed head-on. These leaders also tend to push themselves at least as hard as they push others. Their coworkers know they will be quick to step in and help when needed.

# WHEN DRIVING RESULTS IS NOT ALL IT COULD BE

Leaders' effectiveness in Driving Results can fall short for any of the following reasons.

## Lacking Energy or Drive

Some leaders do not have the energy and drive of their higher-performing peers. Less energetic leaders are more likely to procrastinate on pursuing initiatives or abandon efforts too early. In some cases, the difference between exceptional leaders and less effective leaders involves temperament, which is difficult to change. In other cases, however, a lower energy and drive involve internal conflicts that leaders may have about their initiatives or their roles.

## Underdeveloped Organizational Skills

Some leaders have energy and drive in spades, but their execution falls short because their organizational skills are not well honed. In some cases, leaders' energy levels can mask organizational problems; these leaders are outstanding at putting out fires but fail to recognize how many of these fires they themselves are setting. Common examples of where organizational skills undercut execution include failing to prepare meeting attendees ahead of time, forgetting to consistently monitor progress on goals that have been set with direct reports, and failing to make note of commitments to others and/or set specific times by which they will be completed.

## Developing Ineffective Working Relationships

Success in Driving Results depends on the development of effective working relationships. Some leaders find this part of their roles particularly challenging. A common barrier relates to leaders wanting to be liked. Leaders who are overly concerned about their coworkers liking them often have particular trouble holding people accountable. They may give in too readily to explanations for underperformance, or they may avoid addressing performance issues in the first place.

Even leaders with a more balanced orientation toward their coworkers will fall short if they have not mastered the art of clarifying priorities, setting clear and well-designed goals, and communicating about them on a consistent basis. All of these skills are learnable; leaders can master them most quickly by habitually seeking appropriate feedback (e.g., in times of confusion or underperformance, inquiring about how clear the goals were and how well the priorities and urgency were understood).

---

**When Driving Results Is Not All It Could Be**

- Lacking energy or drive
  - Leaders procrastinate on some agendas and abandon other efforts too quickly.
  - Leaders experience internal conflicts about their roles and initiatives.
- Underdeveloped organizational skills
  - Leaders fail to track important goals and deadlines.
  - Leaders come to meetings unprepared, fail to set clear agendas, or fail to prepare others.
- Developing ineffective working relationships
  - Effective goals are not consistent, clear, or measurable.
  - Excuses for performance shortfalls are accepted too readily.
  - Leaders are overly concerned with being liked by coworkers.

---

## MISUSE AND OVERUSE: HOW DRIVING RESULTS CAN WORK AGAINST YOU

Many of us have had firsthand experience pushing too hard for results at some point in our careers. We learn the lesson, and we adjust our style accordingly. Leaders who never learn this lesson may not see just how awful it can be to work with them. Here are the common patterns we see, and their underlying causes.

### Underemphasizing People

We have already mentioned the danger of letting a people-focus take precedence over a results-focus. There is ample danger in focusing too much on results as well. Some leaders neglect to celebrate successes and instead jump straight to raising the bar again. The consequence is that staff start to pace themselves because any improvements will only call for greater improvements later. Other leaders focus so strongly on individual accountabilities that they foster unhealthy competition among coworkers, undermining effectiveness when teamwork is called for.

Leaders who view their staff only in terms of their productivity tend to foster attitudes among their employees that their work is just a job. Organizational commitment will be lower, and people will be eager to find better arrangements elsewhere. Leaders with this approach may also too quickly dismiss people who have good long-term potential but are underperforming in the near term. These leaders may undervalue coaching and other forms of skill development and may have never mastered these skills.

## Overemphasizing Performance

Even when leaders do well with the people-related aspects of their jobs, they may still overemphasize performance. Some leaders have too much of their own self-concept tied up in achievement at work. This pattern shows up in leaders who consistently focus on the short-term win over the long-term success story. Some leaders will come full-steam into a new position, make a bunch of unsustainable changes, and then leave before that reality becomes apparent.

A related pattern is evident in leaders who focus on performance above all else and expect the same from their direct reports. Leaders who think the ends always justify the means can end up justifying what in hindsight can look overly self-serving or even ethically suspect. Leaders who view their job as the whole of their existence are also at risk for developing dangerous blind spots, not the least of which is a failure to recognize when they are no longer right for the job they have. Classic workaholism has been well described in popular books such as *Chained to the Desk* (Robinson 2014); if you have been told you exhibit these tendencies, they should get attention as part of your professional development.

## Lacking Flexibility

Leaders often find themselves in situations where an initial course of action seems no longer tenable—perhaps the external market has changed, or the leader was working from some misinformation in the first place. Some leaders can effectively admit they were wrong and change course. For other leaders, the very idea of failure is so aversive that they may instead push even harder on their original course of action. The problem becomes framed not in terms of faulty assumptions but as not working hard enough. Patterns like this can end badly, with everyone but the leader recognizing the futility of a given plan, eventually abandoning support and becoming suspicious of the leader's judgment.

**Misuse and Overuse: How Driving Results Can Work Against You**

- Underemphasizing people
  - Staff pace themselves to avoid having their leader raise the bar too often or too high.
  - An overemphasis on individual accountabilities undermines teamwork.
- Overemphasizing performance
  - Leaders focus on short-term wins rather than long-term successes.
  - Performance is pursued at all costs, and ethical issues are not adequately considered.
- Lacking flexibility
  - Leaders may push for results beyond what is best for their organizations.
  - Changing course when necessary becomes difficult.

## HOW TO IMPROVE ON DRIVING RESULTS

### Finding Role Models

Unlike with some of the other competencies in this book, role models in Driving Results are often relatively easy to identify because their accomplishments tend to speak for themselves. Within any organization, strong role models will distinguish themselves as the people whom senior leaders always want to turn to first to take on large, messy projects. They are also constantly at risk of being overcommitted to task forces and special projects because they tend to be nominated more often than others.

If you work as a leader within a specific type of department or profession, you might seek out role models who are your counterparts in similar organizations. Meetings and conferences sponsored by professional associations are good hunting grounds. Look for presenters describing particularly complex turnaround efforts or program expansions. Find opportunities to meet these individuals to learn more about the secrets of their successes.

### Additional Opportunities for Personal Development

If you notice yourself having lower energy or drive around a specific project or process, take some time to think about the ambivalences you may have. The same advice goes for your job: If you feel you are not pursuing it with your fullest commitment of energy, give some thought to the reasons why. Surfacing these internal conflicts can help you work through them, or you may reconsider whether your current role is a good fit for you if these conflicts are more serious.

If your overall energy level is simply sapped, assess your track record of physical activity and outside interests. Gaining balance in life by expanding time spent pursuing family matters or personal hobbies may pay healthy dividends in the workplace. Alternatively, if you have considerable difficulty periodically unplugging from work, or have been described multiple times by coworkers and loved ones as a workaholic, consider reading a book such as Robinson's (2014) *Chained to the Desk* to reflect on the hidden costs this pattern may be having on the people you work and live with.

If you find yourself challenged by tracking and monitoring, consider attending a workshop or course on project management. Most business schools and many graduate healthcare management programs, as well as a number of professional associations, offer these. If you are not using productivity tools (e.g., software-based collaboration tools, such as shared calendars and project sites), look to your more organized peers for advice on technologies that may be useful for you to adopt. If you have an administrative assistant, look for ways he can help you better track and organize your work.

If holding people accountable is a challenge for you, you may need to work on improving your skills and/or your comfort with delivering constructive feedback. Working with an internal or external coach can be very helpful in developing and practicing these skills. Also, be sure to review Chapter 7 of this book, "Giving Great Feedback."

A good general book we suggest is *Getting Results the Agile Way: A Personal Results System for Work and Life* by J. D. Meier (2010).

Several books provide excellent first-person accounts of leaders who are masters at Driving Results. *Who Says Elephants Can't Dance?* describes Lou Gerstner's (2002) dramatic turnaround success story with IBM. Although not about a hospital or healthcare system, the challenges Gerstner faced in many ways parallel ones familiar to health administrators. In *Execution*, Honeywell's Larry Bossidy teamed up with academician Ram Charan (2002) to provide a highly readable, first-person account of his philosophy and successful approach to Driving Results at large, diverse organizations.

## SUMMARY

People have a natural tendency to set performance goals at a level they feel comfortable achieving. Selling staff on higher levels of performance can involve instilling in them a confidence that they are capable of more than they think. Exceptional leaders are able to instill this confidence, while not overdriving to the point where people give up.

> **Think About It**
>
> Consider change management. If you are unfamiliar with the concept, review John Kotter's books on change, including his latest, *Change: How Organizations Achieve Hard-to-Imagine Results in Uncertain and Volatile Times* (Kotter, Akhtar, and Gupta 2021), or review Kotter's eight-step change management process at his website, www.kotterinternational.com/our-principles/changesteps/changesteps.
>
> - Is the competency Driving Results part of change management, or is change management part of Driving Results?

> **Think About It**
>
> The best organizations have a central culture of Driving Results. Small things—such as starting and ending meetings on time, hitting deadlines, respecting budgets, having clear performance standards, giving meaningful evaluations, and using dashboards and scorecards—all add to this type of culture.
>
> - Think of a specific organization that lacks a results-driven culture. Describe how you would begin to develop one.

## REFERENCES

Bossidy, L., and R. Charan. 2002. *Execution: The Discipline of Getting Things Done.* New York: Crown Business.

Gerstner, L. V., Jr. 2002. *Who Says Elephants Can't Dance? Inside IBM's Historic Turnaround.* New York: Harper Business.

Kotter, J. P., V. Akhtar, and G. Gupta. 2021. *Change: How Organizations Achieve Hard-to-Imagine Results in Uncertain and Volatile Times.* Hoboken, NJ: Wiley.

Meier, J. D. 2010. *Getting Results the Agile Way: A Personal Results System for Work and Life.* Bellevue, WA: Innovation Playhouse.

Robinson, B. E. 2014. *Chained to the Desk: A Guidebook for Workaholics, Their Partners and Children, and the Clinicians Who Treat Them.* New York: NYU Press.

# CHAPTER FIFTEEN

# Competency 15: Stimulating Creativity

As they arrived at the conference center, staff and leaders of
perioperative services were clearly tense. They had little idea what
to expect, other than they would be there for the whole morning
talking about how to make their organization a better place to work. What
they found when they got there was huge circle of chairs, with poster boards
and markers next to the walls.

They chatted with each other to ease the tension, until Dr. Bernard
Jacque, the chief quality officer, called for their attention. He introduced a
facilitator, who laid out an agenda that was initially puzzling in its simplicity.
Staff would be asked to identify topics for operating room improvement that
they wanted to talk about; then other staff who were interested in their topic
would join them by one of the poster boards. The person who suggested the
topic would take notes, which would be posted on a central wall. They would
repeat this process several times; at the end of the session, anyone could
volunteer to work on the initiatives when they returned to work.

When it came time to propose topics, the group was quiet for a long
time. Finally, someone broke the silence with the first topic: "getting supplies
on time." Topics got bolder as they went on: "speaking up for patient safety,"
"making scheduling fair," and even "how about a little respect around here?"
and "how do we make our changes actually happen?" When it was time for
the discussions, there was a lot of movement, people switching from one
group to another, and some individuals alone at one of the poster boards
just writing down their own ideas.

At the end of the day, the group had six topics with a lot of interest and
support. Dr. Jacque praised the group for their creative thinking and agreed

*(continued)*

*(continued from previous page)*

to set up quality improvement teams around the six themes. He asked each of the people who suggested the topics to have a progress report ready for presentation at the next quarterly all-staff meeting.

THIS VIGNETTE DESCRIBES an example of "open space," a way of bringing together a large group of people to think creatively and make decisions together. The method is used more commonly in corporate settings than in healthcare, but it shows the kinds of innovative approaches that can be used to unlock people's creative thinking around process improvement. We provide this vignette not as the right way to encourage creative thinking but rather as an illustration of the dynamics associated with an effective approach to the process.

## WHAT IS STIMULATING CREATIVITY, AND WHY DOES IT MATTER?

*Stimulating Creativity* has two parts: being creative and encouraging creativity. We can define *creativity* as using new and different ways to solve problems and make decisions. Stimulating Creativity, then, involves fostering a culture that supports and rewards creative approaches.

**Stimulating Creativity** means you look beyond the typical and are always open to new ideas; you know how to use different techniques to spark group creativity (e.g., brainstorming, design thinking, Nominal Group Technique, scenario building); you look at trends to see what the future might bring and plan for it; you stay well-informed about business and social trends; you understand how strategies work in practice; you seek out information about trends within and outside of healthcare; and you make connections between industries and other trends.

Leaders come to be viewed as exceptional in part for their ability to achieve unprecedented results—in other words, results that are not normally achieved by approaching the work in just the standard ways. Thinking of possibilities that are not obvious requires creative thinking, and the expression of creative thinking by staff requires permission to do so. Organizations that embrace creative solutions are often the first to the market with new services and approaches to care, becoming the places where the best clinicians and employees want to pursue their careers.

## HOW HIGHLY EFFECTIVE LEADERS STIMULATE CREATIVITY

Before we explain what it means to be good at Stimulating Creativity, we should clarify what it does *not* mean. It does not mean that you have to be creative yourself. Some leaders are very creative but not particularly good at fostering creativity in the people they work with. Other leaders are not creative, but they can still be exceptional leaders if they can tap into the creative potential of their teams.

Stimulating Creativity involves the following elements.

### Being Positive About Challenges

When we face significant challenges at work, it is natural to think, "Oh no, how are we going to deal with this?" The challenge becomes a problem that we want to get rid of. Exceptional leaders are able to foster a positive perspective about these challenges. They are quick to ask, "What can we gain from this challenge?" and they help others to adopt a similar attitude.

### Fostering Perspective

Creative approaches require us to look at our work from different angles—from short term to long term, from very narrow to very broad, and from various stakeholders' points of view. Exceptional leaders are good at switching between these perspectives and helping others to do so as well.

For example, consider the topic of "getting respect" from our vignette. The solutions this group comes up with will depend on who chose to participate in that topic discussion: nurses, housekeepers, and anesthesiologists will have different definitions of respect. An effective leader will help staff recognize the missing points of view and encourage people to see from those perspectives—or, better yet, to seek those perspectives out. For our case example, staff may be biased toward defining respect in terms of a specific recent incident in which someone was treated badly. A good leader would help them see that incident not just as an example, but also as a part of the history of the department's culture: "When was the *first* time we saw this kind of interaction? How far back do we think this goes?"

### Drawing Out Creative Ideas

The best leaders are also very good at facilitating brainstorming. Some leaders do not really understand brainstorming; they may just ask people for ideas and then wait a while before shooting them down. But in reality, many creative discussions involve active debate about ideas *while* the ideas are being generated. The key is the climate: People should feel comfortable debating the merits of their ideas without feeling personally attacked. Highly effective leaders are skilled at drawing out creative ideas during brainstorming and keeping the dialogue focused on building rather than debating during this step.

### Building Up to Creative Solutions

A final quality that sets these leaders apart is their capacity to combine people's ideas into a coherent whole. They can identify common themes and trends, and they can effectively articulate them for the group's consideration. They create cycles of divergence (adding new ideas and perspectives) and convergence (summarizing into a new whole) and back again, until they have explored all the possible perspectives or accounted for them.

## WHEN STIMULATING CREATIVITY IS NOT ALL IT COULD BE

Leaders who are not highly effective at stimulating creativity will miss some chances for innovation that their peers may see first. This can happen for different reasons, but these three are the most common.

### Focusing Only on the Presenting Problem

When leaders face a problem at work, most want to solve it quickly and efficiently. The more urgent the problem, the faster they want to fix it. The rapid-response approach is often overdone, and leaders end up "solving" the same problem over and over again without identifying the root causes.

For example, one of us knows a leader who is great at fixing client relationships. He can readily mend just about any client relationship through a combination of owning up to shortfalls, showing willingness to do whatever it takes to make things right, and using incredible charm. He is so good at this that he doesn't have to worry about the root causes of his client-relations challenges (e.g., unclear agreements, disorganization, poor communication). But with additional creative thought, he would probably find much better ways of working with his clients to his own benefit as well as theirs.

## Approaching Problems Too Cautiously

Some leaders stick too much to what has worked for them in the past. These leaders may be very good at developing reliable processes but can also be very reluctant to change them. The surest sign of this bias is when a leader dismisses a suggestion mainly because it has never been tried before, or predicts terrible outcomes that to others seem very unlikely to happen.

## Not Using Integrative Approaches

The vignette that starts this chapter describes a group of people in a situation where their ideas can build on each other. The techniques used recognize the power of group construction and creativity. Some leaders would never use such techniques because they want to keep a tight control over the group discussion outcomes. For example, some leaders feel threatened if the group discussion does not go through them (sometimes called the hub-and-spoke communication model). Other leaders think that coming up with creative solutions is their job and they feel threatened if *any* creative ideas come from their staff. In these cases, staff will learn to keep their ideas to themselves, creating a pattern where leaders will ask for input but not receive any.

In less severe cases, the barriers come from not using the creative ideas effectively through good facilitation and synthesis. For example, ideas may be requested but then turned into a list of items rather than being integrated into a set of themes, or ideas may not be shared back with their sources for further improvement.

---

### When Stimulating Creativity Is Not All It Could Be

- Focusing only on the presenting problem
  - The same problem gets "solved" over and over again.
  - The patterns and root causes underlying the problems are not identified.

*(continued)*

---

*(continued from previous page)*

- Approaching problems too cautiously
  - The bias toward what has worked in the past is too strong.
  - The leader is overly cautious about new approaches.
- Not using integrative approaches
  - Creative ideas from others are discouraged.
  - The leader fails to synthesize others' input and ideas.

## MISUSE AND OVERUSE: HOW STIMULATING CREATIVITY CAN WORK AGAINST YOU

Leaders can also hurt performance by using creativity too much or in the wrong ways. Here are some of the common patterns we have seen.

### Being Creative Instead of Encouraging Creativity

This pattern is often seen in leaders who are creative themselves—those who might be considered role models if they were better collaborators. Some of these leaders are great creative thinkers who don't bring their staff along with them—they may come up with solutions and innovations quickly, but no one can figure out how they got there. They may not have the patience to explain themselves or get buy-in.

Other highly creative leaders do not care enough about real-world constraints. They may enjoy the creative thinking process for its own sake and get annoyed and frustrated when people remind them of reality. While occasionally these leaders may reach brilliant, inventive solutions they would not have otherwise, more often they spend too much time on solutions that don't work.

### Focusing Too Much on Innovation

The pattern of focusing too much on innovation can come from different places, but in each case the process is the same: Innovations are pursued for reasons other than organizational performance. One of these patterns is that of the excitement junkie—leaders who push for innovations to keep themselves from being bored. These leaders may be used to high levels of chaos in their environments and will create this excitement whether it serves the department's goals or not.

Another version of this pattern is the overambitious career-ladder climber. These leaders may push innovation as a way to get attention. The result can be a focus on dreaming rather than planning, or a habit of taking on too much and doing everything poorly.

## Overemphasizing New Ideas

The final harmful pattern is an overemphasis on the idea-development process itself. While thinking about the future can be helpful in generating possible courses of action, some leaders are happiest when they are in a creative brainstorming session, and they block out too much time for these activities. They may find themselves and their staff re-creating their vision of the future more often than they need to or even thinking through change initiatives for departments and domains they have no control over.

Having an overemphasis on ideas is another way that excitement-junkie leaders can misuse the creative thinking process. For many such leaders, this pattern goes along with a tendency to view the necessary day-to-day "administrivia" as so dull that it is not enough to keep them meaningfully engaged in their work. The creative thinking process becomes an escape and is used beyond the point of useful gains. At the senior levels, this pattern can be seen in how leadership teams are structured; a CEO may pay more attention to the creative thinking departments (e.g., strategy and marketing), at the expense of other departments that are vital for running the organization well (e.g., environmental or information services).

---

**Misuse and Overuse: How Stimulating Creativity Can Work Against You**

- Being creative instead of encouraging creativity
  - The thinking processes of creative leaders are not well explained.
  - Ideas are not tempered by real-world considerations.
- Focusing too much on innovation
  - Leaders push change for change's sake.
  - Creativity is used as a tool for personal recognition.
  - Leaders and staff become overextended and thus underperform.
- Overemphasizing new ideas
  - New ideas and approaches are encouraged, while the mundane day-to-day is given short shrift.
  - Creativity in staff is overvalued, and operations are undervalued.

---

# HOW TO BETTER STIMULATE CREATIVITY

## Finding Role Models

Some of the best role models for creative thinking in leadership will be found in areas where creativity is essential for their work: marketing management, communications, and philanthropy departments are good examples. Outside of the health system, you can look for creative organizations, such as advertising agencies and design firms, that have leaders who are skilled at fostering creativity.

If you can, find opportunities to join meetings where creative thinking or problem-solving discussions are on the agenda. Pay attention to the process: How does the leader get everyone involved? How do they react to good ideas? What about ideas that are not so good? How do they combine ideas and move people forward? If the leaders are willing, review the meeting with them afterward. Tell them what you noticed and ask for additional feedback.

## Additional Opportunities for Personal Development

One of the best ways to improve your skills in stimulating creativity is to pay more attention to the creative process and to get more feedback on how you are doing.

A good exercise to start with is to focus on regular meetings where creative thinking or decision making is particularly important for the outcomes, such as a meeting where people are there because of their unique background or experience. At the end of each meeting, make a point to ask the group for feedback. Useful questions include:

- How well did we do in getting each of your ideas out on the table?
- At what point in the process was it most difficult to get ideas out?

For group members who had their ideas rejected, check in with them after the meeting and ask about their experiences with the process. If they are feeling discouraged, give them some positive feedback about their participation and encourage them to keep sharing their ideas in the future.

Sometimes groups develop a habit of not contributing openly, and it can be hard to break. In these cases, bringing an outsider—a process consultant—into a group meeting can help. This person's job is to watch the process of the group: who is talking, who is not, who is supporting whom. Their goal is to bring these patterns to the group's attention so that they can be discussed and changed as needed.

There are many great books that focus on improving your understanding of the creative process. Some of our favorites are *When Sparks Fly: Harnessing the Power of Group Creativity* by Dorothy Leonard and Walter Swap (2005), *Creativity, Inc.: Building an Inventive Organization* by Jeff Mauzy and Richard A. Harriman (2003), and *The Art of Engagement* by Jim Haudan (2008). Some highly accessible books that focus on the design process, and the role creativity plays in it, include Tim Brown's (2009) *Change by Design* and Tom and David Kelly's (2013) *Creative Confidence*. The books of Alex Osterwalder and his colleagues also offer a lot of great tools for human-centered design; some of our favorites are listed in the references section at the end of this chapter.

## SUMMARY

At a time when healthcare is changing like never before, stimulating creativity is growing even more important. When incremental changes are not enough to get us where we need to go, exceptional leaders communicate that innovative thinking is not only welcome, but also essential to success.

---

### Think About It

Assuming that having great perspective and being open to new ideas and approaches are some of the hallmarks of Stimulating Creativity, is it possible that having too much experience may actually inhibit creativity? Consider: Typically, one of the most important requirements when hiring a leader is experience—the more, the better.

- Is this necessarily true?
- What is the possibility that the more experience one has, the less likely one is to have truer perspective?
- Can too much experience cause leaders to fail to examine all the possibilities when confronting a problem?

---

### Think About It

Dave Damron, senior VP of business development; Liam Pak, VP of marketing and PR; and Susan Edwards, VP of planning, were discussing how executives could become more creative. Pak said that the most creative

*(continued)*

---

(continued from previous page)
people she knew had diverse and broad education backgrounds. Damron replied, "So, you think that creativity can be learned? I disagree. I think it is something you are either born with—or not." Edwards joined in, saying, "Well, I think both can have a grain of truth. In any case, I think creativity is a crucial skill most executives need to succeed."

- Detail specific ways in which a leader can become more creative.

## REFERENCES

Bland, D. J., and A. Osterwalder. 2019. *Testing Business Ideas: A Field Guide for Rapid Experimentation.* New York: John Wiley & Sons.

Brown, T. 2009. *Change by Design: How Design Thinking Transforms Organizations and Inspires Innovation.* New York: Harper Business.

Haudan, J. 2008. *The Art of Engagement: Bridging the Gap Between People and Possibilities.* New York: McGraw-Hill.

Kelly, T., and D. Kelly. 2013. *Creative Confidence: Unleashing the Creative Potential Within Us All.* New York: Crown Business.

Leonard, D., and W. Swap. 2005. *When Sparks Fly: Harnessing the Power of Group Creativity.* New York: Harvard Business School Press.

Mauzy, J., and R. Harriman. 2003. *Creativity, Inc.: Building an Inventive Organization.* Boston: Harvard Business School Press.

Osterwalder, A., Y. Pigneur, G. Bernarda, and A. Smith. 2015. *Value Proposition Design: How to Create Products and Services Customers Want.* New York: John Wiley & Sons.

# CHAPTER SIXTEEN

# Competency 16: Cultivating Adaptability

This is how Miguel Jimenez, the COO of the St. Nicholas system's flagship hospital, spent his morning.

*7:00–8:00 a.m.:* Jimenez meets with 15 doctors from cardiology, radiology, and cardiothoracic surgery to talk about creating a new service line that would span several of the St. Nicholas Health System's hospitals. He doesn't say much during the hour; he mostly asks questions, carefully drawing out the doctors' thoughts and discussing potential barriers to collaboration.

*8:00–9:00 a.m.:* Jimenez calls in his key operational vice presidents for a budget meeting. He starts the meeting by telling them that they have lost four key surgeons. He then tells them that because of the expected drop in admissions, he needs to mandate an 8 percent cut on expenses for everyone. "I don't care how you do it, just get it done," he says. The vice presidents leave the room knowing that the next time they get together, their budgets had better reflect the cuts.

*9:00–10:00 a.m.:* Jimenez meets with Josiah Branson, the administrative director of the labs. They discuss Branson's career with the medical center as well as his future plans. Jimenez commends Branson for his leadership on expanding reprocessing and tells him he sees potential for executive leadership one day. He recommends to Branson that he consider enrolling in a master's program in health systems management. He also invites

*(continued)*

*(continued from previous page)*

Branson to join one of the hospital-wide strategic planning task forces Jimenez is setting up, to broaden his exposure to other departments in the hospital.

*10:00 a.m.–12:00 p.m.:* Jimenez meets with the directors of business development and community affairs. They spend two hours together, brainstorming ways they can develop new programs that will involve community physicians and bring additional admissions into their medical center. He shares whatever ideas he can think of and suggests additional people they could contact, always trying to expand the list of options rather than telling them what to do next.

*11:15 a.m.:* Jimenez's meeting is interrupted by his administrative assistant, who has Dr. Rodriquez on the phone. Dr. Rodriquez was very angry to find that the lot his practice tells patients to park in is under construction and no one bothered to tell him. Jimenez steps out of the meeting for ten minutes, listens patiently to the doctor's complaints, apologizes for the lack of communication, and offers to have one of his staff prepare a map with parking alternatives. The call ends with Jimenez thanking him for the feedback, giving the follow-up request to his assistant, and going back into his meeting.

THIS VIGNETTE ILLUSTRATES the kinds of situations healthcare leaders face throughout a typical day. While a general leadership style might get an executive through these meetings, leaders who adjust their style to each situation, based on their goals and audience, will often do better at achieving what they want.

## WHAT IS CULTIVATING ADAPTABILITY, AND WHY DOES IT MATTER?

In leadership roles, *Cultivating Adaptability* involves the mastery of three fundamental skills:

1. reading the environment,
2. assessing the ideal course of action among a number of choices, and
3. responding with an appropriate leadership style.

**Cultivating Adaptability** means you can quickly grasp the essence of issues and problems, effectively bring clarity to situations of ambiguity, approach work using a variety of leadership styles and techniques, track changing priorities and readily interpret their implications, balance consistency of focus against the ability to adjust course as needed, balance multiple tasks and priorities such that each gets appropriate attention, and work effectively with a broad range of people.

Let us look more closely at each of these three skills. The first—reading the environment—means paying attention to the most important aspects of a situation. For example, a leader must determine who is involved, what challenges they are facing, what history may be on people's minds, and the levels of real and perceived urgency. The second skill—weighing appropriate courses of action—involves using good judgment about which approach will work best based on the leader's read on the environment. The third skill—responding with an appropriate leadership style—requires having a variety of leadership styles to choose from and using them skillfully.

Cultivating adaptability is important not only to everyday leadership, but also at the systems level. Everyone working in healthcare during the COVID-19 pandemic had firsthand experience with how vital adaptability is. Beyond pandemics, health system leaders are increasingly being called on to help their communities build resilience, from preparing for natural disasters to addressing the many complex social factors that affect health.

## HOW HIGHLY EFFECTIVE LEADERS CULTIVATE ADAPTABILITY

Exceptionally adaptable leaders have mastered each of the three skills listed above: They are good at reading environments, have a firm handle on the implications of different leadership styles, and have a well-stocked toolbox of practiced leadership styles to choose from.

### Reading Environments

The critical first step in reading environments is taking the time to do it. Exceptional leaders think through their meetings ahead of time to identify the most important aspects related to their role. Some useful diagnostic questions to ask include:

- *Situation.* What is the primary goal of this exchange? What do I want to happen? What do others want to happen? What kinds of time pressures are we facing?

- *People.* How many people will I be meeting with? Are all of the decision makers in the room? Who will be missing, and why? What is each person's role in this meeting? How are they feeling?

- *Relationships.* How do these people get along with each other? How do they feel about me right now? How much leeway will they want, and how much should I give them?

- *History.* What has been the track record for this group? Have they been getting what they want, or have they been turned down for other things recently? Have their departments been stable, growing, or shrinking? What approaches have worked well or poorly with this group before? Do newer members need to know more about the past? Do older members need to move on from the past?

- *Outcomes.* How will the different possible outcomes affect the people involved? Who should be recognized as the decision maker or decision makers? How should these outcomes be communicated, and by whom? How can we use these outcomes to improve our approach in the future?

## Understanding Different Leadership Styles

Exceptional leaders will use their read of the environment to select the style they think will work best. Although this process involves more art and experience than science, some general guidelines are emerging from research. Below we describe some of these styles, and the types of situations that fit them well.

### Autocratic or Coercive

An autocratic or coercive style is when leaders make decisions by themselves and hold their direct reports accountable to them. "Driving Results" (Chapter 14) is an example of a competency that can inform this leadership style. This style is mainly useful when quick action is needed—for example, when facing a natural disaster or a financial crisis. The style is counterproductive in almost all other situations.

### Charismatic or Inspirational

A charismatic or inspirational style involves reaching out to people in a way that gets them excited about a particular vision or agenda. "Energizing Staff" (Chapter 10) and "Communicating Vision" (Chapter 4) are examples of competencies that go well with this style. This style is particularly useful when staff lack a compelling sense of purpose or direction in their work.

### Democratic or Consultative

A democratic or consultative style is when leaders involve staff in the action or decision-making process as equals or advisors. With this style, leaders may let the group make the decisions, and act as a facilitator or additional source of ideas. This style is particularly useful when staff are highly experienced and skilled, when the best actions or decisions are unclear to the leader, or when an employee is given a project as a developmental assignment.

### Encouraging or Supportive

When leaders use an encouraging or supportive style, they focus on the individual needs of their staff or peers. "Earning Trust And Loyalty" (Chapter 5) and "Developing High-Performing Teams" (Chapter 9) are examples of competencies that closely match this style. The style is particularly useful when staff have low morale (e.g., losing a colleague, closing a program they care about) or when trust has been broken.

### Standards Setting

When leaders use a standards-setting style, they focus on the process: how it is measured, how it can be improved, who is accountable, and so on. Used sparingly, this style can be helpful in clarifying roles and goals as well as in improving systems that need immediate attention. Used too often, however, the style will be experienced as fatiguing and micromanaging.

### Coaching

When leaders use a coaching style, they focus on the connection between an employee's development needs and the goals of the organization. Some evidence suggests the style is used less often, which is unfortunate because staff value it and it helps create a positive organizational culture. The style is particularly useful for making sure staff stay loyal to the organization and stay mindful of their development needs and career goals. The "Mentoring" competency (Chapter 8) is closely aligned with this leadership style.

## Developing a Range of Leadership Styles

Leaders who can read the environment and plan their approach accordingly are two-thirds of the way to exceptional adaptability. The last step is to master a variety of leadership styles and get comfortable enough with each to use them effectively when needed. For most leaders, this is a continuous learning process; most of us naturally prefer one leadership style, or a couple at most. Getting better at using a broader variety of styles requires practice, feedback, and more practice.

## WHEN CULTIVATING ADAPTABILITY IS NOT ALL IT COULD BE

Many leaders are less adaptable than they could be because they fall into one or more of the following traps.

### Giving In to Time Pressures

In our experience, time pressure is the most common trap. The dominant theme in health administration roles often seems to be "get it done, get it done!" Leaders can fall into the habit of rushing from meeting to meeting; in the process, they don't take the time to think about the nuances of each situation they are entering. The same problem can happen after: Leaders fail to do even a brief self-check of how their meetings or conversations went and miss these chances to gain a deeper understanding of the interpersonal aspects of these exchanges.

### Lacking Sensitivity to Environmental Cues

For some leaders, reading the environment comes more naturally. Other leaders tend to be more internally focused. These leaders may need to put more conscious effort into attending to environmental cues.

### Sticking to One Leadership Style

A common problem many leaders have is using only one leadership style (or two). For example, some leaders are people oriented; they may create very supportive environments but also fail to hold people accountable. Others may be very process oriented; they are great at making sure things get done on time but may not develop their people well and may also have trouble holding on to them.

## Failing to "Hear" When an Approach Is Not Working

A more serious problem some leaders have is not recognizing when an approach is not working, because they either don't pay attention to the environmental cues or don't care about them. These leaders may not ask for feedback on how well their styles are working, and they may not read others' reactions well—for example, they can't see when things are getting out of hand or when they are crossing a line. Chapter 6, "Listening Like You Mean It," has more information about how to avoid this trap.

### When Cultivating Adaptability Is Not All It Could Be

- Giving in to time pressures
  - Leaders fail to take the time to consider audience, situation, history, urgency, and relevant challenges in planning their approach.
  - Self-assessments to increase one's awareness of interpersonal exchanges are not done after meetings or conversations.
- Lacking sensitivity to environmental cues
  - Leaders have difficulty reading environmental cues.
  - Important facets of situations may blindside leaders.
- Sticking to one leadership style
  - One or two leadership styles tend to dominate; these styles work well in some situations but not as well (or not at all) in others.
- Failing to "hear" when an approach is not working
  - Feedback that a given approach is not working well is not heard.
  - Leaders fail to read others' reactions, so they cannot see when things are boiling over or crossing the line.

## MISUSE AND OVERUSE: HOW CULTIVATING ADAPTABILITY CAN WORK AGAINST YOU

Sometimes, a leader may be seen as *too* adaptable. If that happens, usually one or more of the following problems are present.

### Changing Direction Too Often

Some leaders have trouble sticking to their plans when they face challenges to their approach. For example, leaders using an inspirational style may give up because of staff cynicism; an appropriately autocratic style may be dropped because of resistance. These leaders have trouble following their personal convictions, which is discussed in Chapter 1.

### Switching Leadership Styles Erratically

Some leaders don't keep a consistent style within a particular context. Often this is because they can't read how the people in that context are feeling or reacting. These leaders should work on reading cues and planning for these interactions, using the methods described in earlier parts of this chapter. Other leaders have trouble keeping a consistent style going because it feels monotonous to them. These leaders may like the innovative and creative parts of their job more, and they may change things up to keep themselves more interested. These leaders fail to ask themselves why they are changing styles or evaluate their reasons before switching to a different approach.

> **Misuse and Overuse: How Cultivating Adaptability Can Work Against You**
>
> - Changing direction too often
>   - Leaders abandon leadership styles and waver in their approaches to challenges.
> - Switching leadership styles erratically
>   - Leaders change their leadership style midstream, which creates confusion.
>   - Leaders are too enamored with doing things differently and find a consistent style to be too monotonous.

## HOW TO BETTER CULTIVATE ADAPTABILITY

### Finding Role Models

You will typically find the best role models in positions where adaptability is needed most often. Leaders who work directly with physicians tend to be good at adaptability. Operations executives are also good role models because their daily work often involves many surprises and changes.

In healthcare, another group that is particularly strong in this area is the medical service corps officers in the military. These leaders, many of whom are active within the American College of Healthcare Executives and other professional organizations, are excellent role models to get to know to learn how they adapt and modify their leadership approaches to frequently changing circumstances.

Leaders who are good at understanding different audiences can also be found in marketing and communications departments. These professionals can help you think about the unique aspects of different stakeholder groups. Leaders working in offices of philanthropy often need to have a keen awareness of history and an acute sense of individual interests and needs.

### Additional Opportunities for Personal Development

The best way to sharpen your adaptability is to practice different leadership styles and get feedback on how they work. The resources in this section describe some robust leadership styles that you can learn and practice. Chapter 20 provides additional guidance on developing a feedback-rich environment. We recommend using that chapter and these suggested readings together.

A great resource to start with is Daniel Goleman's (2000) article, "Leadership That Gets Results." This classic article provides a brief, readable summary of research about six leadership styles from the consulting group Hay/McBer. A great book on leadership styles related to the organizational lifecycle is *Risk Taker, Caretaker, Surgeon, Undertaker: The Four Faces of Strategic Leadership* by W. E. Rothschild (1993). Each style is explained in detail, with a focus on how it relates to developing and executing strategy. Yukl and Lepsinger's (2004) book, *Flexible Leadership: Creating Value by Balancing Multiple Challenges and Choices*, provides an in-depth treatment of three leadership styles: efficiency-oriented, people-oriented, and change-oriented. Each style is described in a detailed, behavioral way, and the book includes a chapter on organizational processes that can support and improve the effectiveness of the styles. The book by Keith Ferrazzi and colleagues, *Competing in the New World of Work: How Radical Adaptability Separates the Best from the Rest* (2022), has some unique suggestions post-COVID-19. Lastly, Bob Kaplan and Robert Kaiser's (2013) book, *Fear Your Strengths,* provides an engaging analysis of imbalances in leadership style that can come from relying too much on a particular approach.

## SUMMARY

Cultivating adaptability requires taking a more active role in planning for interactions, and consistently reflecting on how they went. Most leaders do not regularly reflect on their leadership styles and approaches, and it shows over time in a less flexible or imbalanced approach to their roles. Exceptional leadership requires the discipline to keep challenging yourself to improve your adaptability, through a more rigorous and systematic approach.

---

**Think About It**

Chapter 2 talked about emotional intelligence as one of the 16 competencies in the exceptional leadership model. Facets of emotional intelligence include self-awareness, self-management, social awareness, and relationship management.

- Describe how each of these four facets could help leaders improve their adaptability.

---

**Think About It**

The theory of contingency leadership suggests that there is no one best leadership style. Goleman's (2000) article also says that leaders need to be adaptable.

- Research the history of contingency leadership and evaluate whether this approach might be more important in today's organizations than it was before.

---

## REFERENCES

Ferrazzi, K., K. Gohar, and N. Weyrich. 2022. *Competing in the New World of Work: How Radical Adaptability Separates the Best from the Rest.* Brighton, MA: Harvard Business Review Press.

Goleman, D. 2000. "Leadership That Gets Results." *Harvard Business Review* (March/April): 78–90.

Kaplan, R., and R. Kaiser. 2013. *Fear Your Strengths: What You Are Best at Could Be Your Biggest Problem.* New York: Berrett-Koehler.

Rothschild, W. E. 1993. *Risk Taker, Caretaker, Surgeon, Undertaker: The Four Faces of Strategic Leadership.* New York: John Wiley & Sons.

Yukl, G., and R. Lepsinger. 2004. *Flexible Leadership: Creating Value by Balancing Multiple Challenges and Choices.* New York: John Wiley & Sons.

# Part V

# PUTTING THE COMPETENCIES TO WORK

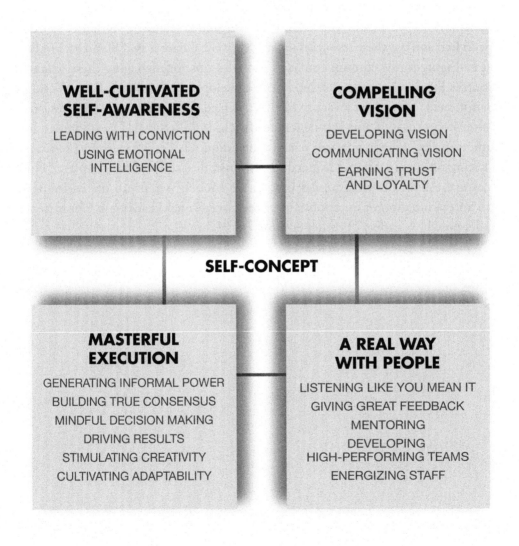

**WELL-CULTIVATED SELF-AWARENESS**

LEADING WITH CONVICTION

USING EMOTIONAL INTELLIGENCE

**COMPELLING VISION**

DEVELOPING VISION

COMMUNICATING VISION

EARNING TRUST AND LOYALTY

**SELF-CONCEPT**

**MASTERFUL EXECUTION**

GENERATING INFORMAL POWER

BUILDING TRUE CONSENSUS

MINDFUL DECISION MAKING

DRIVING RESULTS

STIMULATING CREATIVITY

CULTIVATING ADAPTABILITY

**A REAL WAY WITH PEOPLE**

LISTENING LIKE YOU MEAN IT

GIVING GREAT FEEDBACK

MENTORING

DEVELOPING HIGH-PERFORMING TEAMS

ENERGIZING STAFF

THE FIRST FOUR parts of this book focus on building your understanding of the Dye–Garman Exceptional Leadership Competency Model—the *what* of exceptional leadership. In addition to the specific suggestions in each of the first 16 chapters about how to improve your own leadership competencies, organizations can do many things to ensure leadership strength across their operations. The chapters in this part give you more information about how to apply leadership competencies in your organization, both for yourself and for all leaders, so that your entire leadership team's effectiveness is continuously improving.

Chapter 17, "Systems Approaches to Leadership Development," provides a system-level overview of how to maximize investments in strengthening healthcare leadership. Chapter 18, on "Leadership Coaches and Coaching Programs," explains how to find and use these resources most effectively. Chapter 19, "Mentors: Finding and Engaging for Maximum Impact," provides tips for managing these valuable resources for development. Chapter 20, "Developing a Feedback-Rich Working Environment," overviews a variety of effective feedback-enhancing strategies, such as after-event reviews and 360-degree feedback. In "Physician Development and Competencies," Chapter 21, we consider the unique challenges faced by physicians in taking on organizational leadership responsibilities. The final chapter, "Final Questions About the Exceptional Leadership Model," wraps up the entire book with an examination of questions about the Exceptional Leadership Competency Model posed by readers of earlier editions of this book.

# CHAPTER SEVENTEEN

# Systems Approaches to Leadership Development

LEADERS NEED TO take responsibility for their own learning and growth, but organizations also have important roles in supporting them. Taking leadership development seriously as a strategy requires thinking beyond the needs of individual leaders to look at the bigger picture of leadership needs across the entire organization. It also means developing a discipline around leadership practices, avoiding distractions from the latest trends and gurus, and staying focused on consistency over time.

Over the past decade especially, a robust science about leadership development systems has emerged. System-level studies have revealed relationships between leadership development practices and a wide variety of organizational outcomes, including patient satisfaction (Li et al. 2017), financial performance (Crowe et al. 2017), and hospital bond ratings (Garland et al. 2021).

In this chapter we take an evidence-based approach to describing the components of a high-performance leadership development system.

## CREATING A HIGH-PERFORMANCE LEADERSHIP DEVELOPMENT SYSTEM

Prior evidence reviews (Anderson and Garman 2014; Garman et al. 2022; Lacerenza et al. 2017) have identified leadership development processes with the greatest evidence of impact on important organizational outcomes. We describe eight particularly impactful ones below.

## Strategic Alignment

Leadership development systems need to be clearly aligned with the strategic goals of the organization. Many health systems have tried to implement leadership development from the middle, leaving it in the hands of the human resources or organizational development department or, even worse, to an outside vendor.

A well-aligned leadership development system means, at a minimum, that senior leadership owns the process, even if implementation is delegated to a specific department. Senior leadership should also make sure that the leadership development agenda flows from the organization's strategic plan. Too often, strategic planning focuses too much on the *what* and the *how* and not enough on the *who* of future plans. The gaps in leaders and leadership competencies should guide the selection and development of new talent and prepare them for emerging leadership roles.

Additionally, senior leaders should not just set the direction for leadership development, but also participate in it actively as mentors and learning facilitators for other leaders. In addition to visibly demonstrating the importance of development, this level of engagement provides senior leadership with greater visibility into talent pools and strengthens relationships across leadership teams.

## Attracting and Selecting Leaders

With the benefit of a strategically informed understanding of leadership needs, the next component of a high-performance leadership development system involves finding and attracting people who have the potential to become great leaders. This requires promoting the organization in ways that appeal to high-potential candidates. Organizations that take development seriously tend to be very attractive to high-potential leaders. Communicating these development opportunities your organization provides through channels such as conference presentations, internships, and administrative fellowships can expand your access to high-potential applicants (Garman et al. 2014, 2022; Robbins et al. 2022).

Besides strengthening applicant pools, health systems also need to have a rigorous process for choosing the best candidates for leadership roles. Even though hiring managers may prefer more freedom and flexibility in their selection decisions, research over many decades consistently shows that using more systematic methods leads to much better hires (Sackett et al. 2022; Schmidt and Hunter 1998). As a general rule, the best way to predict future performance is to look at past performance in similar situations, so methods that involve candidates showing their work (e.g., experience-based interviews, simulations, work portfolios) tend to be the most accurate. Competency models, like the one described throughout this book, can be useful tools for making the selection process more consistent, as long as they are tested and validated for the specific contexts where they are used.

## Preparing New Leaders for Success

Organizations differ widely in how they onboard new leaders. Taking a more thoughtful and systematic approach is associated with greater success rates for newly hired leaders, in both job performance and retention (De Vries et al. 2023). Practices that support effective onboarding include scheduled check-ins at 30, 60, and 90 days; planned approaches to meeting people within the organization; and providing coaching support (see Chapter 18).

## Identifying and Developing High-Potentials

Preparing for leadership roles takes time and experience. Senior leadership roles, in particular, can take years to get ready for successfully. The smartest way for health systems to develop leaders is to plan ahead for the leadership needs they will have over time, and start preparing future leaders before they are needed. An important part of this preparation process involves proactively identifying "high-potentials," people who have the talent and interest in preparing for progressively more responsible leadership roles. Competency models like the one described in this book can help prioritize the strengths and gaps future leaders may need to address. Once identified, high-potentials can be developed through a combination of cohort learning programs (or leadership academies) and other types of learning experiences.

As with other types of selection, a more structured approach to the high-potential identification process will outperform one that is based on personal opinions, and adding a structured assessment can help ensure development investments are maximized. Assessment data are also very helpful for tailoring leadership development to specific people's needs.

## Providing Developmental Experiences

Although leadership academies and other formal learning programs can provide the basics for becoming a better leader, most leadership learning happens through experience (Liu et al. 2021). The most effective leadership development systems recognize this fact and emphasize experience-based learning opportunities. Examples include temporary assignments such as leading cross-departmental or systemwide performance-improvement initiatives; participating in building projects or fund-raising campaigns; or even moving to other positions for a while to learn about different parts of the organization and/or system.

### Providing Performance Feedback

Performance feedback is another area where the research is clear: work environments that provide higher-quality feedback have significantly better job performance as well as lower levels of burnout (Katz, Rauvola, and Rudolph 2021), and higher-performing leaders are significantly more receptive to feedback (Katz, Moughan, and Rudolph 2023). Research also shows that more feedback is not necessarily better feedback, and poor-quality feedback can do more harm than good (Kluger and DeNisi 1996). Chapter 7 of this book describes the importance of effective feedback for continuous skill development. Leadership development systems should help ensure leaders are getting the feedback they need and are using it to maximum effect. Chapter 20 describes approaches to cultivating a feedback-rich environment in greater depth.

### Succession Planning

A high-performance approach to leadership development includes keeping an eye on the need for future leaders, as well as the need to replace current leaders who may retire or move on. *Talent management* is a systemwide approach to planning for future needs; *succession planning* usually refers to the narrower activity of planning for specific roles. Having leaders who are ready to take on more responsibility when needed is critically important for making smooth transitions and maintaining organizational momentum (Garman and Glawe 2004). However, industry surveys consistently suggest senior-level succession planning to be the exception rather than the rule, despite evidence that preparing future leaders effectively for top-level roles can take years (Garman and Tyler 2007; Wainwright, York, and Wyant 2021).

### Monitoring Results

Investments in leadership development need to be monitored against a specific set of objectives. In our experience, the best approach is to use a few simple outcome metrics that are easy to explain to senior leadership and other stakeholders. Some common measures include retention of leadership academy graduates over time, percentage promoted within a certain time frame, and perceptions of improvement in leadership effectiveness by the people they work with. For organizations that use leadership development as part of their diversity and inclusion strategy, additional metrics can also include the percentage of leaders from under-represented backgrounds at various levels of the organization.

## REFERENCES

Anderson, M. A., and A. N. Garman. 2014. "Leadership Development in Healthcare Systems: Towards an Evidence-Based Approach." White paper, National Center for Healthcare Leadership.

Crowe, D., A. N. Garman, C. Li, J. Helton, M. A. Anderson, and P. W. Butler. 2017. "Leadership Development Practices and Health System Financial Outcomes." *Health Services Management Research* 30 (3): 140–47.

De Vries, N., O. Lavreysen, A. Boone, J. Bouman, S. Szemik, K. Baranski, L. Godderis, and P. De Winter. 2023. "Retaining Healthcare Workers: A Systematic Review of Strategies for Sustaining Power in the Workplace." *Healthcare* 11: 1887.

Garland, N., A. N. Garman, P. S. O'Neil, and W. J. Canar. 2021. "The Impact of Hospital and Health System Leadership Development Practices on Bond Ratings." *Journal of Healthcare Management* 66: 63–74.

Garman, A. N., and J. Glawe. 2004. "Research Update: Succession Planning." *Consulting Psychology Journal: Practice & Research* 56 (2): 119–28.

Garman, A. N., M. P. Standish, C. Carter, M. A. Anderson, and C. Lambert. 2022. "The NCHL 'Best Organizations for Leadership Development' Program: A Case Study in Improving Evidence-Based Practice Through Benchmarking and Recognition." *Advances in Health Care Management Research* 20: 221–30.

Garman, A. N., J. A. Wainio, D. M. Howard, and M. Rowland. 2014. "Graduate and Fellowship Program Leaders' Perspectives on Administrative Fellowships: Results from Two National Surveys." *Journal of Health Administration Education* 31: 349–59.

Garman, A. N., and J. L. Tyler. 2007. "Succession Planning Practices and Outcomes in US Hospital Systems: Final Report." Report prepared for the American College of Healthcare Executives. https://www.ache.org/-/media/ache/learning-center/research/succession_planning.pdf.

Katz, I. M., C. M. Moughan, and C. W. Rudolph. 2023, in press. "Feedback Orientation: A Meta-analysis." *Human Resource Management Review.*

Katz, I. M., R. S. Rauvola, and C. W. Rudolph. 2021. "Feedback Environment: A Meta-analysis." *International Journal of Selection and Assessment* 29: 305–25.

Kluger, A. N., and A. DeNisi. 1996. "The Effects of Feedback Interventions on Performance: A Historical Review, a Meta-Analysis, and a Preliminary Feedback Intervention Theory." *Psychological Bulletin* 119 (2): 254–84.

Lacerenza, C. N., D. L. Reyes, S. L. Marlow, D. L. Joseph, and E. Salas. 2017. "Leadership Training Design, Delivery, and Implementation: A Meta-analysis." *Journal of Applied Psychology* 102 (12): 1686.

Li, C., P. Barth, A. N. Garman, M. A. Anderson, and P. Butler. 2017. "Leadership Development Practices and Patient Satisfaction: A Study of U.S. Academic Medical Centers." *Patient Experience Journal* 4 (1): 97–102.

Liu, Z., S. Venkatesh, S. E. Murphy, and R. E. Riggio. 2021. "Leader Development Across the Lifespan: A Dynamic Experiences-Grounded Approach. *The Leadership Quarterly* 32 (5): 101382.

Robbins, J., B. Z. Graham, A. N. Garman, R. S. Hall, and J. Simms. 2022. "Closing the Gender Gap in Healthcare Leadership: Can Administrative Fellowships Play a Role?" *Journal of Healthcare Management* 67: 436–45.

Sackett, P. R., C. Zhang, C. M. Berry, and F. Lievens. 2022. "Revisiting Meta-analytic Estimates of Validity in Personnel Selection: Addressing Systematic Overcorrection for Restriction of Range." *Journal of Applied Psychology* 107 (11): 2040–68.

Schmidt, F. L., and J. E. Hunter. 1998. "The Validity and Utility of Selection Methods in Personnel Psychology: Practical and Theoretical Implications of 85 Years of Research Findings." *Psychological Bulletin* 124 (2): 262–74.

Wainright, C. F., G. S. York, and D. K. Wyant. 2021. "Strategic Succession Planning for Healthcare Executives: A Forgotten Imperative." *Journal of Health Administration Education* 38 (3): 809–38.

# Leadership Coaches

THROUGHOUT THIS BOOK we discuss the importance of practice and expert feedback in developing exceptional leadership skills. We also note how difficult it can be to access high-quality feedback on a regular basis, due to the fast-paced nature of executive jobs and the shrinking proportion of senior leaders. As a result, many leaders and healthcare systems have turned to leadership coaching as a supplement to their other leadership development initiatives.

*Leadership coaching* involves a coach with specialized training who partners with clients ". . . in a thought-provoking and creative process that inspires them to maximize their personal and professional potential" (International Coaching Federation 2023). Leadership coaching differs from mentoring (as described in Chapter 19) in two key ways. First, leadership coaching involves a formal agreement between the coach and the person being coached, usually over a specified period of time, outlining a set of learning and/or performance goals they will work on. Second, a leadership coach is expected to have specialized training in the coaching process itself.

Coaching can be an expensive, time-consuming process. But used effectively—for the right purposes, with the right clients matched to the right coaches—it can also significantly accelerate learning and job performance (de Haan and Nilsson 2023). In this chapter we provide guidelines for working with a coach and describe the growing role of centralized coaching programs in health systems.

## WORKING WITH A LEADERSHIP COACH

Can a leadership coach help you become an exceptional leader? The answer may be yes, but it's important to determine whether this is the right step for you based on your goals, readiness, and career stage. Hiring a coach requires a significant investment in time and money, so it's important to carefully consider your decision. It may also be challenging to ask your organization to cover the cost of a coach if it has not done so before.

A leadership coach can be particularly helpful in the following four situations:

1. You are preparing for a new role that requires different leadership skills than you currently possess.
2. You are taking a new position within your organization.
3. You are transitioning to a different organization.
4. You have had concerns expressed to you about a deficit in your leadership skills that may be impacting your performance.

Each of these situations presents a distinct leadership challenge requiring different approaches based on the organizational context, your strengths and weaknesses, and your self-awareness about each. A coach can help you prioritize your development, set specific goals, and stay focused on achieving them.

### Identifying Competencies to Develop

Once you have specific development goals in mind, the next step is to determine the competencies needed to achieve them. Performance evaluations, 360-degree feedback programs (see Chapter 20), and self-assessments from prior development programs can help you identify areas for development. Many leadership coaches begin their engagement with an assessment process, which can help round this out.

Although coaching can be powerful on its own, it is particularly impactful when combined with other developmental options such as workshops and stretch assignments. In general, the more opportunities you have to practice what you are learning on the job, the more effective coaching will be in helping you rapidly develop your skills.

### Assessing Your Readiness for Coaching

A good coach is supportive but may also provide feedback that is direct and difficult to hear. Not everyone responds well to this type of feedback. Some people find it too uncomfortable and may struggle to listen effectively. (The Listening Like You Mean It competency from Chapter 6 is particularly important to coaching.) Kilburg (2001) suggests asking yourself the following questions to assess your readiness for coaching:

1. How *personally* motivated are you to develop these competencies? Is this something you want for yourself, or are you doing it to appease someone else (e.g., a superior, spouse)?
2. Have you tried to work on these competencies before? If so, what approaches have you tried, and how long did you stick with them?
3. What concerns do you have about being coached? Are you optimistic or pessimistic about the potential results?
4. Have you had difficulty following through on developmental assignments in the past?
5. How easy/difficult do you find it to accept constructive feedback?
6. How often have you given up on things because they became too personally challenging?

If you have trouble accepting constructive feedback, give up on efforts that become too personally challenging, have trouble following through, or are pursuing coaching for external reasons, then you are much less likely to see positive outcomes from a coaching engagement. On the other hand, if you tend to be tenacious in following goals, are able to wince your way through constructive feedback, and are pursuing coaching for your own personal growth, you are much more likely to see successful outcomes.

## Finding and Choosing a Coach

Coaching is not a formally licensed activity, and there is no universally recognized learning or certification for professional coaching. This makes the evaluation of qualifications less straightforward. Several different organizations represent and/or certify coaches, including the International Coaching Federation (ICF) (www.coachfederation.org) and the International Association of Coaching (www.certifiedcoach.org). However, certification from these or other organizations will not guarantee that a given coach is ideal for your needs. Conversely, there are also many outstanding coaches—including successful retired health system executives—who do not have any formal certification.

In our experience, the best way to find a coach is often through a referral from someone you trust. You can ask colleagues who have worked with coaches for recommendations and inquire about their coach's experience, style, and availability. The chief human resources officer or head of employee development in your organization may also be able to provide referrals. If your organization is currently contracting with coaches, they are the most likely to know what may be possible through these arrangements.

If you want to expand your search, the American College of Healthcare Executives (ACHE) maintains the Executive Coaches Directory at https://www.ache.org/career-resource-center/advance-your-career/executive-coaches-directory. The directory lists coaches affiliated with ACHE and provides information about their practice, approach, and fees. Although it is a directory and not a screening tool, it can be a useful starting point for identifying potential coaching resources. It is searchable by several fields, including area of expertise and practice location.

The qualifications needed for effective coaching will vary depending on your specific needs. For example, if you need to improve your interactions with senior team members, a coach who has served as an executive and interacted with senior teams may be the best fit. Similarly, many new physician leaders prefer to work with more experienced physician coaches.

In addition to experience and expertise, the quality of the relationship between the coach and client is crucial for a successful engagement (Graßmann, Schölmerich, and Schermuly 2020). We recommend interviewing at least two or three coaches before making a decision. You should feel free to ask questions about their experience, approach, and fees and make sure their answers make sense to you and build trust in the relationship. If a coach tries to avoid your questions or pressure you into working with them, it's best to look for someone else.

### Questions to Ask When Choosing a Coach

1. *How did you become a coach, and what training have you received?* Given the wide variation in backgrounds and experiences among coaches, it's important to find out how they prepared for the role.
2. *How long have you been working as a coach, and how much coaching do you do?* More experience as a coach generally means better skills and a deeper pool of experiences to draw from.
3. *What types of positions have you coached?* Give preference to coaches who have experience working at *and* above your current level in the organization.
4. *How much of your work is focused on healthcare, and what types of healthcare organizations have you worked with?* A coach with relevant experience may better understand the complex environment healthcare leaders face.
5. *What kinds of work did you do before you became a coach?* Coaches who have worked as leaders themselves may have a better understanding of the challenges leaders face.
6. *How would you describe your approach to coaching, and do you have any areas of focus or expertise?* Make sure the coach's approach sounds clear, reasonable, effective, and comfortable for you. Be cautious of coaches who

seem overly captivated with their models or who seem to talk more than they listen.

7. *What types of engagements or arrangements do you offer?* Determine whether the coach and/or their employer has worked with your organization in the past, and if so, whether they have a formal contract with your organization. If they do, you may receive more favorable rates than by contracting individually.

8. *Can you provide client references?* If a coach is unable to provide references to individual clients for confidentiality reasons, see if they can provide the name of a general contact from a client organization (e.g., a vice president of HR) who can comment more generally about the coach's services.

## Other Considerations

1. Coaching is a two-way relationship, and you get out what you put in. A coach can't do the work for you, so it's important to take the process seriously to get the most value from it.

2. Coaching takes time to produce results. If you are working on fundamental changes to the way you work with others, you may need to plan on working with a coach for at least 12 months before seeing significant results.

# ORGANIZATIONAL COACHING PROGRAMS

In many health systems, decisions about the use of executive coaches are decentralized and left to the discretion of individual leaders, with costs covered by departmental budgets. While this approach supports leaders' autonomy and responsibility for their own development, it also means the organization is missing out on opportunities for quality control, leveraged contracting for better rates, and alignment of coaching resources to the areas of greatest strategic importance. For these and other reasons, an increasing number of health systems have developed centralized approaches to identify, contract with, and deploy leadership coaching. In some cases, health systems are creating internal capacity by developing and deploying the coaching capabilities of their own staff. However, these types of programs can involve much more complexity than meets the eye. If you are interested in learning more about internal coaching programs, we recommend the *Handbook of Coaching in Organizations* from the nonprofit Center for Creative Leadership (Riddle, Hoole, and Gullette 2015).

## SUMMARY

When approached wisely, coaching can help leaders quickly improve their skills and maximize the value of their work experience. Well-designed and carefully monitored coaching programs can provide similar benefits across an entire organization. Given the high cost of coaching, it's important to manage these resources carefully. At the same time, few organizations can afford to underinvest in developing their leaders.

## REFERENCES

de Haan, E., and V. O. Nilsson. 2023. "What Can We Know About the Effectiveness of Coaching? A Meta-analysis Based Only on Randomized Controlled Trials." *Academy of Management Learning & Education.* doi:10.5465/amle.2022.0107.

Graßmann, C., F. Schölmerich, and C. C. Schermuly. 2020. "The Relationship Between Working Alliance and Client Outcomes in Coaching: A Meta-analysis." *Human Relations* 73 (1): 35–58.

International Coaching Federation. 2023. "What Is Coaching?" Accessed August 21. https://coachingfederation.org/about.

Kilburg, R. R. 2001. "Facilitating Intervention Adherence in Executive Coaching: A Model and Methods." *Consulting Psychology Journal* 53 (4): 251–67.

Riddle, D. D., E. Hoole, and E. Gullette (eds.). 2015. *The Center for Creative Leadership Handbook of Coaching in Organizations.* San Francisco: Jossey-Bass.

# CHAPTER NINETEEN

# Mentors: How to Find and Work with Them

The term *MENTOR* can mean different things to different people. For our purposes we define it as someone other than your boss who is willing to provide you with support, guidance, and advice for your development. Unlike leadership coaching, which we described in Chapter 18 as a formal and professional service, mentoring relationships are generally more informal and are typically voluntary.

Mentoring can be a powerful resource for leadership development, according to a substantial body of research (Grocutt et al. 2022). Mentors can also benefit from the relationship, as they tend to be more satisfied, committed, and successful in their careers (Ghosh and Reio 2013). Mentoring can also help organizations attract and retain talent (Craig et al. 2013; Payne and Huffman 2005) and support the advancement of women and other diverse groups into senior leadership roles (Murrell, Blake-Beard, and Porter 2021).

This chapter provides some practical tips on how to find and connect with mentors.

## WORKING WITH A MENTOR

To find a good mentor, you first need to clarify what you want from the relationship—career advice, skill development, network development—and what you are willing give to the relationship in return.

If you have a specific career goal, look for people who are similar to you but are further along in their career path. If you work in a large organization, you can meet potential mentors by joining cross-departmental teams. If you are already a senior leader in your organization, then your alumni network or professional associations—like the local chapters of the American College of Healthcare Executives, Healthcare Information and Management Systems Society, Healthcare Financial Management Association, or Medical Group Management Association—can be excellent places to start your search. If you want to improve specific skills, look for people who not only are good at those skills but also have worked hard to master them. Each chapter in this book offers ideas on where to find people likely to be very good at specific competencies.

## APPROACHING A MENTOR

Mentoring relationships can be formal or informal, but if you are hoping for a longer-term commitment from someone, asking for a more formal arrangement may be best. A good approach is to simply say, "I am really interested in learning more about _____. I heard from _____ that you are particularly skilled in this area. Would you be open to meeting with me some time so I could ask you a few questions?" Most people approached in this way will be flattered and will gladly meet with you, but if they do say no, be sure to accept it gracefully before moving on to your next potential mentor.

Once a potential mentor has agreed to meet with you, make the meeting as convenient as possible for them. Offer to go to their office at a time that suits them, or invite them for lunch at a place they like.

When you meet with a mentor for the first time, be prepared and proactive. Have a clear goal, a point of view, and a list of questions. Toward the end of the meeting, ask yourself how well the two of you connected. Is this someone who could help you develop in the future? If you think so, thank them for their time and ask if they would be willing to meet again, maybe every few months (or other interval) for some specific period. If they say yes, then you have found yourself a mentor.

## USING A MENTOR

Always think of time spent with your mentor as a precious resource that you don't want to waste. In each meeting with your mentor, always demonstrate two things: (1) you are grateful for their help and (2) you want to give back to them as much as they give to you, either now or later. The following tips will help you both make the most of this relationship.

# TIPS FOR AN EFFECTIVE MENTORING RELATIONSHIP

## Prepare Well for Your Meetings

Come to any meeting with your mentor as well prepared as possible, and do whatever you can to honor the meetings you arrange. Before the meeting, review your goals for the mentoring relationship. Think about what has gone well and what challenges you have faced since the last time you met. Write these down so you remember to discuss them. Also, note any advice you followed from the last meeting and how it affected your work.

When you talk about challenges, give enough detail so your mentor has a clear sense of the situation. Also, try to formulate specific questions you can ask. These questions should be open-ended enough to allow for dialogue, but not so open-ended that your mentor needs to do most of the work.

For example, say you are working with your mentor to improve on physician relations. In the past month, an incident occurred that you found troubling: You were discussing renovations with a medical director when he suddenly got angry and stormed out of the meeting. Asking your mentor, "Can you believe that?" is probably too vague. It is better to ask, "What do you think might have caused him to react that way?" Even better, however, is asking something even more specific, like this: "In trying to figure out why he got so upset, I came up with three possible reasons. Based on what I told you, do you agree with each of them? How might you deal with each?"

## Use Time Between Meetings Effectively

Before you end a meeting with your mentor, agree on least one specific "homework assignment" you want to do before your next meeting. The assignment can be as simple as applying some specific advice the mentor suggested, or as complex as finding and pursuing opportunities to practice a skill you are working on. In addition to helping you stay focused on the skills you are developing, assignments can add continuity to the mentoring relationship: You are giving your mentor a more compelling reason to see you again, to hear how things worked out.

## Make It a Two-Way Relationship

Even though the main purpose of a mentoring relationship is to help you grow professionally, you will both get more out of the relationship if you find ways to give back. If your mentor is open to talking about their own work, ask questions about what they are doing in their own role, what problems they are facing, and what issues are keeping them up at night. For you, this exchange is a learning opportunity: You get to hear your mentor's own thinking process. For your mentor, it allows them to sound out their challenges and concerns and clarify their views on those issues. Sometimes, you may find that you can offer useful contacts, articles, or other resources that could help your mentor. This type of sharing helps ensure that your mentor is getting something from the relationship too.

### Review Your Progress Regularly

Although some mentoring relationships are open-ended, adding some time limits can ensure that the relationship is productive and progressing toward your goals. It can also be helpful to schedule progress check-ins. For example, if your goal is to improve your influencing skills over the coming year, then review your progress after a year. Check-ins are also useful when considering whether to continue the relationship and, if so, how. For example, if you chose your mentor because of their expertise in a certain area, you can assess your skill level and then decide if you have learned enough or not. You can then make an intentional decision to end or continue the relationship.

### End Well

Sometimes mentoring relationships fade away without a clear end, which can be disappointing for both of you. Meetings may get canceled and not rescheduled, until eventually both parties lose touch. The progress reviews described previously can help you end the mentoring phase of the relationship in a clear and positive way. We recommend having a final meeting to talk about the future or the end of the relationship and to review your achievements. This is also a good time to express gratitude for all the mentor's help.

Even after the formal mentoring relationship is over, we recommend keeping in touch from time to time. For example, you might send an e-mail or a card a year after your last meeting, and occasionally after that. In the message, you can update your mentor on your career and describe how you have used skills you learned. And always, end your note by thanking your mentor for their help.

Historically, the healthcare field has taken a top-down approach to mentoring—that is, encouraging experienced leaders to become mentors, then finding less experienced people to become their mentees. However, research shows that mentoring has greater impact when the mentee takes more responsibility for the whole process—that is, finding a mentor to work with, taking the initiative to work with them, and then finding other mentors as appropriate at other points in their career (Eby et al. 2013; Underhill 2006).

## ESTABLISHING AN ORGANIZATIONAL MENTORING PROGRAM

It's important to distinguish between mentoring and leadership coaching, and also between organizational coaching programs and mentoring programs. Both can be useful for your organization's leadership development and talent management strategy, but each offer different contributions and pose different challenges. Running mentoring programs well can be more complicated. For one thing, unlike with a leadership coaching program, visible senior leadership participation is critical and must be there from the start. Second, because mentors are not professional coaches, you need to pay more attention to preparing them and their mentees. Lastly, because mentors are usually also employees of the organization, you need to manage the relationships differently. If you are interested in starting a formal mentoring program within your own organization, we recommend you read Tammy Allen and colleagues' (2009) book, *Designing Workplace Mentoring Programs: An Evidence-Based Approach*. The authors provide a practical approach to defining mentoring that is strongly grounded by peer-reviewed research.

As we mentioned in Chapter 8, the American College of Healthcare Executives (ACHE) website (www.ache.org) has an online mentorship program called the Leadership Mentoring Network. The ACHE website also provides extensive information on mentoring, including a compilation of articles from *Healthcare Executive* magazine's (2014) "Leadership in Mentoring" column.

## SUMMARY

Exceptional leaders take personal responsibility for their own development, and they also seek out mentoring relationships that can help them develop over time. When you work with mentors, remember that they usually agree to mentor for three main reasons: (1) they feel good about being an expert, (2) they find helping others develop to be rewarding, and (3) they learn from the relationship too. If you make sure these needs are being met, your mentor will stay more fully engaged in the process. Also, look for ways to make these relationships a win–win, both for the mentors you find and the prospective mentees who will ask you for help as your career advances.

## REFERENCES

Allen, T., L. Finkelstein, and M. Poteet. 2009. *Designing Workplace Mentoring Programs: An Evidence-Based Approach.* Malden, MA: Wiley-Blackwell.

Craig, C. A., M. Allen, M. Reid, C. Riemendschneider, and D. Armstrong. 2013. "The Impact of Career Mentoring and Psychosocial Mentoring on Affective Organizational Commitment, Job Involvement, and Turnover Intention." *Administration & Society* 45 (8): 949–73.

Eby, L., T. Allen, B. Hoffman, L. Baranik, J. Bauer, S. Baldwin, M. Morrison, K. Kinkade, C. Maher, S. Curtis, and S. Evans. 2013. "An Interdisciplinary Meta-analysis of the Potential Antecedents, Correlates, and Consequences of Protégé Perceptions of Mentoring." *Psychological Bulletin* 139 (2): 441–76.

Ghosh, R., and R. Reio Jr. 2013. "Career Benefits Associated with Mentoring for Mentors: A Meta-Analysis." *Journal of Vocational Behavior* 83 (1): 106–16.

Grocutt, A., D. Gulseren, J. Weatherhead, and N. Turner. 2022. "Can Mentoring Programmes Develop Leadership?" *Human Resource Development International* 25 (4): 404–14.

*Healthcare Executive.* 2014. "Leadership in Mentoring." American College of Healthcare Executives. www.ache.org/newclub/career/MentorArticles/Mentoring.cfm.

Murrell, A. J., S. Blake-Beard, and D. M. Porter Jr. 2021. "The Importance of Peer Mentoring, Identity Work and Holding Environments: A Study of African American Leadership Development." *International Journal of Environmental Research and Public Health* 18 (9): 4920.

Payne, S., and A. Huffman. 2005. "A Longitudinal Examination of the Influence of Mentoring on Organizational Commitment and Turnover." *Academy of Management Journal* 48 (1): 158–68.

Underhill, C. M. 2006. "The Effectiveness of Mentoring Programs in Corporate Settings: A Meta-Analytical Review of the Literature." *Journal of Vocational Behavior* 68 (2): 292–307.

# CHAPTER TWENTY

# Developing a Feedback-Rich
# Working Environment

THROUGHOUT THIS BOOK we highlight the value of a feedback-rich working environment, which may seem like a daunting task. Changing the quality of feedback in your working environment may require changing the culture of your department or organization (Edmonson 2011). But it can be done, and the benefits are worth it.

The techniques we share in this chapter are proven to improve feedback within organizational environments. They are listed in rough order of relative impact; the first techniques are the simplest and easiest to use. The best way to use each technique is to lead by example—that is, use the technique yourself first, then inspire your staff to follow suit. Then, keep it up until it becomes a habit for your team.

## SPOT DEBRIEF SESSIONS

Spot debriefs are short, ideally habitual, feedback sessions that happen right after a performance. If you or your team don't usually stop to reflect on your work, a simple way to start is to commit to giving spot debriefs at least once a week on an important area of performance. Good subjects for this type of feedback include a presentation to an important group, a negotiation with a vendor, or a joint meeting with a patient's family. To use this technique, a leader (or colleague) first asks the main performer (e.g., the person leading the presentation or the meeting) to share their own thoughts on their performance in two steps: (1) what they think went particularly well, and (2) what they would change if they could do it over again. After the person finishes their self-evaluation, the leader (or colleague) gives their own feedback, building on what the performer already said (what went well, what could be changed).

The structure of this feedback method helps achieve several goals. By starting with the performer's views, the feedback givers can adjust their comments to match the performer's awareness of their own performance. Also, the feedback is more likely to be seen as useful additional knowledge rather than redundant information (i.e., what the performer already knows).

## AFTER-EVENT REVIEWS

The after-event review (AER) is a more structured and formal approach to feedback sessions. First used in the military, this method is now used in healthcare and other fields, and research shows it can be particularly helpful for leadership development (Baron and Boies 2023; DeRue et al. 2012). The method involves a structured team discussion that happens after an activity to find and gain agreement about what worked well and what did not work well. There are many different approaches to AERs, but most involve answering these four key questions:

1. What did we want to achieve?
2. What did we actually achieve?
3. What caused the differences between what we wanted and what actually happened?
4. Based on our experiences this time, what should we keep doing and stop doing next time?

## DEVELOPING A SHARED COMPETENCY LANGUAGE

In environments where people don't reflect on performance with each other very often, staff may struggle to clearly articulate a path to higher performance through their feedback. The meanings of words like *respect, feedback,* or *vision,* for example, may differ across staff depending on their background or experience. By meeting as a team to define leadership competencies for your organization, you can develop a language around performance they are comfortable with. If the development process takes place in a climate of sufficient psychological safety, it can evolve into process improvement meetings in which people can talk about performance openly.

## SHARING INDIVIDUAL GOALS

Too often, individual developmental goals are seen as flaws: We know we need to work on them, but we also try to hide them from everyone else. Sharing your development goals with others, while uncomfortable at first, is often a better way to make real progress in improvement (Harkin et al. 2016). For example, a director who has been told that he sometimes gives harsh and discouraging feedback may be able to improve by just being mindful of his emotions. But he will improve much faster if he tells his development goal to his direct reports. By doing this, he gives himself a chance to get feedback from the people who know his performance best. For instance, he may say to a staff member after giving her feedback, "As you know I am working on giving constructive feedback in a more balanced way. How do you think that went?"

## PERFORMANCE CALIBRATION

Even leaders who are highly experienced with giving feedback can drift over time into their own different views of performance. For example, one leader may think that taking two weeks to fix a payroll issue is okay, but another may view that as extremely insensitive to the affected staff.

Leaders can help each other fine-tune their internal standards through a process of performance calibration. The process involves leaders within a particular department or across a leadership team having a discussion about the standards by which staff are evaluated on performance reviews. The idea is for leaders to compare notes on how they evaluate performance and then get feedback on whether others view their approach as fair, too lenient, or too harsh. Through this process, leaders get a chance to improve their own thinking by listening to their peers' perspectives, and as a group come to greater agreement on a shared approach.

## TALENT REVIEWS

A talent review is a periodic meeting of leaders to discuss employee performance levels in the context of current and future organizational needs. There are many approaches to talent reviews, but all of them usually involve asking questions about how well specific employees fit specific current or future roles. Like calibration meetings, talent reviews can give leaders the opportunity to compare their own thinking about performance-related needs to their peers'. Additionally, the process provides a forum for talking about performance-related needs at the wider organizational and strategic levels. Talent reviews also help to support the idea that leaders are not expected to stay in a role forever; ideally, they should be continuously getting ready for change and succession.

Implementing a talent review process should not be taken lightly. Because talent reviews involve active discussions about whether a person is right for a role, they may feel threatening. Talent reviews usually need top-level support, and sometimes a major culture change, to start.

## MULTISOURCE (360-DEGREE) FEEDBACK

A 360-degree feedback program involves asking for feedback from different people who interact regularly with a given leader—such as peers, direct reports, superiors, and clients, among others—and then giving that feedback to the leader being reviewed in a way that protects the identities of the sources. Following are the eight main steps in a 360-degree feedback process, including the decisions that need to be made and best practices in each step.

### Step 1: Define the Participants and the Goals

A 360-degree feedback process can be done for a single leader, a group of leaders, or the leadership of a whole organization. If many people are involved, starting at the top of the organization and moving down in stages is often best; this lets senior-level executives learn about the process first and also set an example.

In terms of goals, the main decision that needs be made is whether the process is used for development or for appraisal (i.e., will the feedback affect the participant's official performance review?). In general, 360-degree feedback programs are most helpful when used only for developmental purposes; this means that the only people who can see the results are the leader and the feedback facilitator. If used for appraisal purposes, these programs tend to suffer from the same response biases that affect regular performance appraisals (Eichenger and Lombardo 2003).

### Step 2: Choose or Create the Feedback Survey

The survey tool used should meet the needs of the people who will take part in the feedback process. While many ready-made surveys are available, they may not be a good fit for a specific use or for certain leadership roles. Some competencies may be relevant and on point, while others may be irrelevant or not as important. For this reason, many organizations choose to either develop their own survey or adapt an existing one.

When creating a survey, avoid the temptation to include everything but the kitchen sink—in reality, less is often more. Surveys that have 30 items or more risk causing survey fatigue, where responders develop a fixed mindset about the person being reviewed and answer all items similarly. On the other hand, we have seen surveys that asked only for a dozen or so ratings work very well; they often place a lot of emphasis on open-ended questions (e.g., "If this person could improve in one area, what would make the biggest difference in their overall performance?"). Regardless of length, space for open-ended comments should be provided, and their use should be encouraged (or required). The open-ended questions often provide some of the most useful data people receive.

## Step 3: Decide How to Manage the Process

Online surveys are the best choice from an efficiency perspective. Online survey programs (e.g., Google forms, Microsoft forms, SurveyMonkey) can offer low and even no-cost options, especially for small-scale projects. Specialty vendors offer options for larger-scale projects; prices vary a lot so comparison shopping can be useful. Regardless of platform, we strongly recommend that you use an outside party to handle the data-management part of any 360-degree project. Given the potentially very sensitive nature of the feedback, being able to ensure confidentiality in both fact and appearance is crucial. The outside party does not necessarily have to be outside your organization. For example, if you have a well-respected employee/ organization development group in-house, the group may have the capabilities to manage such a project.

If you do go outside the organization for help, consider contacting the industrial psychology department of your local university. Some departments have university consulting practices that can provide high-quality oversight at a fraction of what private-sector consultants charge.

## Step 4: Identify Reviewers

Participants identified in step 1 will need to ask the people they work with to participate in the feedback process. Expectations need to be clear ahead of time about who should be asked to participate (e.g., peers, superiors, direct reports), how many participants should be solicited, and/or whether to allow anyone who wishes to participate.

Here are some general guidelines:

- If people can choose their own reviewers, they should be encouraged to include people (colleagues, direct reports, supervisors) they do not work well with or even have a conflict with. Although their feedback will be less favorable, it often provides insights that we would not get if we only sought feedback from our biggest advocates.
- Having more feedback providers is usually better than having fewer. With more respondents, you can more readily identify common themes across work relationships and will have more confidence in their meaningfulness.

### Step 5: Distribute and Collect the Survey

Set a deadline for getting feedback, but be prepared to extend it at least once and likely twice if needed. Depending on how the survey process is managed, it can be wrapped up in as little as two weeks or as many as four.

### Step 6: Prepare the Reports

Specialized online systems generate reports automatically; generic survey systems may require additional formatting. To protect anonymity, it is usually a good idea to require a minimum number of respondents within categories such as peers and direct reports. If numbers fall below these criteria, categories can be combined within a given report.

### Step 7: Share the Feedback and Plan for Development

Feedback can be delivered in a number of ways. At one extreme is the "desk drop," where people receive their reports without any discussion or expectation for follow-up. At the other extreme is scheduling a meeting between each person, their boss, and a feedback coach to talk through the results, come up with development plans, and set specific goals and a timeline for follow-up.

In our experience, the approach that works best is to have a feedback facilitator (someone outside the person's direct line of management) meet with the person to review the feedback results and explore what they mean for their development. These meetings should usually be at least an hour long so there is adequate time to talk through the results and create meaningful development plans.

## Step 8: Follow Up

People who take part in a 360-degree process should be given clear expectations for how their results should be used. At the very least, each participant should talk with their boss in general terms about the development plan they have developed in response to the feedback. Ideally, they should also follow up with the people who gave them feedback. For example, a participant might take some time during a staff meeting to thank staff for taking the time to complete the survey, and also share the strengths and developmental needs the report revealed. The participant might also tell staff what they plan to do to work on those areas, and ask staff to keep providing feedback on their progress. Taking this extra step has three benefits: (1) it shows the leader's appreciation and openness to feedback from their direct reports, (2) it sets a good example of how to receive feedback constructively, and (3) it holds the leader publicly accountable for making progress.

To track progress, leaders may want to arrange future 360-degree feedbacks to see how they have changed over time. This step can sometimes be helpful, but it can be effective (and much less work) to simply ask colleagues and staff if they have noticed any change in the areas they care about. This approach also helps to create a feedback-rich work environment. If you do decide to arrange additional 360-degree feedbacks, it's important to understand that change is often difficult to measure directly. One reason for this is that people tend to "raise the bar" on performance expectations over time, and even if a leader's skills improve, their average ratings might stay the same or even go down (Martineau and Hannum 2004). For this reason, it's often better to ask the original survey participants to say how they think the leader has changed over time (better, worse, or the same) than to reuse the original survey structure.

## SUMMARY

The best way to keep people developing is to ensure that all staff are regularly receiving high-quality feedback. The techniques we described in this chapter are proven strategies that work well in healthcare and other settings. In places where feedback is uncommon, applying any of these techniques consistently will take some effort. Like working out, you might be tempted early on to skip providing feedback "just this time, because we're so busy right now." Creating a culture where staff can openly talk about their failures as well as successes also takes time. But if you overcome these challenges, you will be well on your way to building a more feedback-rich environment.

# REFERENCES

Baron, L., and K. Boies. 2023. "Workplace Coaching to Develop Leadership Flexibility: The Impact of After-Event Review." *Leadership & Organization Development Journal* 44 (3): 317–29.

DeRue, D. S., J. D. Nahrgang, J. R. Hollenbeck, and K. Workman. 2012. "A Quasi-Experimental Study of After-Event Reviews and Leadership Development." *Journal of Applied Psychology* 97 (5): 997–1015.

Edmonson, E. 2011. "Strategies for Learning from Failure." *Harvard Business Review* (April): 48–55.

Eichenger, R. W., and M. M. Lombardo. 2003. "Knowledge Summary Series: 360-Degree Assessment." *Human Resource Planning* 26: 34–44.

Harkin, B., T. Webb, B. Chang, A. Prestwich, M. Conner, I. Kellar, Y. Benn, and P. Sheeran. 2016. "Does Monitoring Goal Progress Promote Goal Attainment? A Meta-analysis of the Experimental Evidence." *Psychological Bulletin* 142 (2): 198–229.

Martineau, J., and K. Hannum. 2004. *Evaluating Leadership Development Programs: A Professional Guide.* Greensboro, NC: Center for Creative Leadership.

# CHAPTER TWENTY-ONE

# Physician Leadership Development and Competencies

The two top physician executives of St. Nicholas Health System—Dr. Howard James, senior vice president of medical affairs, and Dr. Maria Borman, president of the St. Nicholas Medical Group—were talking about how important it was for their organization to create a better physician leadership development program. "Between the toll COVID has taken on our physicians, the stress and burnout they are currently feeling, and the growth we expect in our western suburbs, we really need to get more physicians into leadership roles," said Dr. James.

Dr. Borman replied, "Yes, and with healthcare growing so complex, we need more physicians at the top. We need more physician leaders to help us do the heavy lifting. But the leadership development programs we have been using from the two outside companies are not getting the job done. Their programs are just outside speakers giving lectures, and that's not enough. We need a new approach for the younger physicians who we see as our future leaders."

Dr. James responded, "I think the new programs that use the leadership competencies that Jim Batten, our HR guy, has introduced could be what we need." Dr. Borman asked, "How so?" Dr. James replied, "Well, if you look at the competencies, they are all about what we need to do as physician leaders—even the ones in part-time roles. They involve behaviors, something that physicians understand very well. Also, when Jim teaches to them, he does it in a real and practical way. He's not a 'death by PowerPoint' instructor. He gives at most a ten-minute introduction, and then people spend the rest of the time actively discussing or solving problems. And Jim uses cases based on the real problems we are facing right now. I think

*(continued)*

*(continued from previous page)*

we could build a big part of our physician development program around applying each of these competencies. Each one could be a course by itself. Let's get with Jim and see what he can do for us."

Two weeks later as the three executives met to discuss the program, Batten said, "I have heard from several physician leaders that they don't like the lecture style our outside firms are using. They want something that is more relevant to us. Also, I know that physicians are not very patient with learning the softer side of management. As scientists, they work mostly with data and think leadership education is subjective and not very useful. They don't care about the theory part if they can't apply it to everyday issues. But I think they will find that using specific leadership competencies will give them a more objective way to define and describe leadership skills and actions. I also think they will quickly understand the need to practice these behaviors and get feedback on them. If we work together, I think we can come up with some realistic examples for them to work on that will illustrate each of the competencies nicely, and give them the initial practice they need to be more effective using them. We could tie the whole program together with an applied learning project participants work on throughout the program, and then have them present their experiences to senior leadership at the end. How does that sound?"

The two physicians looked at each other and smiled. Then James responded, "This sounds like exactly what wanted. Let's get started!"

## WHY A SEPARATE CHAPTER ON PHYSICIAN LEADERSHIP?

As we write this, the healthcare world is changing fast. The field is trying to move on from COVID-19, but the pandemic created huge challenges. COVID caused stress and burnout, and we have serious labor shortages, expense challenges, more public and private payers hiring physicians, clinical integration, population health management, provider shortages, and heightened expectations around health equity and community resiliency. Most of the changes in the industry in the next few years will require more physician leadership. Physicians have a big impact on quality and cost. Also, consumers care more about quality outcomes now. Improving clinical quality and the patient experience is more important than ever. Expert and system-oriented physician leadership will be essential for addressing all of these issues. As Dr. Kevin Casey comments, "Having been relatively new to physician leadership ten years ago, the changes listed at that time were felt to be both significant and real. On the trailing side of the COVID-19 pandemic, they have only been magnified and multiplied. We have even worsening labor and supply chain shortages and increases in cost. Mergers and acquisitions are more common now than before. All of these need to be, and most of them can only be, addressed through equipped, empowered, and engaged physician leaders."

While there has been more focus on physician leadership and developing physician leaders, many organizations are still struggling with it. The first two editions of this book got a lot of feedback from the physician executive community. Many physicians appreciated how we articulated the leadership competencies, which helped them see how leadership could be clearer and more understandable. The idea of leadership competencies also fits well with the scientific nature of physicians. As scientists, physicians are good with numbers and like to deal with objective data. While leadership is not quantifiable to the degree the hard sciences are (e.g., it is wrong to think an assessment can say Leader A is 16.7 percent more effective than Leader B), using competencies still makes leadership easier to understand objectively. Moreover, competencies are about *behaviors*, which can be observed, and this fits well with how physicians think.

Another factor that makes developing physician leaders different is the age at which physicians usually start taking leadership roles. Many nurses take their first leadership roles at age 24 or 25; business executives in healthcare usually have 15 to 20 years of leadership experience by their early 40s. In contrast, most physicians are 45 to 50 years old before they take their first leadership roles. As a result, management and leadership can require a much more substantial shift of professional focus. Understanding leadership competencies can help physician leaders get up to speed quicker. Dr. Saria Saccocio stated, "This is also one reason many medical schools now offer master's programs (MHA, MBA, MPH) in their education options."

Do physician leaders do different things as leaders? In a word, no. They do bring a different perspective to management and leadership than their counterparts without clinical training do. But the functions and practices of leadership are the same. And just because they are physicians does not mean they are qualified to be leaders. Physicians need to get management and leadership training just as nonphysician leaders do. Dr. Lily Henson commented, "I was not taught to lead in medical school—I had to learn it through courses and mentors and making some mistakes."

What does set physician leaders apart is their clinical background. The fact that they know what happens in the care process can give physician leaders an edge as they move to shape strategy and make changes in healthcare organizations. Dr. John Byrnes comments, "The depth of understanding what is done in the clinical setting often lets physician leaders see and comprehend things that nonclinicians will miss." Dr. Kevin Casey adds, "This advantage of clinical knowledge is very helpful and can differentiate a physician leader, but only if all else is equal. Today's physician leader must have knowledge of finance, marketing, strategy, and all the other domains and competencies of other healthcare leaders, and only then does clinical knowledge act as a differentiator."

Dr. Scott Ransom adds, "The key to great physician leadership is balancing all of the various functional skills (e.g., quality, finance, operations) to set the most optimal strategy and solution to move forward. It is not overly helpful to say 'from a clinical perspective' or 'from a finance perspective.' The most optimal approach is to form a completely integrated strategy approach that combines the various functions to create the optimal approach given the specific organizational context and goals."

Most people would agree that having more physicians involved in leadership activities, both part-time and full-time, will improve both patient care and wellness outcomes. Khan, Aziz, and Siddiqui (2022) report that "Literature demonstrates that a clinician's role in the management of an institution is directly related to the overall effectiveness and better-quality parameters. Clinicians in senior management positions improve hospital and company operating outcomes substantially more than those with lower levels of clinician involvement."

Lastly, it must be said that for too long the management and leadership of healthcare organizations have been the domain of professional managers without clinical backgrounds; physicians and other clinicians have often been seen as separate and distinct—us versus them. If management and leadership become too separated from the people working directly with the patients, the ability to work collaboratively and keep up with change will suffer.

## CONTRASTING PHYSICIANS WITH EXECUTIVE LEADERS

"Physicians as leaders are often like fish out of water," wrote Saunders and Hagemann (2009). To be certain, there are big differences between physicians and professional managers. When we think about leadership competencies, we need to remember the background and nature of physicians. Dye and Sokolov (2013) presented a contrast between physician and administrators, as shown in Exhibit 21.1.

Although much has been written about these differences, some points apply particularly to leadership competencies and bear a closer look.

**Exhibit 21.1 Characteristics of Physicians Versus Administrators**

| Physicians | Administrators |
|---|---|
| Science-oriented | Business-oriented |
| One-on-one interactions | Group interactions |
| Value autonomy | Value collaboration |
| Focus on patients | Focus on organization |
| Identify with profession | Identify with organization |
| Independent | Collaborative |
| Solo thinkers | Group thinkers |

*SOURCE:* Dye and Sokolov (2013).

## Science Orientation

To begin with, physicians are scientists by nature. They are quantitative by nature; they seek to solve problems through clearly definable and measurable factors, and avoid making decisions based on hunch or intuition. In contrast, while executives typically use some science and quantitative skills in their work, their decisions are often driven by "good enough" analysis. Choosing a strategic direction for an organization involves subjective feeling as well as objective analysis. And when dealing with people issues, humans are too complex to make this type of leadership completely scientific. Dr. Saria Saccocio observed, "This is why we as physicians often struggle with issues that appear to us as "black and white" or "win or lose."

Another way of viewing this dilemma is V-Thinking versus W-Thinking. In the V-Model of Thinking, physicians take in large amounts of information and then narrow that down to one diagnosis. This approach tends to include only the factors that are relevant to the diagnosis and ignore everything else. It produces a very narrow field of vision. In the W-Model of Thinking, administrators use the information they have to come up with a range of responses and then pick one based on consensus with others. This is bigger-picture thinking, which requires including all the possible factors, whether they are relevant or not. Dr. Lily Henson noted, "It takes time and experience to become comfortable with looking at all the scenarios possible. It's becoming comfortable with the unknown, which is the opposite of what we are taught in our medical training."

The competencies Developing Vision, Communicating Vision, Mindful Decision Making, Driving Results, and Stimulating Creativity are all rooted in science;

physician leaders can often excel at them. These competencies will also be critical as huge changes happen in the next few years in how medicine is practiced.

## Time Perspective

In their clinical work, physicians have short interactions with patients, each one usually lasting 5 to 15 minutes. In that brief time, the physician moves through a process of assessment, diagnosis, outcome identification, planning, and follow-up. One physician said at a board strategic planning retreat, "Look, I do all of my work in 10- to 15-minute increments all day long. Trying to figure out strategy for this organization for the next three years does not fit on my radar screen." Administrative work is rarely done in such a short time. Because a lot of leaders' work is done through collaborating with and coordinating the work of many people, the time span often involves days, weeks, and months. It is easy to see why physicians can get frustrated by this. Another difference is the focus on productivity within many health systems as they work with their employed physicians (see more patients; generate more productivity).

Dr. John Byrnes notes that physicians have been trained with a reactive mindset. "We see one patient at a time, respond to their needs, and move on to the next patient visit. We react to whatever situation or patient need presents itself. We weren't trained to be proactive, to plan, to proactively manage large-scale projects, or to project strategy over several years. This proactive mindset is very foreign to the average physician and must be deliberately learned for physicians to be successful in administrative roles."

The competencies Developing High-Performing Teams, Energizing Staff, Generating Informal Power, Building True Consensus, and Driving Results have significant time elements to them. For many aspiring physician leaders, these competencies are among the hardest to learn and use effectively.

## Personal Versus Organizational Accountability

Another big difference between physicians and administrators is that physicians are held more *personally* accountable for their actions. When a person gets an individual license to practice medicine, that physician is held to specific personal standards *as an individual*. While administrators also have personal accountability for their actions, their responsibility and authority are more tied to the organization. Also, physicians are accountable to the medical standards practiced within a community, and those standards are based on clinical practice within that community. On the other hand, administrators have to answer to either a higher administrator or, in the case of the CEO, to a board of trustees, and the standards are different.

When we think about accountability, the competencies Leading With Conviction, Using Emotional Intelligence, and Earning Trust And Loyalty most closely support this principle within organizational life.

## Time Urgency of Decision Making

Physician decision making is typically immediate, while administrators often deliberate for long periods and require input from many sources, which adds to the time needed to take action. Particularly true of surgeons, emergency medicine physicians, or physicians faced with critical life-saving judgments, physicians have to be able to make quick decisions. One physician remarked, "One thing that drives me crazy is the amount of time it takes for these administrators to make decisions. If I took that kind of time, my patients would die."

Because of the way physicians make decisions in clinical settings, the competencies Listening Like You Mean It, Giving Great Feedback, Developing High-Performing Teams, Building True Consensus, and Mindful Decision Making are often challenging for physicians as they start leadership roles.

However, a final point should be made. Physicians are often unfairly criticized by business leaders when they don't follow administrative procedures. Readers should be mindful that this unfair criticism can be dangerously divisive. We sum up this point by saying, "Don't always blame the physicians." Some organizations tend to point the finger at the physicians and say as one CEO did, "They just are not capable of learning this." Dr. Kathleen Forbes explains this quite effectively:

> It is great to have physician leaders at the table. With the appropriate training, they can have quite an impact on strategy development and execution of organizational strategies. But the misstep that can happen is when physicians are brought to the table as key leaders and then not held accountable for the performance of their areas of responsibility. While they attend the necessary meetings, they may not be fully contributing to the effort since they feel they hold a figurehead role only. Digging deeper into this, you will find this to be multifactorial: Physician leaders may feel that their input doesn't matter since the strategy was developed without their input; the physician leaders are not held accountable to actively participate in key discussions regarding the strategy; the physician leaders may not be invited to the key meetings in which the true planning or execution is accomplished; organizations often assume a lack of business skills by physician leaders

and hire a number of support leaders who work around the physician executives to keep efforts moving forward. Bottom line—bring physicians to the table and engage them. Strong physician alignment is critical, but it is not enough. You must have true physician engagement. This is a big investment and one that needs to be maximized by the organization. Do not underestimate what a well-trained physician leader brings to the table.

## WHERE PHYSICIANS MOST OFTEN STRUGGLE WITH LEADERSHIP COMPETENCIES

Dye and Sokolov (2013) wrote that the cost of firing physician leaders is very high. *Derailment* is the term often used in management and leadership literature to describe situations where people who were doing well suddenly start failing. Dye and Sokolov (2013, 182) wrote that many of these failures are caused by the "inability of physician executives to detect common derailment factors." Often, the reasons for derailment are failures in the 16 competencies. Ready (2005) suggested several causes for derailment, such as not being able to manage teams and others, not executing strategy well, not engaging and inspiring employees, not listening well, and not fitting with the company's values. Clearly, mastering several of the 16 competencies would help avoid these career stoppers.

We suggest reading more about derailment. A favorite resource is *Firing Back: How Great Leaders Rebound After Career Disasters* by Jeffrey Sonnenfeld and Andrew Ward (2007). We also suggest the article "Twenty Years on the Dark Side: Six Lessons About Bad Leadership" by Hogan and colleagues (2021).

Based on the derailment research and what we have seen, we have found that physicians often have problems in several specific areas of the 16 leadership competencies. We are not suggesting that physicians cannot make highly effective leaders. In fact, the opposite is true—physicians skilled in the 16 competencies can be extraordinarily successful leaders. Examining leadership from a competency perspective and considering the challenges physicians in particular often face can be helpful.

### Applying the Competencies in Practice Begins with Deep Self-Reflection

Because of the nature of their work and the way they are trained, physicians often are less self-reflective than other leaders. During the time of life (late teens through the 20s) when most business-oriented leaders are gaining insights from early mentors and learning how to navigate the difficult politics of organizational life, physicians are focused almost exclusively on the rigorous academic study of medicine. Saunders and Hagemann (2009) describe the problems physicians often have with social skills:

> An issue that is not often discussed is that many physicians have personality or character issues due to a prolonged period as a student. Many do not start their careers until their early 30s. They work long hours and study in their off-hours. They have little time to develop social skills. Their social skills often stop developing when they enter medical school. By the time they are asked by the healthcare organization to take a leadership role, they will have bridged some of the social skill gap, but it is very likely that there are still some socialization skills that are significantly lagging.

It is not surprising that physicians focus mainly on growing their clinical knowledge and skills in the first years of their careers. They don't have time to learn or explore business and leadership concepts. Dr. Kevin Casey observed, "The lack of self-reflection is a feature, not a 'bug' of the healthcare structure. After training, very few physicians work in team environments, and even when they do, the hierarchical structure, say in an OR, does not allow for open feedback or discussion. Other physicians of the same specialty are not looking over their care, discussing alternative approaches, or new learnings. Most feedback comes from 'bad outcomes,' which are very rare. The lack of collaborative interaction in the current environment promotes the lack of self-reflection. One can only imagine this will worsen with the physician shortages unless directly addressed."

Drummond (2012) also notes, "What we do pick up automatically in our clinical training is a dysfunctional leadership style based on 'giving orders.' The clinical actions of diagnosis and treatment are simply adopted as our default leadership style. When faced with any practice challenge, we assume we must be the one who comes up with the answers (diagnose) and then tell everyone on the team what to do (treat)."

Dr. Doug Spotts noted, "I suggest the root of burnout lies in those physicians who have lost the ability to acknowledge vulnerability and to ask for help. Training resilient physician leaders for the future and the healthcare problems we are facing requires a sincere and deliberate effort on the part of management to teach vulnerability and self-reflection as key resiliency building tools. If you can 'never fail,' how can you boldly take calculated risks to improve quality and safety healthcare outcomes and break down health disparities?"

Exhibit 21.2 lists the 16 competencies, indicating the ones that physicians most often need to work on. Note that the competencies that are "often a challenge to master" are interpersonal leadership competencies. Deficiencies in these competencies are often derailing factors in leadership jobs.

The reasoning behind Exhibit 21.2 follows.

**Exhibit 21.2 Physicians and the 16 Competencies**

| Cornerstone | Competency | Often a strength among physicians | Usually not well developed among physicians | Often a challenge to master |
|---|---|---|---|---|
| Well-Cultivated Self-Awareness | Leading With Conviction | X | | |
| | Using Emotional Intelligence | | | X |
| Compelling Vision | Developing Vision | | | X |
| | Communicating Vision | | | X |
| | Earning Trust And Loyalty | | X | |
| A Real Way With People | Listening Like You Mean It | X (pediatricians, family medicine, psychiatrists) | | X (most other physician specialties) |
| | Giving Great Feedback | | X | |
| | Mentoring | | | X |
| | Developing High-Performing Teams | | | X |
| | Energizing Staff | | | X |
| Masterful Execution | Generating Informal Power | | | X |
| | Building True Consensus | | | X |
| | Mindful Decision Making | X | | |
| | Driving Results | X | | |
| | Stimulating Creativity | | | X |
| | Cultivating Adaptability | | | X |

**Cornerstone 1: Well-Cultivated Self-Awareness.** If one meaning of *conviction* is "a firmly held belief," physicians certainly possess this characteristic. We see this competency as requiring strong drive and being confident in actions. Most physicians have these skills. But when it comes to emotional intelligence, many physicians fall short—often because of the relative inattention to socialization we described earlier. Moreover, when they begin clinical practice, physicians rarely get direct feedback on how they interact with others.

**Cornerstone 2: Compelling Vision.** Because of the shorter-term nature of their work, physicians often have difficulty developing longer-term vision. Strategic planning can be frustrating. Beckham (2010) writes, "For physicians, strategic planning is a bureaucratic and amorphous undertaking run out of a hospital administrator's office. There is usually a flurry of interviews, some retreats and then lofty commitments. Physicians rightly ask, 'What has that got to do with me?' And, too often, the answer may be, 'Very little.'" The experience of many physicians is that they are invited to strategic planning retreats (which may happen every three years or so), asked for their input, and then sent "back to the clinical factory" while over the next few years, the executives of the organization change or even undo that strategy—all without any further consultation with those same physicians who participated in the original planning retreat. Dr. Lily Henson expresses it well: "Physicians in their clinical work typically deal with one patient at a time and in short bursts of time. And they do not leave a patient without a clear path of activity set forth. But when they move into leadership roles, they are usually faced with longer-term time frames and the path of activity is often unclear."

**Cornerstone 3: A Real Way With People.** Gartland (2007) says it well: "A frequent criticism of physicians expressed by patients is that the rigorous scientific training required for their medical educations depersonalizes some of them to the extent that effective medical technicians are produced who, upon entering the clinical practice of medicine, have fewer communication and interpersonal skills than they had upon entering medical school." This is true not only for interactions with patients, but also for other workplace interactions.

One difference in the competency Listening Like You Mean It is between specialties. Specialties that require intensive listening to patients—such as pediatrics, family medicine, and psychiatry—often transfer those effective skills into leadership positions. Dr. Doug Spotts noted, "It is ironic that we have more tools than ever in which to communicate with colleagues and team members, and yet, more communication breakdown than ever for the lack to simply discuss a difference or issue with another individual. You can't 'bubble chat' or text your nuanced leadership perspective, and the EHR [electronic health record] often flattens communication into two dimensions rather that the multidimensional organism that is needed to solve real problems in healthcare, health, and well-being."

More and more medical education and practicing clinician communities are recognizing that teaching team skills is critical for medical students, residents, and new physicians. In his commencement address to the Harvard Medical School, Dr. Atul Gawande (2011) described a "skill that you must have but haven't been taught—the ability to implement at scale, the ability to get colleagues along the entire chain of care functioning like pit crews for patients." Although Gawande talks about people working directly with patients needing this skill, the same holds true for physician leaders who work with leadership teams running today's healthcare organizations. Dr. Doug Spotts had an interesting observation: "When I practiced as a family physician, the bulk of the work and decision-making was totally on me. But even in family medicine that is changing, and working in teams has become more prevalent. And this is even more true for me as a physician leader."

**Cornerstone 4: Masterful Execution.** Similar to their view on strategic planning, many physicians are not accustomed to practices such as generating informal power, stimulating creativity, cultivating adaptability, and building true consensus. They come from a more controlled environment where they are the experts and their orders are final. *Execution* for physicians means following the orders of the clinician in charge. Orders are to be carried out—and are usually not questioned. But this "command and control" culture does not work well with modern approaches to decision making.

Despite shortcomings they may have in the 16 leadership competencies, physicians are often quick to see their gaps when it comes to themselves personally. In a paper written for his doctoral thesis in management, Deegan (2002) writes, "As a consequence of the way American physicians have been selected, educated, and socialized during their training, many are highly competitive, relatively independent practitioners. They often eschew teamwork and collaboration and other affiliative behaviors. Their education and socialization fosters pacesetting or commanding leadership styles that may be appropriate in certain clinical circumstances, e.g., a busy emergency department or a critical care unit, but could be counter-productive when used in other care settings."

Finally, Kirch (2011), former CEO of the Association of American Medical Colleges, discussed how important teamwork and relating to patients are: "When I entered medical school, it was all about being an individual expert. Now it's all about applying that expertise to team-based patient care."

## HOW CAN PHYSICIANS DEVELOP FURTHER IN EACH COMPETENCY?

Physicians are typically fast learners. They can use the 16 competencies as a guide to learn and practice leadership well. This section has some suggestions for physicians to improve their leadership skills as they think about moving into part-time or full-time leadership and management positions. Dr. Kathleen Forbes commented, "Almost all physician leaders start in part-time leadership roles. This is good because it gives them a chance to 'try out' leadership decisions before many move on to full-time and more senior leadership positions. Having the chance to test out leadership decisions as well as having some leadership education is essential for success."

Organizations need to lay some groundwork to ensure that physicians successfully grow as leaders. Some of this involves structure, and some of it is about the willingness of other senior leaders to personally help physician leaders develop. Dr. Lily Henson stated, "Dyad structures can be very helpful for physicians in learning leadership." And Dr. Doug Spotts observed, "In developing physician leaders, intentional focus should be made through mentoring and understanding highly matrixed organizations with their inherent politics and bureaucracy. These challenges can quickly become insurmountable barriers to the newly appointed physician leader without a sage guide invested in guaranteeing their colleague and team's ultimate success."

### Get Adequate Assessments and Feedback

Physician leaders often have trouble getting effective feedback. Dr. Saria Saccocio agrees, stating, "As physicians, we often struggle with openly receiving constructive feedback and processing how we can improve as leaders." We think this happens for several reasons. First, because most physician leaders are older when they start leadership positions, others may hesitate to provide input on their leadership or interpersonal behaviors. Second, physician leaders often move into high-level positions as their first roles. In these settings, like board rooms or senior management meetings, discussion focuses mainly on organizational matters and only rarely on specific personal styles and approaches to leadership. Third, physicians typically hold the "captain of the ship" position and are not questioned much as a result. The Dye–Garman Competency Model can be used for 360-degree feedback (see Chapter 20), which can be a good way to get past these feedback barriers. But to reach the level of exceptional leadership, it is essential that physician leaders listen, understand, internalize, and act on the feedback they receive. Dr. John Byrnes adds:

> It's critical that physicians actively reflect, internalize, and study the results of feedback and link this information directly to a formal plan of study to gain needed competencies. I remember my training on the surgical side of the house—it was a very combative and aggressive environment, and I quickly learned the behaviors needed to succeed. However, in my first management role, I quickly found that the behaviors that served me well in the OR were the exact opposite of what I needed as an administrator. The bottom line: I needed to drop many of my surgical behaviors and consciously replace them with the 16 competencies. Yearly feedback has become an invaluable tool in this journey.

Dr. Kevin Casey stresses, "The point made about 'unlearning' cannot be overstated in today's environment. We cannot 'do more with less' but will have to 'do differently with what we have.' We first need to 'unlearn' much of what we thought was absolute over the past decades in medicine and embrace changes in how, where, and what care is provided. Physicians are the only ones who can lead us successfully through this."

## Learn by Doing

Leadership is best learned by doing—and doing when the outcomes matter. Dye and Sokolov (2013) discuss how important crucible experiences are for learning leadership, where the learning happens when real-world situations or problems come up, not classroom examples or case studies. While classroom time is important, it is more powerful when used as a supplement to applied work, not the other way around. Dr. Scott Ransom adds, "Regular active mentorship by excellent physician and nonphysician leaders together with 360-degree feedback with specific goals facilitated by an outside facilitator is also an excellent path to development as physician leaders."

## Use an Executive Coach

Physician leaders are increasingly using leadership coaching, as described in Chapter 18. One reason a coach can be so effective is that by the time physicians come into leadership positions, they are often at an age when getting feedback on leadership competencies is uncommon. Use caution, however, to make sure that the coaches chosen have prior experience in relevant settings and, ideally, with physician clients.

## Avoid Overconfidence

Physicians train and work in a culture where confidence is paramount. Not knowing something or to being unable to do something are often seen as signs of weakness. Great leaders, in contrast, recognize that they can only know and do so much themselves, so they surround themselves with strong and capable people and focus on coordinating the work of those people. Physicians in leadership positions must remember that they do not need to have all the answers to every problem and that letting others take the lead is appropriate at times. For a deeper understanding of the risks of overconfidence and other derailment risks, we recommend *Why CEOs Fail: The 11 Behaviors That Can Derail Your Climb to the Top and How to Manage Them* by David Dotlich and Peter Cairo (2003). Dr. Kevin Casey observed, "In my work of developing physician leaders, I often reinforce the approach of 'humility, brevity, and curiosity.' If physician leaders can approach most situations with these three in mind, they are often more successful."

## SUMMARY

Dyche (2007) said it well when he wrote, "An understanding physician must be able to tolerate ambiguity because science's clear solutions often do not match people's lives." Leadership is extremely complex, but a good competency model can provide a helpful guide to the terrain. As more physicians become leaders in healthcare organizations, they will benefit themselves and their organizations by learning and using a competency-based approach to leadership.

The essence of this chapter is summarized well by Dr. Lily Henson: "Effective leadership is all about appropriate behaviors—competencies—and the best physician leaders will learn and model these."

## NOTE

The authors are grateful to the many physicians who shared their insights in this chapter. As nonphysicians, we felt it important to get input from these outstanding physician leaders. We sincerely thank each of them for their special review and contributions to this chapter.

## REFERENCES

Beckham, D. 2010. "Physician Involvement in Hospital Strategic Planning." *Trustee* 63 (6): 6–7.

Deegan, M. J. 2002. "Emotional Intelligence Competencies in Physician Leaders: An Exploratory Study." Presented at Academy of Management Annual Meeting, Denver, CO. http://digitalcase.case.edu:9000/fedora/get/ ksl:weaedm139/ weaedm139.pdf.

Dotlich, D., and P. Cairo. 2003. *Why CEOs Fail: The 11 Behaviors That Can Derail Your Climb to the Top and How to Manage Them.* San Francisco: Jossey-Bass.

Drummond, D. 2012. "The Frustrating Gap of Physician Leadership Skills." KevinMD.com. Published June 18. http://www.kevinmd.com/blog/2012/06 /frustrating-gap-physician-leadership-skills.html.

Dyche, L. 2007. "Interpersonal Skill in Medicine: The Essential Partner of Verbal Communication." *Journal of General Internal Medicine* 22 (7):1035–9. doi: 10.1007/s11606-007-0153-0.

Dye, C., and J. Sokolov. 2013. *Developing Physician Leaders for Successful Clinical Integration.* Chicago: Health Administration Press.

Gartland, J. 2007. *Better Physician Writing and Speaking Skills.* London: Radcliffe Publishing Ltd.

Gawande, A. 2011. "Cowboys and Pit Crews." *The New Yorker*, May 26.

Hogan, R., R. Kaiser, R. Sherman, and P. Harms. 2021. "Twenty Years on the Dark Side: Six Lessons About Bad Leadership." *Consulting Psychology Journal: Practice and Research* 73 (3): 199.

Khan, R., A. Aziz, and N. Siddiqui. 2022. "Clinicians as Leaders: Impact and Challenges." *Pakistan Journal of Medical Science* 38 (4Part-II): 1069–72.

Kirch, D. 2011. "Doctors Must Now Pass Social Skills Tests to Attend Medical School." Tradeschool.com. Published July 21. https://blog.tradeschool.com/doctors-must-now-pass-social-skills-tests-to-attend-medical-school.

Ready, D. A. 2005. "Is Your Company Failing Its Leaders?" *Business Strategy Review* 16 (4): 21–25.

Saunders, C., and B. Hagemann. 2009. "Physicians as Leaders: What's Missing?" *Health Leaders Media*. Published April 15. www.healthleadersmedia.com/content/PHY-231588/Physicians-as-Leaders-Whats-Missing.htm.

Sonnenfeld, J., and A. Ward. 2007. *Firing Back: How Great Leaders Rebound After Career Disasters.* Cambridge, MA: Harvard Business Review Press.

# CHAPTER TWENTY-TWO

# Final Questions About the Exceptional Leadership Model

IN THIS LAST chapter, we answer some common questions that frequently came up from earlier editions about how the Exceptional Leadership model relates to healthcare management in the broader context:

- "Does the Exceptional Leadership model cover everything I need to know to be an exceptional healthcare leader?"
- "Where does _____ fit in the model?"
- "How do I adopt a leadership competency model in my organization?"
- "Can the Exceptional Leadership model help me with hiring decisions?"
- "What are the potential pitfalls of using a competency model?"

## DOES THE EXCEPTIONAL LEADERSHIP MODEL COVER EVERYTHING?

The Exceptional Leadership model (or the Dye–Garman model as it is sometimes called) was created with two main goals in mind. The first was to identify the characteristics that most consistently distinguished exceptional healthcare leaders from those who are performing well (just not exceptionally so).

The second was to create a model that would be practical and useful for the field. At the time, many leadership competency models were too long and cumbersome to be useful. For example, Lombardo and Eichinger's (2004) model included 67 competencies; other models from top consulting firms and professional associations had even more. Models like these can work okay for university programs settings, but they are not well suited to applied settings. Can you imagine a CEO search committee trying to realistically compare candidates on 50 or 60 leadership competencies? Or a manager doing a performance review on each of her direct reports on 50 competencies?

With competencies, as with other assessment tools, more is not always better: You reach a point where people lose interest and focus. We didn't want our model to have that problem, so we deliberately limited it to just the top 16 and defined the scope of each competency accordingly. The model is not meant to be complete. In fact, some competencies that are clearly associated with the healthcare management profession are not in the model at all: process improvement, project management, financial management, and information systems, to name just a few. Learning more management competencies would almost certainly strengthen any leader's toolkit and should be considered by anyone who wants to rise up the leadership ranks.

With that in mind, we can say, based on our experiences over the past several decades, that many healthcare leaders have found the model helpful for their own growth and the growth of the people they work with. Many readers have told us how they have used specific competencies in their work and how this has made them more effective in their leadership roles. We gratefully accept these comments and hope that more leaders will benefit from this work in the future.

## WHERE DOES _____ FIT IN THE MODEL?

Readers who know other leadership models sometimes ask us how some parts of those models connect to the Exceptional Leadership model. Because many of these models keep changing, the answer to this question is not fixed. We will explain this in more detail in the discussion on competency mapping. For now, we will answer four of the more common questions we get.

1.  Some have asked where the "drive to achieve" (from McClelland's Achievement Motivation Theory) is in the Exceptional Leadership model. We think it is closest to the competencies Leading With Conviction, Driving Results, and Stimulating Creativity.
2.  We have also been asked why the model does not include oral and written communication, since surely these must be very important to highly effective leadership. While we agree that communication is very important, in our experience, what makes exceptional leaders stand out is not communication skills themselves, but instead how they get used. In particular, communication skills are essential to the competencies Developing Vision, Communicating Vision, Giving Great Feedback, and Mindful Decision Making.

3. We often get asked about problem solving. Like communication, problem solving is a broader idea that relates to many of the competencies in the model, and mastering those competencies will make a leader a better problem solver. For example, most complex problem-solving tasks involve the competencies Using Emotional Intelligence, Earning Trust And Loyalty, Building True Consensus, and Driving Results.

4. Many have asked where improving performance fits in the model. We would say that many of the 16 competencies help with this, for example, Developing High-Performing Teams, Energizing Staff, Mindful Decision Making, Driving Results, and Stimulating Creativity.

Another important note is the distinction between leadership competencies and functional/technical competencies. Functional/technical competencies match a specific job and show skills and abilities that are needed for that job. For example, a chief financial officer needs to have competency in reading financial statements. Or a chief nursing officer must have certain clinical competencies to do the job well. The point of this brief discussion is not to suggest that one or more of the 16 competencies cover every possible leadership competency imaginable. But it does show that the 16 competencies cover almost all other competencies. Instead of getting into a debate about semantics, we hope that readers can use the model fully and apply it to their leadership needs.

## HOW DO I ADOPT A COMPETENCY MODEL IN MY ORGANIZATION?

As discussed in Chapter 17, adopting a competency model for your whole organization can help you align your talent investments with organizational strategy. To do this, you should involve a wide range of people in creating the model you use. This will make it easier to implement it later. Also, since competencies are much more widely used these days, if your organization has not adopted an organization-wide leadership competency model, it is likely that some leaders, departments, or professional groups within your organization are already using their own model. Be sensitive to the good work that may already be going on in your organization, and try to include as much of it as possible in the broader organizational efforts.

One approach that can be particularly helpful in pursuing an organization-wide model is to create a cross-walking or cross-mapping of competency models already in use. Cross-mapping involves comparing two or more models side-by-side to identify points of overlap and then collapsing the models into a single one. Although this is often done by hand, computer-assisted approaches can help facilitate this process, especially when there are multiple models to compare (Garman, Standish and Kim 2018; Garman, Standish, and Wainio 2020).

Exhibit 22.1 shows an example of a competency cross-map. In this example, the left column lists two specific leadership competencies from an unnamed health system that are not described with the same words or in the same way as the competencies in this book. The second column shows those competencies from this book that map or match up with those from the health system.

## Exhibit 22.1 Competency Mapping

| Competency from Organization A | Competencies from the Exceptional Leadership Competency Model |
|---|---|
| | **Leading With Conviction**<br>◆ Knows and is in touch with one's values and beliefs<br>◆ Is not afraid to take a lonely or unpopular stance if necessary<br>◆ Is comfortable in tough situations<br>◆ Can be relied on in tense circumstances<br>◆ Is clear about where he/she stands<br>◆ Faces difficult challenges with poise and self-assurance |
| **Showing Trust and Respect, Practicing Collaborative Behaviors** | **Building True Consensus**<br>◆ Frames issues in ways that facilitate clarity from multiple perspectives, keeps issues separated from personalities, and skillfully uses group decision techniques<br>◆ Ensures that quieter group members are drawn into discussions<br>◆ Finds shared values and common adversaries, and facilitates discussions rather than guides them |
| | **Generating Informal Power**<br>◆ Understands the roles of power and influence in organizations<br>◆ Develops compelling arguments or points of view based on a knowledge of others' priorities<br>◆ Develops and sustains useful networks up, down, and sideways in organizations<br>◆ Develops a reputation as a go-to person<br>◆ Effectively influences the thoughts and opinions of others, both directly and indirectly, through others |

## Exhibit 22.1 Competency Mapping *(continued from previous page)*

| Competency from Organization A | Competencies from the Exceptional Leadership Competency Model |
|---|---|
| Showing Trust and Respect, Practicing Collaborative Behaviors | **Listening Like You Mean It**<br>• Maintains a calm, easy-to-approach demeanor<br>• Is patient, open-minded, and willing to hear people out<br>• Understands others and picks up the meaning of their messages<br>• Is warm, gracious, and inviting<br>• Builds strong rapport<br>• Sees through the words to express the real meaning<br>• Maintains formal and informal channels of communication<br><br>**Using Emotional Intelligence**<br>• Recognizes personal strengths and weaknesses<br>• Sees the links between feelings and behaviors<br>• Manages impulsive feelings and distressing emotions<br>• Is attentive to emotional cues<br>• Shows sensitivity and respect for others<br>• Challenges bias and intolerance<br>• Collaborates and shares<br>• Handles conflict, difficult people, and tense situations effectively |

Other examples of mapping might include:

| Competency Not Listed in the Model | Corresponding Competencies from the Model |
|---|---|
| Critical thinking | Developing Vision, Stimulating Creativity |
| Resilience | Leading With Conviction, Driving Results |
| Influencing others | Listening Like You Mean It, Energizing Staff, Generating Informal Power |
| Persuasion | Developing Vision, Communicating Vision, Earning Trust And Loyalty, Driving Results |
| Judgment | Using Emotional Intelligence, Earning Trust And Loyalty, Mindful Decision Making |
| Showing passion | Leading With Conviction, Energizing Staff, Driving Results |

## HOW THE EXCEPTIONAL LEADERSHIP MODEL HELPS IN HIRING DECISIONS

Besides identifying areas for development, competency models can also help you make better hiring decisions. Dye and Sokolov (2013) show a method for hiring where leadership competencies are one of nine criteria used to evaluate candidates for leadership roles.

Many organizations don't use leadership competencies in their assessment process. This often happens because the qualifications section of many job descriptions is vague or because there is no clear leadership competency model. Consider the following list of qualifications from a real job description:

- Ability to manage and make independent decisions
- Strong interpersonal communication skills
- Ability to function as a leader
- Exhibits creative, positive problem-solving abilities
- Experience coaching and developing senior-level leaders
- System thinker

The problem with this list is that some of the items are not well-defined or easy to understand—what is a system thinker, what are strong interpersonal skills, what does it mean to be able to function as a leader, what makes someone creative? They may mean different things to different interviewers. One interviewer might think a candidate is a good system thinker while another interviewer might think this same candidate is weak. Think about how similarly unclear the qualification "ability to function as a leader" is.

To improve the assessment process, each of the required competencies should be more specific and, as explained throughout this book, linked to behavioral indicators. Each competency should have some observable actions or behaviors that show how the competency is used. Since the first edition of this book came out, many organizations have found using competencies helpful in their hiring processes. But in every case we are aware of, these organizations developed more detailed descriptions that made the competencies more meaningful and clearer. Then when they evaluated candidates, the competencies were used as standards in the decision process that led to selection. Exhibit 22.2 shows how this process works.

You can also use the leadership competencies to create specific behavior-based questions for interviews. Appendix C has examples of questions that go with each of the 16 competencies.

**Exhibit 22.2  Making Competencies More Meaningful in Assessment**

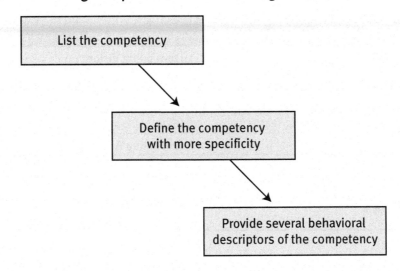

**Operational Focus Versus Strategic Focus**

Lastly, a deeper look at the 16 competencies shows that some are more about operations and others are more about strategy. For example, a system CEO would likely need to be more skillful in Developing Vision, Building True Consensus, Stimulating Creativity, and Cultivating Adaptability than would a chief operating officer of a smaller acute care hospital (who would probably need more skills in Listening Like You Mean It, Developing High-Performing Teams, Energizing Staff, Mindful Decision Making, and Driving Results). Similarly, a leader who has to turn around an organization financially would need competencies that are more focused on operations. Exhibit 22.3 shows these distinctions. We also note, though, that some of the competencies may fall into both categories.

We also think that Leading With Conviction and Using Emotional Intelligence are "must-haves" or core competencies that *all* exceptional leaders need, no matter what their title or position in the organization or what their work goals are.

## POTENTIAL PITFALLS WITH COMPETENCY MODELS

While competency models can be helpful, we have seen users run into trouble in at least three common ways. One is when models are too vague in their definitions. For example, listing "communications" as a competency may at first seem sensible,

### Exhibit 22.3 Contrast of Operational and Strategic Competencies

| More Operations-Oriented Competency | More Strategy-Oriented Competency |
|---|---|
| Listening Like You Mean It | Developing Vision |
| Giving Great Feedback | Communicating Vision |
| Mentoring | Stimulating Creativity |
| Developing High-Performing Teams | Mindful Decision Making |
| Energizing Staff | Cultivating Adaptability |
| Generating Informal Power | |
| Building True Consensus | |
| Driving Results | |

but then most of a leader's activity involves some form of communication, so which types of communication are we referring to? The same confusion can happen for many other competencies, such as "leading teams," "respecting dignity," or "getting results." It is important to define competencies in clear, detailed, and observable terms.

On the other hand, we have also seen competency models get too complicated. Effron (2013) described today's typical competency model as "an all-encompassing, multi-layered monstrosity whose complexity far outweighs its value. And, even with its verbosity and heft, it still doesn't tell managers exactly how to succeed." The length of the list can be a problem, as can the usual human resources rules about how to use the competencies. As Roberto (2012) writes, "Senior executives have to boil down their expectations to a simple list of behaviors and capabilities that they value and wish to cultivate in aspiring leaders. Simplicity and brevity will breed behavioral change much more quickly and effectively than complexity and comprehensiveness."

A third challenge comes from leadership competency lists that are just handed down from higher-level management without enough attention to preparing people for their use and making sure they are implemented. See Chapter 17 for specific tips on how to successfully include competencies in the organizational culture. In these cases, models tend not to reach their full potential or, worse, become forgotten over time. Many competency lists like these are seen as the "management du jour" for the organization and are met with great skepticism.

## SUMMARY

This final chapter shows some ways that leadership competency models can support performance improvement. But this review only scratches the surface. For example, competencies can also help with succession planning to better identify the competencies needed for specific roles and to find out the gaps that high-potential candidates may have. Competencies can also help with onboarding by clarifying the expectations for the new leader. Even strategic planning can be helped by defining the leadership competencies that will be needed to carry out the plan. We hope that this review has opened your eyes to the value of creating a common language of performance in your organization, and that you will be motivated to keep learning about competency-driven approaches to performance improvement—both for yourself and your organization.

## REFERENCES

Dye, C., and J. Sokolov. 2013. *Developing Physician Leaders for Successful Clinical Integration*. Chicago: Health Administration Press.

Effron, M. 2013. "Life After the Competency Model." The Talent Strategy Group. http://talentstrategygroup1.com/wp-content/uploads/2013/01/Life-After-the -Competency-Model.pdf.

Garman, A., M. Standish, and D. Kim. 2018. "Enhancing Efficiency, Reliability, and Rigor in Competency Model Analysis Using Natural Language Processing. *Journal of Competency-Based Education* 3 (3): 1–4.

Garman, A., M. Standish, and J. Wainio. 2020. "Bridging Worldviews: Toward a Common Model of Leadership Across the Health Professions." *Health Care Management Review* 45 (4): E45.

Lombardo, M., and R. Eichinger. 2004. *FYI: For Your Improvement, A Guide for Development and Coaching*, 4th ed. Minneapolis, MN: Lominger Ltd Inc.

Roberto, M. 2012. "The Problem with Competency Models." Published January 25. http://michael-roberto.blogspot.com/2012/01/problem-with-competency -models.html.

# Appendix A:
## Self-Reflection Questions

THE FOLLOWING SELF-REFLECTION questions can help you identify areas you need to improve on to enhance a specific leadership competency. Read each question and think about an honest answer, making notes as needed. After you have gone through the questions, review all question sets to determine which area you felt most strongly about. You may also want to share your answers with a trusted confidant.

### Chapter 1: Leading With Conviction

- To what extent are you driven by a clear set of values, principles, and goals?
- To what extent are your convictions based on ethical guidelines?
- How well do you understand how your values, principles, and goals developed?
- How widely have your values been influenced? Were they developed by gaining perspective on a broad understanding of living and the issues of the world (as opposed to developing them from narrower experience)?
- How effective are you in recognizing when your fundamental belief systems are challenged? How systematic are you in reconciling these challenges?
- How hesitant are you to state your point of view?
- Are your convictions aimed at matters that count and are important to your organization (versus simply being selfish ones that serve to benefit only you)?

### Chapter 2: Using Emotional Intelligence

- To what extent are you aware of your emotions? To what extent do you understand rationally why you react the way you do?
- Do you see the link between your emotions and feelings and your behavior?

- To what extent can you manage your emotions? Can you control anger? Can you channel frustration? How effective are you at engaging others even when you are upset or irate?
- To what extent would you describe yourself as open, approachable, and sincere?
- Are you successful at developing rapport with others? With others who are different than you?
- Would others describe you as a respectful person?

## Chapter 3: Developing Vision

- Are you intellectually curious? Would you describe yourself as having broad interests?
- What do you read? Do you spend enough time reading professional journals and/or articles about trends and developments in business, science, and society? To what extent can you translate or apply those trends into your daily healthcare leadership roles?
- Are you able to analyze data and statistics and understand their broad implications?
- How often do you visit with people from other industries and walks of life to hear about their work and learn from their perspectives? How often do you visit communities outside of where you work and live—especially the ones your organization's patients and employees live in?
- How successful have you been at dealing with novel problems and challenges?

## Chapter 4: Communicating Vision

- How effectively do you balance working on day-to-day challenges with developing longer-term strategies?
- To what extent can you develop compelling arguments for change? How persuasive are you?
- How well can you simplify and summarize a strategic vision into something that can easily be communicated?
- Do you have effective techniques for getting others engaged?

### Chapter 5: Earning Trust And Loyalty

- What is your do/say ratio—the number of times you actually do what you say you will do? Would others agree with your self-assessment?
- Would others say that you are concerned about their needs and affairs?
- Are you passionate about follow-through, particularly when it comes to getting back to others on their questions and concerns?
- Do you lead by example? Do you help out on routine tasks when you can? Are you a roll-up-the-sleeves person? How easily can others access you when they need you?
- To what extent would others say that you use your power and influence for the benefit of the organization and for others (versus selfish purposes)?

### Chapter 6: Listening Like You Mean It

- Are you approachable? (Ask yourself this question again.)
- Do you typically understand where others are coming from? To what extent do you care about their concerns?
- To what extent can you get to the heart of someone's verbal message to you?
- Do you often use questions to gain greater clarification?
- How open are your channels of communication? Do you have multiple informal and formal channels of communication and ways to discern what is happening in your organization?
- Do you sometimes (or even frequently) interrupt others or finish their sentences?
- Are you aware of the mechanical aspects of good listening (e.g., making eye contact, avoiding distractions such as smartphones, keeping the right physical distance from the speaker) and, more importantly, do you practice them?

### Chapter 7: Giving Great Feedback

- How clear and direct is your communication style?
- How well do your direct reports understand their performance goals? Do they have a clear understanding of their performance appraisals, or do they feel surprised after an evaluation?

- How consistent are you in providing feedback regularly?
- How well balanced is your feedback (positive and negative)?
- Would others say that you sometimes give mixed messages?
- To what extent might your feedback be undermined by "tee-up" phrases (such as "Don't take this the wrong way, but . . ." or "I'm just saying" or "As far as I know" or "To be perfectly honest" or "I'm not saying, but. . .")

## Chapter 8: Mentoring

- How strongly do you believe in career development? Do you have former staff who have gone on to higher-level positions?
- Would others describe you as a boss who regularly provides them with stretch assignments and opportunities to work outside their area of responsibility or to gain exposure at higher levels of the organization?
- How supportive are you of others' needs to attend educational programs? Have you encouraged subordinates to earn advanced degrees?
- How often do you provide teaching moments—brief, informal, and unplanned explanations during the workday about a situation or event at hand?
- Can you point to others who have advanced their careers because of your support and guidance?

## Chapter 9: Developing High-Performing Teams

- How well do you support the concept of teaming (as opposed to dealing with people on a one-on-one basis)?
- Do you encourage cohesiveness by identifying common vision, goals, and threats among team members or by establishing team rules?
- What steps do you take to prevent small, subgroup cliques; team role ambiguity; and emotions from driving debate?
- Are your team members clear on their mutual accountability to one another?
- Would your team members indicate that they are closely connected in purpose and in esprit de corps?
- When your team meets, does it exhibit a passion about its purpose?
- To what extent can (does) your team function when you are gone?

## Chapter 10: Energizing Staff

- How often do you show personal energy and enthusiasm about your work and your achievements?
- Would others describe you as goal driven and passionate about achievements and accomplishments?
- Do you regularly use humor, wit, and levity in the workplace?
- To what extent do you inject spontaneity into the workday or workplace?
- How often do you make a point of recognizing the accomplishments of others and celebrating their achievements?
- Do you avoid bureaucratic rules and regulations that can create a disengaged workforce?
- Do you use daily huddles to instill purpose and focus into the workday?
- Do you have a practice of finding innovative ways to engage and enthuse staff?

## Chapter 11: Generating Informal Power

- How often are you sought out by people (besides direct reports) for your opinions?
- How strong are your informal networks? How well informed do you feel through these networks?
- How openly do you share information?
- If others do favors for you, how conscientious are you in reciprocating?
- To what extent do you understand power and sources of power in the organization?
- A wise CEO once said, "Informal power is directly related to the amount of care and concern you show for others multiplied by your visibility within the organization." To what extent do you practice this?
- Do you take the lead in informal settings?
- If you are the leader of a team that has just had a success, do you share the recognition with your team members?
- Do you make the time to congratulate others on their achievements, both inside and outside the workplace?

## Chapter 12: Building True Consensus

- How familiar are you with group decision-making techniques (e.g., NGT, parking lot, brainstorming, affinity mapping, straw polls)? How comfortable are you with using them?
- How effectively do you make use of agendas, outlines, handouts, and the like when managing a meeting?
- How regularly do you provide opportunities for all group members to voice their thoughts and opinions during meetings? How effectively do you reach out to members who are visibly silent?
- To what extent are you able to keep a group focused on a solution to an issue or problem?
- Once a group decision is made, do you clearly summarize the conclusion so that everyone knows what was decided?
- During conflict situations, have you ever used silence or a brief break in the action to help the group decompress and get back to refocusing on the issue at hand?
- Do you have strong rules for engagement that define appropriate behavior during debate within the group?
- Have you mastered the ability to bring underlying causes of a conflict or problem to the surface so the conversations can have better focus?
- Do you have a record of honoring commitments once a group decision is reached?

## Chapter 13: Mindful Decision Making

- How well do you know what drives your decision making? Have you ever mapped your decision-making process in writing?
- How much are ethics, values, goals, facts, alternatives, and judgment incorporated into your decision-making processes?
- To what extent are you able to analyze and evaluate choices and choose the best one? Do you have a method for weighing various alternatives?
- How familiar are you with decision-making tools (e.g., force field analysis, cost-benefit analysis, decision trees)? How comfortable are you with using them?
- When making decisions, do you hear out opposing viewpoints, or do you tend to focus on developing arguments in favor of your own viewpoint?
- When making important decisions, are you equipped to use mindfulness to focus with clarity on the issue at hand?

- To what extent are you able to focus on the real issue involved in a decision versus making a series of other decisions that do not relate to it?

## Chapter 14: Driving Results

- How effectively do you keep people focused and on task?
- If team members are derailing movement toward an objective, how comfortable are you with stepping in to take action?
- How frequently do you set a higher bar for your team's performance and help them see it as an achievable goal?
- Do you fully understand the need to recognize that each team member likely has different motivations, and thus your leadership toward results must be customized for each one?
- Do you regularly use scorecards, scoreboards, or dashboards to show progress on major goals?
- Are the number of key goals and objectives reasonable (no more than nine or ten)?
- Are you adept at breaking key objectives into small achievable pieces so progress can be felt?
- Do you show the ability to demonstrate calmness and poise during extremely active times?

## Chapter 15: Stimulating Creativity

- How often do you pause before an important interchange (e.g., meeting, negotiation session) to think reflectively about the situation and people involved?
- Do you occasionally do something radically different? Read some book in an area in which you know very little? Explore new opportunities? Learn a new language?
- Have you gotten to know individuals who are very different from you?
- It is often said that fear of making mistakes is one of the greatest inhibitors of creativity. To what extent do you agree with this belief?
- How often do you create opportunities for your staff to mix and mingle with others outside of your team?
- When exploring new ideas for addressing a problem, to what extent are criticism and debate encouraged?
- Do you create an equal playing field for your team when they debate an issue?

## Chapter 16: Cultivating Adaptability

- Do you have one primary style of leadership? If so, in what situations might this style be less useful?
- To what extent are you able to read and assess the environment and to develop an appropriate leadership style of action?
- Do you understand the various styles of leadership?
- How comfortable are you with leading people to look at problems with fresh eyes?
- When the people you work with seem stuck in a rut, what kinds of approaches do you use to break them out of it?
- How often do you come up with new initiatives or solutions to problems that bring people together in new ways?
- To what extent are you comfortable with unpredictability or changing work settings?
- To what extent are you a person who prefers to live life by the book (typically a policy-driven individual)?
- Have you ever asked yourself, "If I were to leave my job today, what things would my successor change?"
- Do you frequently update your skills and knowledge?

# Appendix B:
# Sample Self-Development Plan

THINK OF A self-development plan as a business plan for your career growth. Like a business plan, it should state your desired goals (both short-term and long-term), your objectives, and the resources you need. (Some development plans even include a calculation of return on investment, based on market rates of salaries associated with promotions, although this is not necessary.) All elements of the plan should be specific enough to allow you to self-monitor your progress. The following is a sample outline for a development plan that you can modify for your own use. A copy may be accessed on the Exceptional Leadership website: https://www.exceptional-leadership.com.

Name _____

Date _____

**Part 1: Career Goals.** In this section, state the direction you want your career to take. It is often most helpful to have at least three milestones—three, five, and ten years are used here, but you can choose different milestones as you see fit for your situation. *Note:* If you are unsure about your career goals, then identifying them should be your first step.

Answer the following questions for each of the numbered items below: What would you like to be doing, and where would you like to be? What would be your ideal work setting, position, lifestyle, etc.? If you are planning to remain in your current position, how would you improve the way you work or the way your position is structured?

1. Steps I will take to identify my career goals:

*What I need to learn*     *Whom I can learn this from*     *My action plan*     *Due date*

_____          _____          _____          _____

_____          _____          _____          _____

_____          _____          _____          _____

_____          _____          _____          _____

2. Three-year goals: _____

3. Five-year goals: _____

4. Ten-year goals: _____

**Part 2: Developmental Needs.** In this section, prioritize the developmental steps you will need to take in pursuit of your career goals. *Note:* If you do not have a clear sense of your developmental needs, then clarifying them should be your first step.

1. Steps I will take to clarify my developmental needs: _____

2. Competencies I need to develop: _____

*Competency*          *How I will develop*          *My action plan*          *Due date*

_____          _____          _____          _____

_____          _____          _____          _____

_____          _____          _____          _____

_____          _____          _____          _____

*Final Note:* If you don't write and develop your Self-Development Plan in full detail, it won't be as useful to you.

# Appendix C:
## Sample Interview Questions
## Based on the 16 Competencies

| Exceptional Leadership Competencies | Interview Questions |
|---|---|
| **Competency 1: Leading With Conviction** | 1. Describe a specific situation in which you felt pressure to compromise your integrity.<br>2. What is the most courageous action you have ever taken?<br>3. Describe two situations in which you had to fight a specific battle with a key physician. How did the conflict start and escalate, and how did you manage through it?<br>4. Describe a specific situation in which you confronted unethical behavior and chose not to say anything in order to not rock the boat. |
| **Competency 2: Using Emotional Intelligence** | 1. In the most recent feedback you have received about yourself (e.g., annual evaluation, coaching, 360-degree), what did you learn?<br>2. How much feedback do you like to get from people you report to, and in what form (e.g., written, face to face)?<br>3. Describe some of the specific techniques you use to get feedback about how others perceive you.<br>4. What have you identified as your principal developmental needs, and what are your plans to deal with them?<br>5. What have been the most difficult criticisms for you to accept?<br>6. When were you so frustrated that you did not treat someone with respect?<br>7. How would you describe your sense of humor?<br>8. Tell me about a situation in which you were expected to work with a person you disliked.<br>9. What do you do to alleviate stress?<br>10. Describe a time in which you did not handle yourself well under stress and pressure.<br>11. Describe a time in which you lost your cool.<br>12. Describe a situation in which you were the angriest you have been in years. |

| Exceptional Leadership Competencies | Interview Questions |
|---|---|
| **Competency 3:**<br>**Developing Vision** | 1. What is your vision for your job? How did you develop this vision?<br>2. What professional development programs do you attend? What is the best program you have attended in the past year?<br>3. In the past year, what specifically have you done to remain knowledgeable about the competitive environment, market dynamics, technology trends, and clinical practices?<br>4. Are you more comfortable dealing with concrete, tangible, short-term issues or more abstract, conceptual, long-term issues? Please explain.<br>5. Provide an example of a time when you played a key leadership role in developing the vision for an organization.<br>6. Describe your experience in strategic planning.<br>7. What professional development programs do you attend? |
| **Competency 4:**<br>**Communicating Vision** | 1. Give an example of when you had to present complex information in a simplified manner to explain it to others.<br>2. Give an example of when you built a business case or new program proposal and presented it to an audience. How did it turn out?<br>3. Give a specific example of when you had to reverse strategic direction and had to communicate the change.<br>4. Describe a situation in which you were most effective selling an idea.<br>5. Describe a situation in which your persuasion skills proved ineffective. |
| **Competency 5: Earning**<br>**Trust And Loyalty** | 1. Give an example of when you have maintained good relations with a person even when you could not agree on certain issues.<br>2. Give an example of when others readily followed your lead and one when they did not.<br>3. If we were to ask others to comment about your personal leadership, what would they tell us? |
| **Competency 6:**<br>**Listening Like You**<br>**Mean It** | 1. Describe your specific methods and practices to ensure that another person feels you are listening to him/her.<br>2. How do you practice active listening?<br>3. What would coworkers say regarding how often and how effectively you use active listening?<br>4. How have you developed informal and formal channels of communication in the past? |

| Exceptional Leadership Competencies | Interview Questions |
| --- | --- |
| **Competency 7: Giving Great Feedback** | 1. Describe the specific methods you use to evaluate the job performance of those who report to you.<br>2. Detail the specific methods and practices you use in conflict situations. Detail one situation where your approach failed.<br>3. What are the techniques you use to clarify obscure message meanings?<br>4. Describe a situation in which you had to terminate someone. What approaches were used? Would this person indicate that you had given them regular, honest feedback and sincere coaching efforts to help the situation? |
| **Competency 8: Mentoring** | 1. Describe a situation in which you acted as a mentor.<br>2. How would subordinates you have had in recent years describe your approaches to training and developing them?<br>3. (If adequate time in career has provided for this) How many individuals who have worked for you have moved on to higher positions? Describe some of those you are most proud of.<br>4. What processes have you put in place in the past to ensure that members of your team/organization have a development/career plan? |
| **Competency 9: Developing High-Performing Teams** | 1. Describe a situation in which you had to maintain peer relations with a team member when you could not agree on certain issues.<br>2. Describe your most recent teams and how you have led them.<br>3. What specific techniques have you tried to build teamwork? Which ones have worked well, and which have not?<br>4. Which of your teams has been the biggest disappointment in terms of cohesiveness or effectiveness?<br>5. Describe a situation in which you actively tore down walls or barriers to teamwork.<br>6. Describe situations in which you prevented or resolved conflicts.<br>7. Describe two to three situations in which subordinate team members were fighting, and describe what you did as the team leader.<br>8. Give examples of how you celebrate team and/or individual successes. |

| Exceptional Leadership Competencies | Interview Questions |
| --- | --- |
| **Competency 10: Energizing Staff** | 1. Describe how you keep team members involved and motivated. <br> 2. Give examples of steps you have taken to make team members feel important. <br> 3. Describe a situation in which you were most effective selling an idea. <br> 4. Describe a situation in which your persuasion skills proved ineffective. <br> 5. Describe what hands-on management means to you. If contacted, what would your subordinates say about your degree of micromanagement? |
| **Competency 11: Generating Informal Power** | 1. Describe a situation where you had no organizational authority but had to be persuasive in getting a point of view accepted. <br> 2. Give a specific example of a situation where you were able to convince independent physicians to change their minds about a situation (perhaps a joint venture proposal or a business deal). <br> 3. Describe one or two political situations you have faced and detail how you worked through them. <br> 4. I am curious about your style of interacting with others over whom you have no authority. Do you believe in collecting favors (for example, trading one action for another)? Give me some examples. <br> 5. Can you describe a time when you actually had to pull strings via your influence with others to get something accomplished? <br> 6. Is your ability to accomplish objectives in your current position tied a great deal to issues of favoritism? |
| **Competency 12: Building True Consensus** | 1. Describe a situation where you had to generate an agreement among parties who originally differed in opinion, approach, and objectives. <br> 2. Describe a time when you had disagreement from another person or group but were able to persuade them to change their minds. How did you do it? <br> 3. Give a couple of examples of how you facilitated discussions to guide a group that had people with different values to reach a common conclusion. |

| Exceptional Leadership Competencies | Interview Questions |
|---|---|
| **Competency 13: Mindful Decision Making** | 1. Give two examples in which you had to make an immediate decision—one with a positive outcome and one with a negative outcome. What process did you follow?<br>2. Describe a time in which you reached a decision when additional information would have changed the action steps. Do you have a process to use when you have to make decisions without complete information?<br>3. Describe the decision-making approach you used when you faced an extremely difficult situation.<br>4. Describe a time in which you reached a decision when you were decisive and quick and the outcome was perfect. Now describe one in which the outcome was negative.<br>5. What is the most difficult decision you have made? |
| **Competency 14: Driving Results** | 1. Give an example of a successful change you helped implement.<br>2. Give an example of a change initiative that was less successful.<br>3. (For each job the person has held) Describe the three or four key challenges you faced in your new job and how you changed them to the positive.<br>4. Describe a situation where you raised the bar for others in getting things done. Explain your tactics, the problems you encountered, and the outcomes.<br>5. Describe your communication methods when you are announcing a critical decision for your organization. |
| **Competency 15: Stimulating Creativity** | 1. Give an example of a creative solution to an unexpected situation when your leadership skills were needed.<br>2. Give an example of an innovative solution you created to solve a problem.<br>3. Assuming you see yourself as a creative person, exactly what do you do to stimulate your creative thinking?<br>4. What processes or approaches do you use to drive creativity in your staff?<br>5. Discuss the differences you see in developing creative ideas versus implementing them. |
| **Competency 16: Cultivating Adaptability** | 1. Describe a situation when you saw a problem no one else had identified. Detail the problem. Describe how you found out about it and what you did about it.<br>2. Describe one to two situations in which your negotiation skills proved effective or ineffective.<br>3. What would other leaders with whom you have worked in the past several years say about your ability to adjust and adapt to changing circumstances? |

# Index

Confidentiality: feedback surveys and, 210
Conflicts: working through, 104
Consensus. *See also* Building True Consensus: appropriate attention paid to factors related to, 137–38; building unnecessary, 140; definition of, 136; uneven approach to, 138–39
Conservative approach to problems, 169, 170
Consistency: acting with, 148
Consultative leadership style. *See* Democratic (or consultative) leadership style
Consumer-driven care, xv
Contingency leadership theory, 184
Control: teams and, 105, 106
Convergence: creating cycles of, 168
Conviction: physicians and, 223
Coolidge, Calvin, 70
Core self-evaluations, xxxii
Cost-benefit analysis, 146
"Country club managers," 19
"Country club" teams: creating, 107, 108
Courses of action: assessing, 176, 177
COVID-19 pandemic, 34; cultivating adaptability during, 177; energizing staff post-COVID, 119–20, 121; healthcare challenges related to, xv; leadership references in era of, 183; physician leadership challenges and, 213, 214–15; upending of leadership development and, xiii
*Creative Confidence* (Kelly and Kelly), 173
Creative ideas: drawing out, 168
Creative process: books on enhancing understanding of, 173
Creative solutions: building up, 168
Creativity: being creative rather than encouraging creativity, 170, 171; definition of, 166; design process and, 173; experience and, 173, 174; group construction and, 169
*Creativity, Inc.: Building an Inventive Organization* (Mauzy and Harriman), 173
Credentialing: of coaches, 195
*Credibility: How Leaders Gain and Lose It, Why People Demand It* (Kouzes and Posner), 60–61
Credit: assigning to wrong person, 56, 57
Critical thinking: competency mapping for, *235*
Critiques: reluctance around, 83, 84
Cross, R., 120
Cross-departmental roles: informal power and, 132
Cross-mapping (or cross-walking): of competency models, 233–34
*Crucial Accountability* (Patterson, et al.), 86
*Crucial Conversations* (Patterson, et al.), 86, 97, 154
Crucible experiences: learning leadership and, 226
Cultivating Adaptability (Competency 16), xxvii, *xxviii*, 175–84; definition and importance of,

176–77; highly effective leaders and, 177–80; misuse and overuse of, 181–82; personal development and, 183; physicians and, *222*; role models and, 182–83; sample interview questions based on, 255; self-reflection questions on, 248; St. Nicholas Health System vignette, 175–76; strategic focus and, 237, *238*; when it is not all it could be, 180–81
Cult of personality, 59
Culture of safety: feedback-rich working environment and, 211
Curiosity, 227
Customized leadership competency models, xvii; foundation for, xvii
Cynicism: staff, inspirational leaders and, 182; tolerating, 117, 118

"Dark" side of self, understanding, xxxiii
Data analysis: overzealous focus on, 36, 37
Decision making. *See also* Mindful Decision Making: consensus and, 136; creativity and, 172; evaluating best approach to, 145–46; keeping biases in check, 153; teams and avoidance of, 107, 108; time urgency of, physicians *vs.* executive leaders and, 219–20
Decision-making methods: lack of, 149
Decisions: analysis of, 147; for decisions' sake, 150–51; fear of making mistakes, 148, 150; mindful approach to, 153; overanalysis of, 151
Decision trees, 146
*Decisive: How to Make Better Choices in Life and Work* (Heath and Heath), 141
Deegan, M. J., 224
Democratic (or consultative) leadership style, 179
Demosthenes, 42
Derailment risks, references on, 220, 227
*Designing Workplace Programs: An Evidence-Based Approach* (Allen), 203
Design process: creativity and, 173
Design thinking, 166
Developing High-Performing Teams (Competency 9), xxvi, *xxviii*, 101–11; definition and importance of, 102; encouraging (or supportive) leadership style and, 179; highly effective leaders and, 103–4; misuse and overuse of, 107–8; operations focus and, 237, *238*; performance improvement and, 233; personal development and, 109; physicians and, *222*; role models and, 109; sample interview questions based on, 253; self-reflection questions on, 244; St. Nicholas Health System vignette, 101–2; time elements and, 218; time urgency of decision making and, 219; when it is not all it could be, 105–7

and, *xxviii*, 124, 135–43; competencies related to, *xxviii*; Cultivating Adaptability competency and, *xxviii*, 124, 175–84; Driving Results competency and, *xxviii*, 124, 155–63; Generating Informal Power competency and, *xxviii*, 124, 125–34; Mindful Decision Making competency and, *xxviii*, 124, 145–54; physicians and, *222,* 224; Stimulating Creativity competency and, *xxviii*, 124, 165–74

Master's programs: offered at medical schools, 215

Mauzy, Jeff, 173

Maxwell, John C., 64

McChrystal, General Stanley, 109

McClelland, David, xxi

McClelland's Achievement Motivation Theory: Exceptional Leadership Model and, 232

MD Anderson Cancer Center: vision statement of, 49

Medical schools: master's programs offered by, 215

Medical service corps officers, 182–83

Meese, Katherine, 120

Meier, J. D., 162

Mentoring: leadership coaching *vs.,* 193, 199, 203; leadership development and, 199; physicians and, 225, 226; self-concept and, xxxii; undervaluing, 92–93, 94

Mentoring (Competency 8), xxvi, *xxviii*, 89–99. *See also* Mentors; Role models; coaching leadership style and, 179; definition and importance of, 90; developing business case, 98; highly effective leaders and, 90–92; misuse and overuse of, 94–96; operations focus and, *238*; personal development and, 97; physicians and, *222*; role models and, 96; sample interview questions based on, 253; self-reflection questions on, 244; St. Nicholas Health System vignettes, 89, 98; when it is not all if could be, 92–94

Mentoring programs: organizational, 98, 203

Mentoring relationships: effective use of time between meetings, 201; ending engagement well, 202–3; exceptional leaders and, 203; formal or informal, 200; informal, voluntary nature of, 199; periodic reviews and, 202; preparing well for your meetings, 201; as two-way, 201–2

Mentoring skills: lacking, 93–94

Mentors, 10. *See also* Mentoring competency; Mentoring relationships; Role models; approaching, 200; benefits for, 199; communicating vision and, 47; definition of, 199; energizing staff and, 120; finding, 120; senior leaders as, 188; using, 200; working with, 199–200

Mergers and acquisitions, 215

Message: understanding the why beneath, 67

Messenger: valuing, 67

Metrics: in leadership development, 190–91

Microsoft forms, 209

*Microstress Effect, The* (Cross and Dillon), 120

Mindful Decision Making (Competency 13), xxvii, *xxviii*, 145–54; communication skills and, 232; competency mapping for, *235*; definition and importance of, 146; highly effective leaders and, 146–48; misuse and overuse of, 150–52; operations focus and, 237; performance improvement and, 233; personal development and, 152–53; physician decision making and, 219; physicians and, *222*; role models and, 152; sample interview questions based on, 255; science orientation and, 217; self-reflection questions on, 246–47; St. Nicholas Health System vignettes, 145–46, 153–54; strategic focus and, *238*; time urgency of decision making and, 219; when it is not all it could be, 148–50

Mintzberg, Henry, 133

Mistrust, 19, 20, 52

Mobile phones: inattentive listening habits and, 68

*Modern Healthcare,* 31

Money: not always a motivator, 121

Monitoring platforms: for leadership development, 190–91

Moralism: personal conviction and, 9, 10

Motivation: definition of, 114; intrinsic, 121; undervaluing, 116, 117

Motivational skills: underdeveloping, 117

Multisource (360-degree) feedback. *See* 360-degree feedback

Natural disasters: cultivating adaptability during, 177

Network building: ineffective approaches to, 129–30

Networks: involving the wrong people in, 129, 130

New ideas: overemphasizing, 171

New leaders: preparing for success, 189

*New Scientist, The,* 32

*Noise: A Flaw in Human Judgment* (Kahneman), 153

Nominal Group Technique, 136, 141, 166

Noninterpersonal work aspects: avoiding, 21, 22

Nurses: typical age leadership roles assumed by, 215

Office politics, 134

Onboarding: leadership competency models and, 239; new leaders, 189

Role models (*continued*)
and, 60; enhancing emotional intelligence and, 22; feedback skills and, 86; finding, 10; generating informal power and, 132; Listening Like You Mean It competency and, 71; Mentoring competency and, 96; Mindful Decision Making competency and, 152; personal conviction and looking for, 10; Stimulating Creativity competency and, 172
Rothschild, W. E., 183
"Rules of engagement": in group interaction, 154
Russo, J. Edward, 153

Saccocio, Saria, 215, 217, 225, 228
Saunders, C., 216, 221
Scenario building, 166
Scenario sketching, 141
Schein, Edgar, 75
Science orientation: physicians *vs.* executive leaders and, 217–18
Scope: of coaching programs, 193–97
Selective memory, 145, 151
Self-assessments, 194
Self-awareness, 2, 12; Compelling Vision competencies and, 28; cultivating, 17; developing, xxv; emotional intelligence and, 184; Goleman's definition of, 24
Self-concept: critical importance of, xxx–xxxi; Exceptional Leadership Competency Model and, *xxviii*; healthy, xxiv; listening and, 77; overemphasizing performance and, 160; positive, xxxii; strengthening, xxxii–xxxiii; successes and failures and, xxxi; working with others and, xxxi–xxxii
Self-confidence, xxx
Self-development plan, sample: career goals, 249–50; developmental needs, 250
Self-esteem, xxx
Self-interest: balancing with selfless interest, 17
Self-management: emotional intelligence and, 184
Self-reflection: physician application of leadership competencies and, 220–21, *222*, 223–24
Self-reflection questions: for leadership competencies, 241–48
Self-worth, xxx
Senior healthcare leaders, xxiii; shrinking proportion of, 193
Senior leadership: strategic alignment in leadership development and, 188
Senior leadership teams: collective goals in, 102; dynamics commonly found in, 103–4
Senior management positions: clinicians in, 216
Shanafelt, Tait, 120
Shared calendars and project sites, 162

Shared competency language: developing, 206
Shock: listening derailed by, 73
Shoemaker, Paul, 153
Siddiqui, N., 216
*Signals Are Talking, The* (Webb), 38
Simulations: high-performance leadership development and, 188
Six Sigma specialists, 141
Skill development: guidance in, xvii; high-quality feedback and, 211
Smaller groups: scheduling time with, 74
Smallwood, N., xvi
Social awareness: emotional intelligence and, 184
Socialization skills: physicians and, 221
Socrates, 2
Sokolov, Jacque, 216, 220, 226, 236
Sonnenfeld, Jeffrey, 220
Specialties: Listening Like You Mean It competency and, 223
Sports coaching approaches, 97
Spot debrief sessions: definition of, 205; feedback-rich working environment and, 205–6
Spotts, Doug, 221, 223, 224, 225, 228
Staff development: mentoring and participating in, 91–92; undervaluing, 93, 94
Standards-setting leadership style, 179
Star performers: overemphasizing, 95, 96
Stimulating Creativity (Competency 15), xxvii, *xxviii*, 165–74, 232; competency mapping for, *235*; definition and importance of, 166–67; highly effective leaders and, 167–68; misuse and overuse of, 170–71; performance improvement and, 233; personal development and, 172–73; physicians and, *222*; role models and, 172; sample interview questions based on, 255; science orientation and, 217; self-reflection questions on, 247; St. Nicholas Health System vignettes, 165–66, 173–74; strategic focus and, 237, *238*; when it is not all it could be, 168–70
St. Nicholas Health System Case Study, xviii, xxvii; Building True Consensus competency and, 135, 142; business, xli; Communicating Vision competency and, 41, 48–49; Cultivating Adaptability competency and, 175–76; demographics and community, xl; Developing High-Performing Teams competency and, 101–2; Developing Vision competency and, 29–30, 39–40; Driving Results competency and, 155; Earning Trust and Loyalty competency and, 51–52, 61–62; Energizing Staff competency and, 113–14; Generating Informal Power competency and, 125–26; Giving Great Feedback competency and,

# About the Authors

**Carson F. Dye, MBA, FACHE,** is president and CEO of Exceptional Leadership, LLC, a leadership consulting and executive search firm. He conducts CEO, senior executive, and physician executive searches for a variety of organizations. His consulting experience includes leadership assessment, organizational design, and physician leadership development. He also conducts board retreats and provides counsel in executive employment contracts and evaluation matters for a variety of client organizations. He is certified to work with the Hogan Assessment Systems tools for selection, development, and executive coaching.

Prior to starting his own firm, he served for 15 years as a senior partner with Witt/Kieffer. Prior to that, he worked in executive search with Lamalie and TMP Worldwide. His consulting career began with Findley Davies where he was a partner and director of their Health Care Industry Consulting Division. Prior to his consulting career, he served 20 years in executive-level positions at St. Vincent Mercy Medical Center, Toledo, Ohio; The Ohio State University Wexner Medical Center; Children's Hospital Medical Center, Cincinnati, Ohio; and Clermont Mercy Hospital in Batavia, Ohio.

Dye serves as a faculty member for The Governance Institute and is a physician leadership consultant expert on the LaRoche National Consultant Panel. He served on the adjunct faculty of the graduate program in management and health services policy at Ohio State University from 1985 to 2008, and has also served as adjunct faculty at Xavier University and the University of Cincinnati. He has also taught the leadership and human resources courses for the University of Alabama at Birmingham (UAB) in their executive master of science in health administration program.

Since 1989, Dye has taught several programs for the American College of Healthcare Executives (ACHE) and is a frequent presenter at the ACHE Congress on Healthcare Leadership. He has won the James A. Hamilton Book of the Year three times—for *The Healthcare Leader's Guide to Actions, Awareness, and Perception*

(Health Administration Press 2016) in 2017, *Developing Physician Leaders for Successful Clinical Integration* (Health Administration Press 2013) in 2014, and for *Leadership in Healthcare: Values at the Top* (Health Administration Press 2000) in 2001. The latter book was revised and released as *Leadership in Healthcare: Essential Values and Skills*, 4th edition (Health Administration Press 2023), and is used by many graduate programs in health administration as a leadership text. With Andrew Garman, PsyD, he has also written *The Healthcare C-Suite: Leadership Development at the Top* (Health Administration Press 2009). Other publications include *Enhanced Physician Engagement Volume 1: What It Is, Why You Need It, and Where to Begin* (Health Administration Press 2022), *Enhanced Physician Engagement Volume 2: Tools and Tactics for Success* (Health Administration Press 2022), *Winning the Talent War: Ensuring Effective Leadership in Healthcare* (Health Administration Press 2002), *Executive Excellence* (Health Administration Press 2000), and *Protocols for Health Care Executive Behavior* (Health Administration Press 1993). Dye has also written several professional journal articles on leadership and human resources.

Dye earned his BA from Marietta College and his MBA from Xavier University.

**Andrew N. Garman, PsyD, MS,** is professor in the Department of Health Systems Management at RUSH University in Chicago and director of the RUSH Center for Health System Leadership. At RUSH, Garman facilitates a variety of graduate courses and executive workshops on topics including leadership competencies, organizational change, strategic human resource management, and environmental stewardship. In addition to his role with RUSH, Garman also serves as senior advisor for leadership development for the International Hospital Federation's Geneva Sustainability Centre, where he contributes to a portfolio of innovative executive education programs and leadership simulations delivered around the world.

Dr. Garman is a recognized authority in evidence-based leadership assessment and development practice, as well as long-term trends affecting the future of healthcare. His research and applied work have been published in more than a hundred peer-reviewed journals and trade publications. His books include *Healing Our Future: Leadership for a Changing Health System* (Berrett-Koehler) as well as two others with Health Administration Press: *The Healthcare C-Suite: Leadership Development at the Top* (with Carson Dye) and *The Future of Healthcare: Global Trends Worth*

*Watching.* For his work in leadership competency modeling and CEO succession planning, he has received three Health Management Research Awards from the American College of Healthcare Executives.

Dr. Garman's prior work experience includes a variety of practitioner and faculty roles with organizations including the Federal Reserve Bank of Chicago, the Illinois Institute of Technology, the University of Chicago, and the National Center for Healthcare Leadership, as well as a variety of behavioral health organizations. Dr. Garman received his BS in psychology/mathematics emphasis from Pennsylvania State University, his MS in personnel and human resource development from the Illinois Institute of Technology, and his PsyD in clinical psychology from the College of William & Mary/Virginia Consortium.